MYSTERIES AND HISTORIES:
Shipwrecks of the Great Lakes

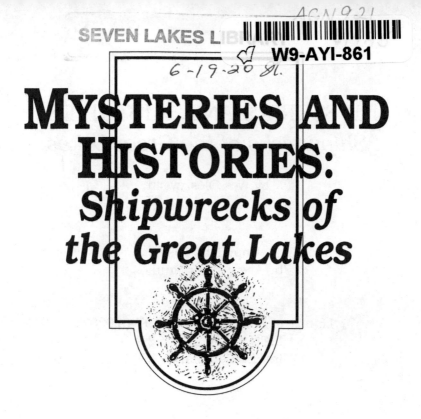

by Wes Oleszewski

Avery Color Studios

Marquette, Michigan 49855
1997

MYSTERIES AND HISTORIES:
Shipwrecks of the Great Lakes

by Wes Oleszewski

Copyright 1997
by Avery Color Studios

Library of Congress Card # 97-070282
ISBN # 0-932212-92-1
First Edition March 1997

Published
by Avery Color Studios
Marquette, Michigan 49855

Dedication

To Dave "D.J." Story

There are so very few truly Good People in this world, and D.J. is one of those people. An undiscovered master of vessel photography, D.J. represents all of the best in the folk who live in the Great Lakes region, and absolutely none of the worst—he is a nice guy in the most pure sense of the word. I am proud to call him my boat buddy and all around good friend.

Other Books by Wes Oleszewski

Stormy Seas—*Triumphs and Tragedies of
Great Lakes Ships*

Sounds of Disaster—*Great Lakes
Shipwrecks*

Ice Water Museum—*Forgotten Great
Lakes Shipwrecks*

Ghost Ships, Gales & Forgotten Tales—
True Adventures on the Great Lakes

Table of Contents

Glossary

ABEAM—Beside the boat.

AFT—Behind a vessel.

AGROUND—Running into very shallow water.

BACK—A vessel's spine or keel.

BALLAST—Something, other than cargo, taken aboard a vessel so as to load it down.

BARGE—A vessel with no power of its own

BARK- Sailing vessel with mizzen-mast fore and aft rigged while other masts are square rigged.

BEAM—The width of a boat.

BEAM ENDS—A vessel's sides.

BRIG—Two masted, square rigged sailing vessel.

BULKHEAD—Vertical walls that divide a hull width-wise.

CANALLER—A vessel designed to fit a specific lock size.

CAPSTAN—A large spool-like device used for pulling lines or chains

CUT DOWN—Removing cabins, decks or both to facilitate the use of a vessel in another manner.

DAVIT—Boom-like supports for the lines used in lowering lifeboats.

DONKEY BOILER—Used to create steam for uses other than propulsion, such as heating or steering.

FATHOM—Six feet.

FIREHOLD—The area where coal is shoveled to feed the vessel's fires.

i

FLOTSAM—Floating wreckage.

FO'C'SLE—The deck below the elevated portion of the bow, (derived from the term Fore Castle).

FOREPEAK—The upper tip of the bow.

FOUNDER—To sink.

FUNNEL—Smoke stack.

GALE—Winds between 40 and 74 miles per hour.

HAWSER—A very heavy line used to pull another vessel.

HEEL—To lean to one side.

JIB—A triangular sail rigged to the forward-most end of a sailing vessel.

KEEL—A beam running the length of a vessel at the bottom upon which the structure is based.

LIGHTER—To remove the cargo from a boat, also a name attached to vessels used for that task.

LIST—Leaning to one side.

LYLE GUN—A small cannon-like device used to shoot a projectile and attached line across a great distance.

PORT SIDE—Left side.

SCHOONER-BARGE—A former sailing vessel now used as a tow-barge.

SCREW—Propeller.

SHOAL—Shallow area that presents a hazard to navigation.

SPAR—Mast.

SPAR DECK—The main deck of a vessel where the masts are mounted.

STEERING POLE—A long thin boom-like device with one end attached to the vessel's forepeak. The boat's wheelsman uses the free end as a sight aimed at buoys or land-marks in order to steer the vessel.

TEXAS DECK—The deck upon which the pilothouse is mounted.

TILLER—A long handle-like extension attached in a hori-zontal fashion to the upright portion of the rudder-post in order to facilitate steering.

WING ON WING—Having one sail extended out over the port side and the other over the starboard side in an effort to best catch a wind coming directly from behind.

YAWL—A small lifeboat or rowboat.

Foreword

*T*o some people the Great Lakes are only an abstract slash of blue on the map of North America with names they were forced to memorize in elementary school and can now scarcely recall. To others who happen to visit the lakes they are a startling expanse of gem-like blue water that appears beyond the trees and stretches past the horizon. To those who vacation annually along the lakes they afford hours of pleasant recreation, where fond memories are made in the months when the fresh water seas are on their best behavior. To the residents who live year-round along the lake shores they are places of ever-changing temperaments that range from shimmering indigo summers to gray winter ice. And to nearly all who visit the Great Lakes those distant vessels moving like snails on the horizon are simply taken for granted. But, for those of us who are compelled to peek into the history of these distant vessels and the people who have sailed their long-forgotten courses, the lakes are a giant treasure chest of history and sometimes mystery. Thousands of tales are there. All we need do is open the lid and peer inside. This book will do just that.

Beneath the keels of the giant modern lakeboats that crawl the distant horizon the lake bottoms are littered with the bones of shipwreck history. The visitor to the lake shore would probably be shocked to know that, with more than 5,000 shipwrecks on the fresh water seas, the odds are good that while they stand and ponder the sparkling

waters, they may be looking directly at the site of a long forgotten adventure. Sadly, most of these harrowing tales
have been overlooked or misplaced, but within these pages
we will recall and reconstruct some of those events. It is
best for the reader to be prepared at this point—because
the tales contained here are all true and have been recon-
structed in terrifying reality. With only occasional dialogue
being synthesized for color, every fact has been checked
and cross-checked for truth. In some cases speculation on
circumstantial evidence was made but it is always presented and clearly identified by the author as conjecture. In
every case the greatest pains were taken to insure that
when the reader does visit the locations of these stories, his
view will be factual.

In this text we will have the rare opportunity to set
straight some of the inaccuracies in history. For example,
in the case of the steamer THOMAS CRANAGE, it was discovered that every single written account concerning that
vessel's final trip (up to this book) was wrong! In the chapter concerning that vessel, we will set right the boat's point
of departure. In the initial news reports that announced the
CRANAGE's predicament, the media of the day mistakenly
stated that the boat was bound from "Duluth to Tiffin."
From that point on, the error was picked up and published
in one text after another each referencing the other for eight
and one-half decades. In researching the story for this
book, it was found that the CRANAGE did not appear in the
upbound or downbound passages at the Soo in the appropriate time-frame, nor was her name listed as passing in or
out of Duluth. By chance I stumbled across the vessel's
name in the passages for Mackinaw City listed the day prior
to the wreck. On the hunch that 85 years of resource material may be incorrect and that the boat may actually have

come off of Lake Michigan rather than Lake Superior, I e-mailed fellow historian and author Dave Swayze and asked him to check the vessel passages for Lake Michigan. At the speed of light Dave e-mailed back that my hunch was correct and those passages did show that the CRANAGE had indeed departed Chicago, and not Duluth. Since 1911 everyone had taken for granted that the newspapers were correct and no one had bothered to work backwards and look closely. Such pains-taking effort may seem a trivial endeavor simply to sort out a single fact of a vessel passage nearly a century into the past, but clarifying confused facts is one of the main reasons for writing a book such as this. Getting the story straight may not matter to some, but I feel it is an important tribute to the people who once worked the vessels about which you will be reading.

Confusion of the facts sometimes obscures the adventures as much or more than the depths and sands of the lakes. For example, on the beach of Michigan's Tawas Point state park there is an official historical marker stating to all who stroll by that sandy place that just a few yards out in the lake rests the wreck of the schooner KITTY REEVES, lost in November of 1870. According to the best efforts of Great Lakes maritime historians, however, that vessel never existed. So, when the tourists ponder the wave-tossed distance they are contemplating the concocted story of Frank Black and Julius Roth circa 1941. A one-time resident of the Tawas area, Black wrote a letter to Roth spinning the tale of the wreck of the REEVES, and Roth took the hearsay as pure fact. Following in Roth's wake newspaper reporters and Great Lakes authors alike picked up on the story that Roth continued to embellish. To this day no evidence of the existence of the KITTY REEVES has ever been found, but Julius Roth's fib lives on. Meanwhile, directly across the state, the bones of the schooner GRANADA rest in the beach sands off Muskegon state park—without notice at all. There is no marker, and few records. The park rangers did not even know of the wreck until they were informed by this author. Each summer the sunbathers spread blankets and children scoop buckets of sand upon the very spot where the vessel met her doom. They have not a hint as to the wreck that may lie in the sands beneath them. Yet another problem exists as to where information may be found. In the case of the wreck of the schooner-barge JOSEPH G. MASTEN, off Two Rivers Point, Wisconsin, for example, one would expect to find reams of information concerning the wreck at the Manitowoc Maritime Museum which is located just a few miles south of the wreck site. Digging in the museum's files, however, there is not a single mention of the vessel to be found. Only by going to other repositories in Ohio and Minnesota can information concerning this wreck be uncovered. Then there are the occasions when the facts simply are confused at the time of the occurrence. Looking back at the events surrounding the steamers PHILADELPHIA and ALBANY, at least one source exchanges the names of the captains of the two vessels. That same source, however, gives sensational details of human carnage that are later debunked in the very same publication. Lastly there are the reports that were never recorded in print and cannot be verified, such as the report that the remains of the steamer GEORGE W. MORLEY were "removed" in 1929. There is no good reason or outstanding evidence to support such a removal—it is my conclusion that this single source is incorrect and that she is still where she wrecked. This is the paradox of Great Lakes shipwreck history. Until very recently it was prone to fiction, concoction, oversight and just plain confusion. The effort within this text will always be to eliminate those elements with fact.

Then we have those tiny mysteries—events that when looked at with a research eye only leads us to ask more questions. Such are the tales that comprise a great deal of this text. It is this author's hope that the readers will be so challenged by these stories that they will gaze across the lakes with a new sense of wonder and perhaps be inspired to set out in quest of answers that I have not yet found.

Researching a text such as this varies to the same degree as the availability of the information. At one point this author found himself seated in front of a micro-film viewer reading three months worth of a local newspaper, in a fruitless attempt to gain any new facts concerning the THOMAS CRANAGE. At the other extreme, when a single fact concerning the wreck of the MABEL WILSON was missing from my own files, a quick e-mail was sent via the internet to fellow author and historian Dave Swayze. His answer, containing the final bit of information needed to make the story complete, was received the same day and the story was completed. Such is the method through which we pursue history and provide you the reader with your vehicle to travel through time.

Finally, there is the overall purpose of a text such as this. That purpose is to inform and entertain. As always it is important to keep in mind that there are as many ways to tell a story as there are story tellers, and every individual has his or her own outlook. Additionally, the writer of this text is not beyond making mistakes—that is why they put erasers on pencils and "back space" keys on computers. Of course—there are always those who get their greatest pleasure from picking your work apart. Thus, for all those who open these pages to learn, explore, ponder, enjoy and just plain pick apart... that is why it has been written. Just remember that no matter how much you may enjoy doing those things with this text, you will never find a fraction of the fun that I have found in writing it.

Entanglements

Often the events that wrap around a Great Lakes adventure become so tangled that even the most basic of facts are confused. A case in point was the fate of the steamer H.C. AKELEY on Lake Michigan in November of 1883. The confusion surrounding this vessel and her crew appears to go on without end. In hind-sight it is important to keep in mind that this was an era when news was dispatched by telegraph in the clicks of Morse code, decoded into written notes and put into print by hand-setting type one letter at a time. Considering all of this it is easy to see how records of events such as those of the AKELEY could have a number of errors within their text. But in this particular case even the actual chain of events is difficult to decipher. Within the news accounts of the day not only are there five spellings of the vessel's name, but even the captain's name has at least three different spellings. Within this story we shall attempt to set straight the entanglements of the H.C. AKELEY. Not an easy task considering that the web involves not only the AKELEY, but the schooners CLARA PARKER, DRIVER and ARAB as well the tug PROTECTION. Remove any of these vessels from this story and the ending would have been different in the extreme—because what happened to one had dramatic consequence on each of the others.

A blizzard howled all around as the residents of Saugatuck, Michigan, and Captain O'Brian's lifesavers trudged along the beach north of the harbor in search of what Lake Michigan might decide to give up. The lifesavers from St. Joseph had already spent many cold exhausting hours working the tug PROTECTION. Snow had been falling so heavily that it now totaled 20 inches and the beach combers were forced to wade through three to four foot drifts. It was Thursday, November 15th, 1883 and the gale that had been churning the lake for nearly a full week continued to roar from due west. What no one here could possibly know was that the gale would keep blowing for two more full days. It was amidst this maelstrom that Captain Edward Stretch came ashore.

"There!" one of the searchers shouted pointing toward the frigid surf in the distance, "Look! There's something out there."

Lifting their knees as high as they could in an attempt to make haste through the drifted snow, the searchers were thwarted by the white peaks. In the surf beyond, the waves playfully tossed a lifeless body onto the snow-garnished sand. Dressed in dark blue pants, a brass-buttoned uniform jacket and cork lifebelt, the figure was obviously that of Captain Stretch—a well known friend to most of the searchers. Juggled like a rag-doll the corpse seemed to beckon to the approaching beach-combers as the lake shoved it higher onto the beach. Then, just as they seemed within a few steps of recovering Captain Stretch's remains, Lake Michigan teasingly sent a big wave that crashed down over the body and pulled it back out into the surf. For a long shivering moment the searchers stood watching as the uniform-clad cadaver tumbled in the white-caps and then vanished. The lake gave Captain Stretch up long enough to allow a morbid salutation to those ashore and then it took him back—forever.

The forgotten steamer H.C. AKELEY   —*Author's concept*

Ten days before Captain Stretch made his ghoulish appearance on that Saugatuck beach, he stood in the pilothouse of the steamer H.C. AKELEY. November is never a pleasant time on the lakes, but in this the first week of that wicked month in 1883 it seemed as if the autumn Vilnius was intent on going out of her way to be particularly foul. On Tuesday the sixth day of the month Captain Stretch had the AKELEY headed across western Lake Michigan's agitation toward the port entrance of Milwaukee. Secured to the steamer's stern and tugging on the thick towing hawser as each wave slapped her bow was the schooner-barge W.H. BARNUM. Both boats were loaded to capacity with coal that had been hauled from Buffalo. It had been a rude trip all of the way and as the harbor entrance came into view it is doubtless that Captain Stretch was just a bit relieved that the trip was coming to an end.

Unfortunately, Captain Stretch's troubles were just beginning. No sooner had the AKELEY reached the calm waters of the Milwaukee harbor than she promptly ran hard aground on the port's muddy bottom. Water levels were down at the end of the 1883 season, but coal rates were up in anticipation of having to stock-pile for the coming winter. With the combination of these two elements, it is not difficult to picture how Captain Stretch's boat became stuck. For the better part of the next two days the steamer sulked with a lighter barge at her beam scooping away at her load. By Friday the boat had been lightered, moved to the coal dock, unloaded and promptly departed for Chicago without cargo. A load of 54,000 bushels of corn consigned to a Buffalo elevator was waiting to slide down the chutes into the AKELEY's hold.

Practically brand new, the H.C. AKELEY was only two years old. Having been launched in 1881, the edges on her planking were still sharp and the ice-scars on her bow were few. Although there is no reliable record as to exactly when she slid from the builder's ways at Thomas W. Kirby's Mechanic's Dry Dock Company in Grand Haven, Michigan, the best bet is that it was in the spring of that year. Some $200,000 had been invested in the expansion and renovation of the facility where the 240 foot steamer had been constructed. Her completion was certainly an exclamation point on the effort. As official number 95639 the H.C. AKELEY was to be put under the immediate command of Captain Stretch. At 1,187 tons the AKELEY cost $110,000 and was an oak monster that seemed to dominate the Grand River when she floated free of the builder's ways. It was only fitting that the mighty vessel would come under the command of the 43 year old Captain Stretch who was considered to be one of the best local mariners. To his credit the master navigator had taken the brig PAMLICO from Chicago to Europe, a tremendous undertaking in the mid 1800s. Additionally he had commanded the schooners MONTPELIER and SUNRISE as well as the brig MARY of which he was owner.

Doubtless that Healy C. Akeley himself was present at the birth of his namesake lakeboat. Akeley had arrived in Grand Haven in 1858 and aside from a stint in the Union Army during the Civil War had spent most of his life working at being the town's leading citizen. Lumber and shingle mills, schools and churches were all a part of the Akeley touch. He would even serve as mayor of Grand Haven from 1882 to 1884. From clever business dealings in nearly every corner of the city to community leadership—Akeley did it all. Indeed it was proper that the grandest vessel ever constructed on the Grand River, and one of the largest boats on the lakes to boot, should be named for Mr. Akeley. Now, two seasons after her birth the AKELEY continued under Captain Stretch's able authority as he headed her for Chicago.

About the same time as the AKELEY was entering the port of Chicago, the tug PROTECTION was working at towing the schooner ARAB across the surface of Lake Michigan. Autumn had not been kind to the ARAB this season. She had stranded 200 yards southwest of the lifesaving station at St. Joseph, Michigan, on the last day of October. Station Keeper William L. Stevens mustered his storm warriors and went to the rescue of the schooner's crew. All six of the crew were safely removed from the boat and taken into the warmth of the St. Joseph station where they were treated to the hospitality of the lifesavers.

Even when stuck aground the 158 ton ARAB was a sight of elegance. Constructed in 1854 she had all of the stylish curves that represented the pride of the shipwrights of her day. With her hull painted coal-black and her deck and cabins painted red, the boat was pleasing to the eye regardless of from what angle the boat-watcher viewed her. On November 10th the lifesavers and the ARAB's crew had removed her deck-load of lumber and secured a towline to the PROTECTION. The tug then hauled the leaking schooner into the harbor where two steam pumps were placed aboard to keep the water out of her. In order to man the pumps two firemen and two engineers were added to the ARAB's crew, making her total complement ten in number. At half past six o'clock that same evening the tender schooner was tugged from the harbor at the end of 500 feet of the tug PROTECTION's towing hawser and headed across Lake Michigan. The sky was clear and the stars sparkled— only a shallow swell bent the surface of the sweet-water sea.

On Saturday night, the three masted schooner CLARA PARKER departed Chicago headed to Collingwood, Ontario. In her hold was piled 29,500 bushels of corn shipped at the employ of Johanna Lindbren of Evanston, Illinois. Captain Lewis was in command and found the prevailing southwest winds to be much to the advantage of his wind-grabber. In tow of one of the harbor tugs, the schooner casually passed the steamer H.C. AKELEY, now securely moored at her loading elevator. A short time later the PARKER was released on the open lake and Captain Lewis watched as sailors Don and William Oleson, Henry Tunville, Andrew Nelson, Robert Zindre, Henry Francis and Charles Stewart set the boat's sails in a routine they had performed a thousand times. By the time Mate William Peterson reported all was in order, the schooner was plowing ahead wing on wing making "good way" up the lake. No doubt, the Lindbren concerns were going to make a tidy profit on this trip.

There was once a superstition in the Great Lakes maritime community that predicted no good would ever come from a trip that was started on a Sunday. As Saturday the 10th of November, 1883 turned into Sunday, the barometer in the AKELEY's pilothouse was beginning to drop. About an hour's loading remained, followed by the trimming of the corn cargo, the closing of the hatches and tarpaulining of the planks. First Mate John Kingston of Port Colborn was supervising the loading activities as deckhands James Crawford and George Murray went about the work. In addition to their normal chores the deckhands were burdened with the task of introducing the ways of the AKELEY to the two new deckhands who had just come aboard at Chicago. Why or if the AKELEY had come up short two deckhands is not on record, all that is known for sure is that Charles Kurts and Charles Smith were added to the crew while at the grain dock. Now all of the boat's deckcrew began to feel an unstated sense of urgency in their toil. The captain wanted to get under way, and soon before whatever weather that was on the way would strike. Although no one probably said it aloud, they all knew that this meant starting the trip on a Sunday, and "no good can come from a trip started on Sunday."

A blustery wind picked up the dust left behind by the sliding corn and slung it at the deckcrew—November was cooking up a brew and Captain Stretch wanted little of it. With that in mind he threw the "Sunday hoodoo" aside and started his trip to Buffalo. Casting off her lines in the first hours of Sunday morning, the AKELEY's crew set her free of the Chicago grain dock. Standing at the steamer's forepeak, watchman David Lark kept a sharp lookout as the big oak steamer churned from the slip. At half past two o'clock in the morning, the AKELEY cleared the harbor and was plodding her way onto the expanse of Lake Michigan. From the southwest came the winds and Captain Stretch ordered Chief Engineer John Driscoll to "let 'er go." Firemen Charles Sward and Bernard Kelly had kept the fires up on their respective shifts so once the throttle was opened the boat started to make good headway. Wheelsman Samuel Martin pointed the steering pole a little more northward at the captain's direction so as to keep her a bit more in the lee of the western shore. Through the night Second Mate Henry Paulson would see to it that she stayed there just in case November's temper came suddenly down upon them. Once on the lake the AKELEY and crew found the winds to be blowing with a strength that could not be felt in the confines of the harbor. At near gale force the southwest winds built waves that grew larger as the steamer moved farther from the southern shore. Running in the following sea was going to be awkward, but the boat would surely make good time.

In our modern world weather is plotted by armies of government meteorologists, photographed by satellite, modeled by super computers and dumped into every American's lap by radio and television every hour of every day. In 1883 the best form of weather forecasting was essentially the "Farmer's Almanac." As a result, no one on the Great Lakes on this fitful Sunday had the slightest inkling as to what November was actually brewing up. The media of the day used terms such as "unsettled" and "look out for squalls" to give indications of the weather ahead. Such reports were much like horoscopes—so general in nature that they could be called correct no matter what happened. Armed with the very best of weather reporting of the day the mariners of 1883 pressed on—come what may.

Just over 60 miles north of where the AKELEY was routinely plowing through the autumn mess, the story was substantially different for the tug PROTECTION and the schooner ARAB. It was just after four o'clock in the morning when the watch aboard the tug noticed cries for help coming from the schooner. A closer look indicated a great deal of commotion on her deck, then her people could be seen rushing aft. A moment later the boat tucked her bow under and rolled sharply onto her starboard side. She sank until only about 10 feet of her port quarter remained above water. In haste the tug went into reverse and backed toward the sinking schooner. The cause of the boat's sudden foundering was the pumps that had been put aboard to help keep her afloat. Apparently, shortly after leaving port, it had been determined that just one pump would be enough to keep the ARAB afloat, so the starboard pump was shut down. By the time it was discovered that a single pump was not enough, the ARAB was doomed. Now the tug hustled to the rescue of her consort. Unfortunately, as she churned aft her screw ingested the tow-line. After a brief rhythmic thumping, the engine screeched to a dead stop. Lowering the tug's yawl, the crew went to work at freeing her propeller. It was at this critical time that the lake reached out to take the wounded boats.

As if inspired by a distant cataclysm the winds came rolling ahead of the storm and with them came the seas. The yawl of the PROTECTION left her stern and headed toward the ARAB. Nine of her crew were plucked from the hull and taken to the tug. Only one man, William Kelly, was missing. Kelly, an engineer, had been desperately attempting to start the port pump when the ARAB rolled. The heavy pumping machinery ripped loose and tumbled over the side taking Kelly with it to the bottom of Lake Michigan.

Having the winds and seas at her heels the H.C. AKE-LEY made substantial headway, and just before nine o'clock Sunday morning she was already abeam of Milwaukee. Cook John Babbitt had served another of his best Sunday breakfasts and cabin-boy William Stanley was busy cleaning the mess. Meanwhile second cook Robert W. Mack busied himself with baked goods; it all seemed to be a stormy routine morning aboard the steamer. That was when the disabled tug PROTECTION was sighted ahead rolling violently in the seas. Easing up to the tug, the crew of the AKELEY tossed a line and waiting hands quickly pulled a towing hawser over. With no small sense of relief the tug PROTECTION was taken in tow of the AKELEY. Apparently the tug and her people had been rescued, and with what appeared to be relative ease. Such an impression was a grave misunderstanding because the worst of what the lake had to offer was yet to be seen. What the two boats were now sailing into was an arctic hurricane complete with an eye!

The brunt of the storm would pass directly over Lake Superior where the eye of the storm showed all of the classic signs of a hurricane. Witnesses reported that as the eye passed the winds calmed and the skies cleared. Then the winds suddenly came back with greater intensity from the southwest. The big passenger propeller MANISTEE was obliterated on Superior when her master, Captain John McKay was suckered out of port by the passing eye. All of this conflagration took place four days after the leading edge of the storm found the AKELEY and PROTECTION. Shortly after taking the crippled tug in tow Captain Stretch's H.C. AKELEY was overtaken by the icy hurricane's leading disturbance. The winds unexpectedly swung from out of the north northwest and roared a full gale.

Suddenly, Captain Stretch found himself hauling directly into the most foul blow that he had ever seen, and it was rapidly getting worse. That once-helpful following sea was given no time to become confused. It simply rose up before the wind in giant frigid waves. It was all that could be done just to keep the AKELEY headed into the wind as the seas loomed ahead and broke green over the steamer's bow rail. Having the powerless tug in tow tended to pull the steamer off of her course, forcing wheelsman John Sinclair to lead the wind gusts by spinning her wheel. Nearly two stories tall, the boat's giant oak rudder worked heavily in command of the steering gear. The combination of the laboring steamer and the loads imposed on the rudder soon reached their limit.

In answer to a particular gust of wind and a faceless wave the AKELEY's wheel spun, useless, in the wheelsman's hands. Agonizingly, the steamer fell from her course and into the sea trough. The tug was immediately cut loose and left to her own devices as the crew of the AKELEY reacted to save their own boat. By this time the snow was falling so heavily that the tug was swallowed from sight shortly after the line was axed. Chief Driscoll and his second engineer James Connell quickly made their way to the "tween-decks" area at the steamer's stern where her steering tiller was swung. There they found the gears and cast workings shattered and damaged to the point where repair was out of the question. As the two engineers crawled about in the dark recesses of the steamer's heels, the oak decking began to roll beneath them in a fearful manner. Before word could be sent forward as to the condition of the steering gear, Captain Stretch set the boat's storm sail in an effort to pull her from the troughs. His effort was thwarted as the winds blasted the canvas to rags before the boat could change her posture by as much as a degree. Now the gale held the AKELEY tightly in its clutches nearly in the middle of Lake Michigan's expanse and, unknown to everyone but us, the storm had seven more days to blow.

Twisting and flexing with the roll of every wave, the steamer's oak timbers moaned loudly. Helpless as a log, she wallowed at one moment atop a giant sea and next deep in the valley of doom between. Snow pelted with the wind so thick that at times it was hard to see the stern from the pilothouse, but she still had steam and with that—heat and hope. If Chief Driscoll could just get her rudder-post rigged with a temporary tiller, she might yet be saved. As a plan of attack was being hatched, the lake dealt another card. The rolling motion of the AKELEY shifted her corn cargo giving her a pronounced list and allowing the waves to sweep the deck to cause an even greater rolling of the boat. It was the twisting of her hull that caused Chief Driscoll's next headache. So radical had been the flexing of the wooden vessel that the steel machinery could not keep up. At about half past 10 p.m. a defining roar accompanied a billow of steam as the "pony-feed" pipe was ripped from the port boiler. Engineers Driscoll and Connell fought their way through the scalding cloud to the heart of the AKELEY's latest problem. Not only did she blow off steam from the compromised fitting, but water to the port boiler was interrupted. Should the boiler run out of water, the resulting explosion would blast the AKELEY into kindling.

There was no time to cool the well-stoked fires beneath the boiler, so Chief Driscoll reckoned that he could hold water in the port boiler simply by changing the throttle from right to left. The answer was not that simple. The port boiler continued to hemorrhage. An entangled maze of pipes, tubes, valves, gauges, shafts, gears and ducts has

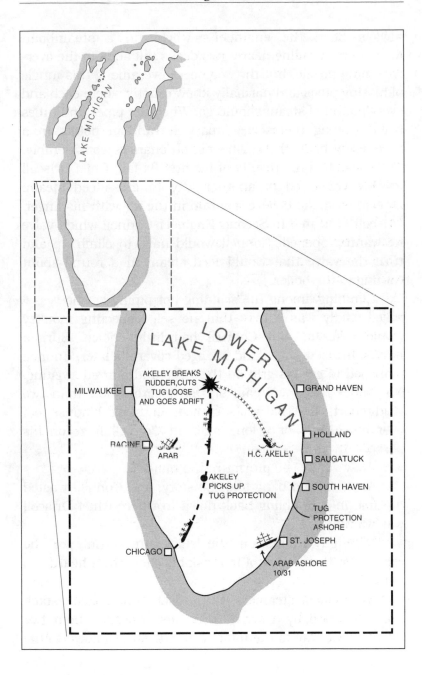

always been the engineer's world on a steamboat. Machinery standing nearly two decks tall adds to the overwhelming puzzle, but the engineers live among this jungle of hissing pipes and normally know exactly where each and every pound of steam should go. When the pipes and tubes begin ripping themselves apart at random points in a foundering boat, the engineer's job changes considerably. As he watched the results of his first fix fail, Chief Driscoll quickly conceived of another way to cross-feed steam. Drawing a make-believe diagram in the air with his finger, Driscoll indicated to Second Engineer Connell which valve he wanted opened. Connell would have to climb up and turn the valve that would feed steam in a round-about routing to the boiler.

Climbing among the scalding hot piping as the vessel rolled wildly was a task that no self-respecting monkey would take on, but Connell had little choice. Burned hands, bruised knees and snagged coveralls later, Connell managed to get his grip on the valve and started twisting. No sooner had the steam started to cross-flow than two loud reports, like rifle shots, came from the deck house roof over his head. For a long moment Connell froze on his perch.

"Now what?" he murmured to himself.

Another loud bang told the story, and Connell wasted no time in scrambling back down to where Chief Driscoll was waiting.

"The guy-chains on the stack are lettin' go," he reported with no attempt to mask his concern, "I heard 'em partin'"

As on most steamers, the AKELEY's tall smokestack was supported by a series of chains attached about two thirds of the way to the top and tightly strung down to the deckhouse roof. These guy-chains supported the stack which was nothing more than a long pipe stood on end over the boiler. With the groan of a steel tree falling, the AKELEY's funnel slowly toppled. At 11:30 Sunday evening the smokestack rolled over the side and sank to the sandy bottom of Lake Michigan. Now, no draft could be formed and the AKELEY's fires and steam pressure died together— the boat was completely helpless. Pitching and groaning as she wallowed in the waves, the men of the battered steamer no longer asked if she would go down; they all knew it was a question of when the end would come. Ice formed in the rigging and gray seas came foaming aboard to frolic on the decks in a stormy celebration of Lake Michigan's next prize. Like a cat with a bug the lake wanted to play with the AKE-LEY—until it was dead.

As the night dragged on the unending waves came aboard to smash doors and slap at the windows. The crew forward were isolated from those aft by an impassable expanse of swirling ice water and a blinding curtain of snow. As if the lake had not dispensed enough woe on the beaten lakeboat, it now sent a wave to pluck away one of the AKELEY's two lifeboats. By daylight the helpless laker had drifted about 40 miles to the south southeast, but was still nearly in the middle of the lake.

Noon Monday brought signs that the end was very near. The rolling of the boat grew lazy and it appeared as if her seams were giving way. Feeling that he was about as close to land as he would get while still afloat, Captain Stretch played his only remaining card in the stormy game. With orders to heave the anchor deckhands Crawford, Murray, Kurts and Smith went to the cat. Putting the massive stock anchor over the side would be no easy task with towering seas exploding over the bow. Choreographing

their moves with the coming of each wave the team suc-
ceeded in their desperate chore and the hook went over.
Taking the greatest of care Mate Kingston paid out the
chain allowing the anchor to bite without the chain parting.
As her chain pulled taut the AKELEY's bow was brought
head to the seas, but now the waves no longer simply
climbed aboard. With the force of dynamite the combers
exploded against the bow throwing spray high into the air.
Just how much of this pounding the already tender boat
could take, no one could tell.

During a time when the prevailing weather had forced
nearly every vesselman from the lake Captain David Miller
was running the schooner DRIVER among the gale winds
bound from Chicago to Grand Haven. The storm had
brought him to a point about 15 miles southwest of
Holland, Michigan at about half past one p.m. on Monday,
November 12, 1883. It was there and then that his path
entangled with that of the AKELEY. Through the snow and
seas the crew of the DRIVER spotted the disabled steamer.
At about the same time, those aboard the AKELEY saw the
approaching schooner and a crew once united in survival
suddenly divided in their decision as to how to meet their
fate. Some were of the opinion that the steamer would not
last another moment and that the only option was to take
to the lifeboat and escape. They would be forced to take
their chances in the gray seas until the DRIVER could come
near and pull them one-by-one to safety. Others of the crew
felt that their best bet would be to stay aboard the AKELEY
until the DRIVER could come along side. Such was the
opinion of Captain Stretch. Little discussion took place, but
Second Mate Paulson expressed the opinion that he and
some others wanted to take to the remaining yawl.

"All right then," the captain said resignedly, "go aft and look out for yourselves."

Mustering at the lifeboat davits, Chief Driscoll, Second Engineer Connell, Mate Paulson, wheelsmen Martin and Sinclair, firemen Sward and Kelly, oiler McDernott, watchman Lark, deckhands Crawford and Murray and second steward Mack all prepared to abandon the AKELEY. In short order the dozen expatriates of the H.C. AKELEY were drifting clear of their sinking boat. At the bow Captain Stretch was kept company by Mate Kingston as well as the two new deckhands from Chicago, Kurts and Smith. Additionally, cook John Babbitt and cabin boy Willie Stanley had elected not to take to the lifeboat and remained aboard the AKELEY. As the DRIVER drew near its crew watched the desperate decision unfold. Now all that Captain Miller had to do was get there in time and decide which group to rescue first.

Before Captain Miller could make any judgment, the H.C. AKELEY made the decision for him. Right in front of the disbelieving eyes of everyone on the scene, the one time pride of Grand Haven suddenly foundered and took all aboard with her. Now the DRIVER's mission was clear—rescue those in the lifeboat. The problem was that the tiny yawl was often lost among the tall waves and the on-going snow squalls. Searching with a sailing vessel in the middle of one of the worst gales in Great Lakes history was no easy matter. Through the schooner's rigging the sailors scurried as Captain Miller took the wheel himself and the vessel worked through the tempest. Darkness began to settle in and everyone knew too well that once the night swallowed the yawl, none of the AKELEY's people would come off of the lake alive.

While the last act of the AKELEY's drama was being played in the snowy distance off Saugatuck, local residents there had telegraphed St. Joseph to summon Captain Stevens and the lifesavers. Their call was not in concern for the AKELEY; she was out of sight over the horizon and behind a 15 mile thick curtain of snow. The call was for the lifesavers to come to the rescue of the tug PROTECTION which had been blown ashore at eight o'clock Monday morning just one half mile south of Saugatuck. The crew had lashed an oar to the bow with a sheet of awning tied upon it as a flag of distress. Originally the lifesavers at Grand Haven had been telegraphed, but they were away from their station on another rescue. So the St. Joseph lifesavers—some sixty miles distant—were summoned. Boarding their gear onto the Chicago and West Michigan Railway, the lifesavers sped toward the site of the PROTECTION's distress. At three o'clock in the afternoon the train came to the village of Richmond and the lifesavers were transferred to the tug GANGES and steamed down the Kalamazoo River and toward Lake Michigan. So shallow was the river in spots, that the tug repeatedly smacked bottom. At half past five Monday evening the storm warriors arrived and went to battle over the lives of those aboard the PROTECTION. Using the Lyle gun, a line was eventually shot aboard the tug, a breeches buoy rigged and an interesting reunion begun. The St. Joseph lifesavers found themselves again entangled with the crew of the schooner ARAB that they had rescued just 14 days earlier only this time they were coming from the schooner's tug. One by one familiar faces were seen coming across in the breeches buoy as the lifesavers managed to rescue the crew of the ARAB twice in just two weeks.

At 11:30 Monday evening, as the tug's crew as well as the survivors of the ARAB gathered on the storm-raked beach, the lifesavers received another call. This one puzzled all of the castaways. The message was from Captain Robbins of the Grand Haven lifesaving station requesting assistance with an urgent rescue. According to the telegram the lifesavers were requested to move to a position just over nine miles south of Grand Haven in order to assist in effecting the rescue of the crew of the schooner ARAB which, it was reported, had blown ashore at that point. As Captain Stevens read the telegram aloud, one of the ARAB's shipwrecked sailors looked over his shoulder,

"But..." the drenched crewman insisted, "...we're the crew of the ARAB."

Meanwhile in the distance out on Lake Michigan— using every bit of skill at his disposal, Captain Miller had managed to find the AKELEY's lifeboat. No matter how well he maneuvered the schooner, however, he found that the winds would not allow him to come within reach of the lifeboat. The night was quickly closing upon the scene and would certainly bring with it the end of all aboard the yawl. With this in mind, Daniel F. Miller, Captain Miller's brother and also the DRIVER's First Mate, and Patrick II. Daly conceived a desperate plan to save the castaways. They volunteered to take the DRIVER's yawl with a line attached and drift over to the floundering lifeboat. Once attached to the AKELEY's yawl, all would be hauled back to the DRIVER and safety. Considering the situation, such a venture was madness, but there was no debate. With fellow mariners on the brink of an icy doom the two crewmen did not give a second thought—they simply went to the rescue. Pitched and tossed like a paper cup, the DRIVER's yawl and its two occupants were also often lost from sight as they worked toward the AKELEY's people. The line was paid out from the schooner as benumbed and callused hands gripped it, holding 14 lives at its end. Snow blasted from the low gray clouds and the tops of the whitecaps were ripped by the wind, but the yawl managed to reach the lifeboat and the line was made secure. Thankfully, this particular thread in the AKELEY's saga did not become entangled—hand over hand the DRIVER's crew pulled their shipmates and the survivors of the AKELEY from the clutches of Lake Michigan.

There was no chance to make the ports on the Michigan shore, so once the survivors were aboard, the DRIVER headed to Chicago. For this selfless act of bravery, on June 2, 1885, Daniel Miller and Patrick Daly were awarded gold medals for distinguished service in the saving of life from the United States lifesaving service. Silver medals were awarded to Captain David Miller. Charles Miller and C.S. Pertekson were the rest of the crew of the DRIVER.

By Tuesday morning reports were in indicating that a black hulled schooner with red cabins was sunken off Racine—apparently the ARAB. If that was so, then who was ashore below Grand Haven? At dawn, when the lifesavers went to work on the stranded schooner this thread of the entanglement was untied. The wrecked schooner was the CLARA PARKER and her crew were more than happy to finally see the lifesavers. She had been pounced upon by the gale when just off of Big Sable Point at about the same time the AKELEY was assaulted. So sudden had been the wind shift that most of the boat's canvas was blown out and she was forced to turn and run with what sail remained. After being beaten for more than a day, she started to spring her butts and leak badly. Captain Andrew

Lewis did the only thing he could. He turned her for shore and beached her. His action meant the end of the PARKER but allowed for all of her crew to be rescued by the life-savers.

Most Great Lakes maritime buffs will tell you that the worst storm in lakes history was the "Great Storm of 1913" where over a three-day period, 12 big lakers were wrecked and 25 others tossed ashore. Between 250 to 300 mariners were killed. So far we have viewed the storm of 1883 through a key-hole focused on a few vessels that found their fates peculiarly entangled. Stepping back we can see the over-all view of a storm that had many of the characteristics of the 1913 storm, but blew twice as long. In the worst upheaval since 1867, 23 vessels, (4 steamers and 19 schooners) were totally wrecked and another 23 lakers, (6 steamers, 16 schooners and 1 tug) were tossed ashore and later returned to service. The winds of the 1883 storm did not start to subside until the 17th of November, meaning the storm's duration was just over six days. By the 21st a peculiar calm settled over the lakes and a spooky fog hung over many of the waterways. The ARAB was left on the bottom about 35 miles off Racine. Of the AKELEY's crew, all of those who elected to stay with Captain Stretch perished with the steamer. To this day the AKELEY herself rests in Lake Michigan somewhere to the west, northwest of Saugatuck, anchored to the sandy bottom by about a hundred yards of chain.

This single storm left behind hundreds of stories, just like this one, many of which are yet to be written. It also left behind one final coincidence. On the same day that saw Captain Stretch's ghostly appearance in the surf off Saugatuck, there was a startling discovery in Muskegon, Michigan. At nine o'clock in the morning a worker at the

Davies Brothers lumber mill found that a fire had broken out among one of the piles of cut lumber. Immediately the alarm went out but it was already too late. Fanned by the hurricane winds, the fire proceeded to consume 200,000 board-feet of fine lumber. Through the use of the best fire-fighting equipment available in 1883 at Muskegon, Michigan—the hand-pumped hose, horse-drawn steam pumper and bucket brigade—the blaze was brought under control after an 11 and one half hour battle. The obliterated lumber was owned by Mr. H.C. Akeley's Roscommon Lumber Company of Grand Haven. For Mr. Akeley it had been a very bad week to say the least.

Over the years much has been written concerning the players in this narrative and sorting out the events was no easy matter. The AKELEY's name, for example, can be found spelled as "Akley," "Akely," "Ackley" and even (with some real digging) "A. Keley." In order to untie this strand of the entanglement the key was to find out more about the man for whom the boat had been named, "the honorable Healy C. Akeley." Fortunately, there was far more information available on Mr. Akeley than had been written about his namesake vessel, including the proper spelling of his name. Finding the proper spelling of the AKELEY's master's name was quite another matter. Captain Stretch's name can also be found as "Strech" and "Streck" depending on where you look. For this story the spelling as "Stretch" was taken from what the author considers to be a good source of the AKELEY's era, an 1883 painting of the wreck of the vessel done by William Jorgerson in Chicago. But, even this string remains slightly entangled because on the painting the vessel's name is misspelled "Akley." Then there is at least one account of the events that lists the wrecks of the PROTECTION and CLARA PARKER two days apart. To

CAPTION ON OLD PRINT READS:

Steam Barge H.C. AKLEY of Grand Haven, Michigan
Capt. Ed Stretch, Commander
Foundered off Saugatuck, Michigan, November 13, 1893;
Captain and five men drowned.

L.W. FELT, Photographer

untangle this a number of different sources were used, most prominently the United States Life-Saving Service's "...Table of Wrecks..." all of which listed these events as given here. The only remaining loose end to this entanglement is the location of the AKELEY herself. Certainly the AKELEY rests on the bottom of Lake Michigan with her anchor chain paid out waiting to be found. Or, with the growing popularity of research diving, has already been found with her location either being kept secret or put aside as insignificant. At least now there is a story to aid in the unwinding of the H.C. AKELEY's entanglements. Once more the sleuthing into a long forgotten adventure on the lakes opens questions that we can not readily solve here. Perhaps the answer rests in a scratchy spool of microfilm at Racine, or at the bottom of Lake Michigan. It is just the type of highly obscure entanglement that "puts the hook in us." It is the final thread in the entangled tale of the wreck of the H.C. AKELEY.

Through the Cracks in History

*T*hermometers mounted in the shade read 95 degrees as the sun hovered in the hazy sky over the port city of Bay City, Michigan. Almost everywhere around the city a holiday atmosphere was in the air as throngs of residents, garbed in their best summer fashions, headed toward the Saginaw River. Extra cars were added to the electric trolleys, particularly on the Salzburg line which lead to the West Bay City shipyard of James Davidson. This event was far more than simply another birth of one of Captain Davidson's oak lakeboats, and a special air of excitement seemed to loft around the city. The whole day seemed bigger and much more delightful than the launchings of the CITY OF VENICE, CITY OF GENOA and CITY OF NAPLES, the previous summer—and for good reason. It was the last Saturday of July, 1893 and the crowd was gathering to watch the launching of the largest wooden steamship in the world.

Every ten minutes a trolley stopped and unloaded another bunch of festive passengers. Soon the shipyard was a mass of white cotton hats and bright parasols intermixed with gray suits and bowler hats. A uniformed band played an all-day concert as a part of the celebration and among the musical brass tones the lemonade and iced tea flowed in generous quantities. Across the river at Wenona Beach, and overshadowing the colorful banners that were draped from every overhang at the Davidson yard, was a towering hot air balloon manned by the famous aeronaut

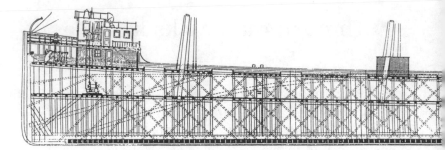

*Longitudinal section of the wooden lake steamship THOMAS
CRANAGE, built by Thomas Davidson, Bay City, Michigan.*
Marine Engineering Drawing, 1898

"Professor Hogan." Standing on his soapbox the daring
aeronaut bellowed toward the milling crowd that at four
o'clock in the afternoon he would make his ascension to the
dizzying altitude of 2,000 feet. Boisterously he added that
he fully expected to one day be killed while up in the air and
that his only hope was to be high enough so as to die
instantly in the inevitable mishap. Many of the listeners
gasped with shock at the daring aeronaut's taunt with
death, and later returned to plunk their money down so as
to get a good look at the ascension. On both banks of the
Saginaw River, the setting for the big steamer's launching
rivaled the Fourth of July festivities.

Poised on the launching ways at Davidson's boat yard
was the steamer THOMAS CRANAGE, sporting three tall
masts with a giant American flag waving elegantly from the
top of the after most spar. Wobbling up the ladders and
planks that formed the scaffold at the steamer's beam, a
small parade of V.I.P.s climbed toward the CRANAGE's
deck. Lead by Captain J.S. McNeill, the line of dignitaries

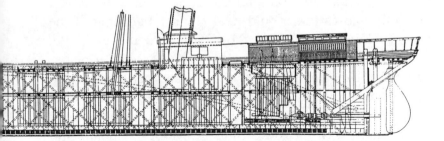

This detailed cross-section shows many of the fascinating features of the THOMAS CRANAGE—including the diagonal steel cross-strapping.

consisted of Thomas Cranage, J. Will McGraw, H.H. Norrington, S.P. Cranage, and Edward Smith, all of whom were to be aboard the colossal oak laker as she made her first meeting with fresh water. Waiting at the rail was Chief Jenkins, the CRANAGE's engineer. Both he and Captain McNeil would guide the cartel of owners on their pre launching tour of the new laker.

Starting in the forward quarters, the V.I.P.s were shown the officer and guest accommodations. All of the forward rooms were paneled in mahogany, trimmed in polished oak, and sported elegant furnishings and tall mirrors. The Master's quarters, the guest stateroom and a parlor-type sitting room were all located on the Texas deck, with the rest of the officers' accommodations being one deck below. The Texas deck was not only accessible at the bulkhead, but also via two companionways that ran along the boat's beam. As her investors strolled around her spanking-new quarters, they could not help but be impressed by fixtures that would make comfortable the most prominent of lumber barons.

Curving with grace, the CRANAGE's hull stretched 325 feet in overall length and a fat 43 feet in beam with 23 feet of depth, figures that would rival any steel steamer of the day. Timbers of five inches by 12 inches made up the CRANAGE's bottom and sides, with the exception of her garbord strakes and the timbers where her bottom rounded upward to her beam, which were made up of planking of six inches in thickness. Spar decking was of two shelves, seven inches apart with the lower timbers five by 11 inches and the upper shelf three by five inches. When looking at a cross section of the CRANAGE's hull, it was apparent that she was somewhat "double bottomed" with a space between her outer hull and inner structure that ranged from a maximum of 17 inches at her keel to about six inches at her rail. Nine hatches of seven feet by 28 feet on centers of 24 feet were cut into the steamer's spar deck with combings that were built up only eight inches above the deck. Davidson had used the finest Michigan white oak to form the entire vessel with the exception of the decking for which he employed the state's fragrant white pine.

Amidships on the CRANAGE's spar deck a doghouse of sorts was placed and would be the quarters for the firemen and deckhands as well as being the storage area for the boat's lamps. Just forward of the boat's after cabin sat the only steel structure on the vessel, her boiler house. Observing that many wooden steamers were consumed by fires that were literally, "sparked" by their own steam plants, Captain Davidson decided to separate the boiler works of his boats by encasing them in a housing of number 10 steel. Aft of the boiler house was the number nine cargo hatch followed by the aft deck-house which contained the galley and dining room. Overall, the CRANAGE

On a sweltering summer day, the THOMAS CRANAGE is launched.

was by far the most elegant and the most grand wooden steamer on the Great Lakes as well as the world.

As the hour of four o'clock passed on that muggy after-noon, the Davidson yard workers took their sledge ham-mers in hand and made their way into the launching ways beneath the CRANAGE. At twenty minutes past four, the last wedge was driven and hull number 57 slid sideways into the narrow slip adjacent to her launching ways. The splash of the steamer's birth turned the rude water into a tremendous white billow as nearly 10,000 Bay City resi-dents looked on. A cheer came up from both sides of the Saginaw River, Professor Hogan waved from his balloon and the hatted ladies gasped as the THOMAS CRANAGE rocked to a stop. Aboard the hatchling oak giant the V.I.P.s gave a relieved belly laugh, slapped one another on the back and lit up cigars. Through the day the celebrating would continue with the people of importance being entertained at selected lumber barons' mansions and those of labor pressing into assorted stuffy taverns. Doubtless, more than a few of the laboring class men would awake the next day in the care of the local constable due to an excess of indulgence. Boat launchings were a glorious affair in this era, and on extremely hot summer days it was just too easy to be overtaken by strong drink in the shadow of months of hard labor finally gone afloat.

Following abbreviated sea trials on Saginaw Bay, the largest wooden vessel on the lakes was ready to go to work. Only a few days were spent tied to the pier at the Davidson yard before the CRANAGE was on her way to haul her first cargo. As the steamer's bow was pointed toward the expansion of Saginaw Bay, Captain McNeill called down through the speaking tube to Chief Jenkins. Upon the order to "let her go," the chief ran her steam pressure up to 160 pounds and the CRANAGE started to make a wake. Her fore and aft triple expansion engine with cylinders of 20, 33 and 54 inch diameters with a 42 inch stroke would drive the wooden beast across the lake surface at 14 miles per hour when she was running light with steam up to 160. A cargo of 110,000 bushels of wheat was waiting in a Chicago elevator for the CRANAGE, and the maiden vessel would make good time in getting to it. From the shore of Saginaw Bay the fine lines of the steamer soon faded into a silhouette as she moved off onto the hazy summer, indeed she was off to a good start.

Just over 100 years after her birth, somewhat of a bewilderment hangs over the THOMAS CRANAGE and her final dispatch. There are the yellowing photos of the giant wooden laker impaled on a submerged reef and the same basic paragraph repeated time after time in the newspapers of various port cities supposedly accounting the event. "The steamer THOMAS CRANAGE with grain from Duluth to Tiffin has run aground in Georgian Bay..." would be a good paraphrase for such, "...her bow is out 6 feet and it is thought that she will be a total wreck." Again and again the same basic account is found passed by wire service from one newspaper to another. Spooling through the microfilm time-machine the researcher will zoom ahead nearly a month to another series of dittoed news-bites that simply state the vessel as "given up for lost" or "gone to pieces." End of the story, perhaps not—for some reason the THOMAS CRANAGE seems to simply drop from the pages of history nearly as soon as she went on the rocks and information concerning her fate becomes suspiciously scarce, redundant or at the same time, conflicting. Contact with the Transport Safety Board of Canada returns a terse response which states flatly that "...we are advised that no records exist of such an occurrence." Normally, in this era the loss of a vessel such as the CRANAGE would produce as a by-product, reams of information. There is usually the eyewitness account of the master, mate, owner, or crewmember detailing the event, but in the case of the CRANAGE the marine news columns are abnormally empty. Even records of vessels' movements immediately prior to her entanglement are unusually devoid of her name at the times when she should be listed. She is absent from both the upbound and downbound passages at the Soo, and likewise is missing from the passages in and out of Duluth in the same time-frame. Any vessel hauling a cargo between Duluth and Tiffin must pass through the locks at

Seen here passing downbound at the Soo, the THOMAS CRANAGE was the largest wooden steamer on the lakes.

the Soo, and should have been noted by the ship reporter. But the passages are devoid of the CRANAGE's name. She seems to simply pop up in the marine columns as unexpectedly as she grounded. No matter how one looks at it the question appears to form—just what did happen to the THOMAS CRANAGE?

Using what circumstantial evidence can be found, we can synthesize a probable chain of events. This, however, only creates more questions. Additionally, we must keep in mind that without the benefit of first-hand written accounts there can only be conjecture as to the exact events. Most importantly, however, is that until this text, every book, report, historic listing and newspaper account says that the THOMAS CRANAGE was bound from Duluth to Tiffin... and they are all wrong!

Perhaps no one took particular notice as the haze of grain-dust began to dissolve around the Chicago elevator and the chutes were pulled back. Squatting below the elevator, the massive wooden form of the sovereign of the white oak oreboats was now stuffed with oats. One at a time the hatch-planks of the THOMAS CRANAGE were slapped across the openings to her hold by one group of her crew as others worked at her lines in preparation for departure. It had been 18 years since that humid July day when she first tasted fresh water and much had changed in the Great Lakes maritime universe. Steel-hulled lakers had taken over the job of hauling the ore from the head of the lakes to the blast furnaces on the shores of the lower lake ports. Some of these steel oreboats were now exceeding 600 feet in length and 15,000 tons in capacity. Such competition relegated the wooden hulls to other tasks, and many of the Davidson boats found profit and efficiency in the hauling of grain.

September of 1911 was just beginning to see the full weight of the annual fall grain rush and the CRANAGE's burden was bound for the port of Tiffin, Ontario at the southern tip of Georgian Bay, adjacent to the famed port city of Midland. Looking at the steamer's mighty oak bow, the casual boat watcher would have thought she had seen better days. It was, however, still easy for the common observer to be overcome by the laker's size. Even when fully packed with cargo, the CRANAGE loomed at the dockside, dwarfing the men who worked her lines. Steam hissed from vents and the muffled sounds of the equipment used to work her occasionally resounded from deep within the hull. Although surpassed in size and capacity by her steel kin, she was no less the mighty oak sea-monster than she had been on launching day.

Arriving without cargo on September 22nd, the CRAN-
AGE took just under 24 hours to load and around one
o'clock on the morning of the 23rd was ready to head off for
Ontario. With her screw churning mud from the bottom,
the CRANAGE shuddered as Captain L.H. Powell began to
slowly back from the slip. At her launch, Captain Davidson
had boasted that the CRANAGE could do 14 miles per hour,
but in reality her loaded speed was right around 12 miles
per hour. Nosing onto the open lake, the boat and crew
would spend the next 27 hours plowing up Lake Michigan.
After passing through the Straits of Mackinac and entering
upper Lake Huron, the CRANAGE's crew would initially
wheel the boat onto an east, southeast course for just
under seven hours bringing the steamer below Great Duck
Island. From a point 10 miles south, southwest of the
island, the heading would be directed slightly more to the
north on a course of 102 and three quarter degrees for the
61 and one quarter mile haul to the entrance of Georgian
Bay nearly due west of Cove Island. This, however was the
easy navigation—the hard part was yet to come.

Georgian Bay is a place poorly named, as it is much
more like another great lake than a simple bay. In many
places the water is deeper than the greatest depth of Lake
Erie. In fact, if the North Channel is taken into account,
Georgian Bay is very close to the area taken up by Erie.
North Channel included, the bay is over 240 miles long and
more than 50 miles wide. To make matters worse the bay
is ringed with scores of islands of all sizes from rock out-
crops to mountain-like isles carpeted with thick forests.
The entire bay as well as its surrounding shoreline is
Canadian territory and even in modern times consists of
some of the most isolated and rugged real-estate on the

Great Lakes. It is a navigation nightmare that does not know the difference between modern times and 1911.

Threading the CRANAGE past Cove Island and through the rocky shoals that surround the entrance to Georgian Bay, Captain Powell felt his way toward open water. As best can be calculated it was just about dinner time on September 24th, 1911 when the largest wooden steamer on the lakes threaded her way into the bay with Captain Powell checking her back to half speed. Once passing Bear's Rump Island he would shout down the speaking tube to open her throttle once again and direct his boat on a 101 degree heading that would bring him within spitting distance of the Cabot Head light. Then assuming a 113 degree course, there were 46 miles of deep water ahead before the steamer would come upon the Western Islands and the Western Island lighthouse. Like many things on the bay of misnomer, the "Western Islands" were hardly that at all and appear to have been ill-named. Located on the south eastern tip of the bay, they are more like a group of large ice-age rock deposits than islands. The fact is that there are three groups of rocks and the western most of these has the lighthouse planted upon it—hence the name. After passing the Western Island light, there would be just over a dozen miles to run before Hope Island would be passed off of the starboard rail. With the hard part behind, an even more challenging part was now at hand.

If all went well, upon passing Hope Island, a turn of six degrees more to the south on the CRANAGE's compass would set Captain Powell up for a eight and one half mile run into the zigzag passage toward Tiffin. First Giants Tomb would pass on the port then a gap of just 200 feet wide in the shallows followed by the squeeze between

Pinery Point and Beausoleil Island followed by Dalton Point and finally the bay off the port of Midland and the rail-head to Tiffin. Much the same as every other master who sails the bay, Captain Powell would rightfully have considered this part of the trip to contain the greatest hazard. He was wrong.

Sometime after passing the Cabot Head light, and with the expanse of Georgian Bay stretching beyond her steering pole, the THOMAS CRANAGE strayed from her course. The night was calm and the weather was fair; it was perfect weather for sailing as the steamer left Cabot Head in her wake. Five and one half hours later the oak timbers of the steamer's bow slammed into the submerged boulders of Watcher Reef. Although no written records can be found to pinpoint the exact time, the best time-speed-distance calculations that can be done indicate that she impacted the reef around half past one o'clock on Monday morning the 25th day of September, 1911. So severe was the impalement that the big steamer came to a stop with her bow six feet out of the water. Exactly when and how the boat came off track was never recorded and is likely lost forever, but there are several probable causes that we can look at. From September 23rd through the 26th, the weather in the area saw a steady barometer and only a few localized autumn showers. This eliminates wind and wave as the possible cause of the grounding and leads to a number of other probable causes.

The first possible explanation is simple compass error. From the Cabot Head light the safe passage course is 113 degrees, but an error of just three degrees north would run the boat directly onto the unmarked reef. Considering that compass equipment was under-inspected in this era, such a tiny but critical error seems plausible. Additionally, there

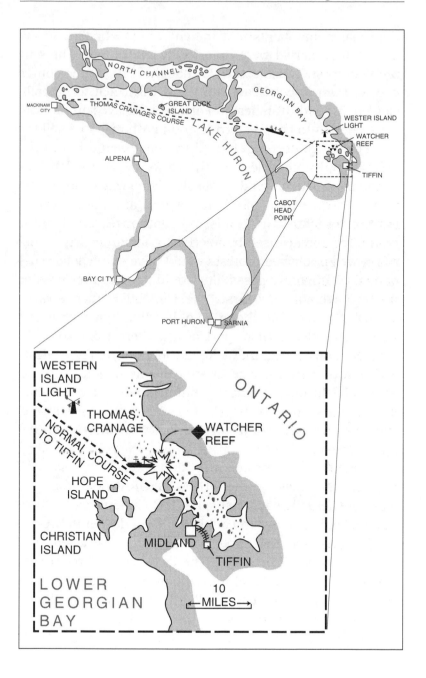

were many complaints that the charts of Canadian waters in this time period were notoriously inaccurate. The only problem in such conjecture is that the 110 degree course needed from Cabot Head to put the CRANAGE on a collision course with Watcher Reef also would have run the boat close enough to the Western Island lighthouse to smell the keeper's coffee brewing. Indeed the boat would have been only a few hundred feet off the rocks below the Western Island light. There would be absolutely no way to stray onto the 110 degree course for Watcher Reef and not be alerted to the error by the Western Island lighthouse. And, had the grounding been caused by inferior Canadian charts a chorus of well published protests would have surely followed—none did. The other possibility would be that after passing Western Island, on course, the CRANAGE then strayed toward the reef. This alteration of heading, however, would have required a turn to port of anywhere from 10 to 27 degrees! Considering that lake mariners normally navigate with the precision of one quarter of one degree, such an accidental heading change is unimaginable. The elimination of those possibilities leaves only one other line of explanation... deliberately or carelessly—someone ran her on the rocks.

The act of deliberately wrecking a vessel was so common in the days of the THOMAS CRANAGE that the mariners actually had a name for it. Commonly called "selling the boat," the action could vary from deliberately scuttling the vessel, to simply abandoning a stricken boat before all hope had run out. The term "selling" referred to the transfer of the vessel from the owner to the insurance underwriters, so when one "sells" the boat, they wreck it in order to gain the insurance value. In this same era, however, such a dirty deed carried a very heavy penalty—death!

Indeed it was considered a capital crime for a master of vessels to wreck his boat intentionally. With this in mind it is hard to imagine Captain Powell running his boat on the rocks so as to gain insurance money for the owners.

Then there is another possible explanation as to what would cause someone to steer the CRANAGE onto Watcher Reef—"demon rum." Drunkenness on duty was a very common problem in the era of the CRANAGE. In fact in modern times one of the items most restricted from being taken aboard a lakeboat is any type of alcohol—(a carry-over restriction from the drunken events of the early 1900s). It is quite possible that both parties on the pilothouse watch were intoxicated at the time of the grounding. Finally there is the possibility that those in charge of navigating the boat were simply asleep at the wheel. This was also a time when pilothouse officers and crews stood long boring watches with little to break the monotony. On a calm autumn morning it is not hard to picture the pilothouse watch dozing off. All of the above situations would go far toward explaining the unusual lack of information concerning the circumstances surrounding the grounding of the boat. In the vessel's home port of Bay City, S.P. Cranage was a powerful businessman and could easily mute information concerning the grounding. Most of the wire services tended to pick up such stories at a single source and in this case the Bay City papers would have been that point. If the grounding of the vessel had the potential to embarrass the owners, or worse, cost them an insurance claim due to negligence— Cranage would have been wise to put a gag on the outgoing information. Surely, the boat was in a location remote enough to allow only that information which Mr. Cranage saw fit to circulate.

Regrettably, there are some stories whose conclusions, even with the greatest of digging, we are unable to find, and this is one such tale. Likewise, the puzzle of the THOMAS CRANAGE's loss has not left behind enough pieces to allow us to solve it. Looking at the faded picture that is Great Lakes maritime history we begin to see that it is tattered and cracked in some areas. The section that is Georgian Bay in the autumn of 1911 seems to have the largest number of cracks, and the THOMAS CRANAGE seems to have slipped through them. Less than two decades after the throngs of Bay City residents cheered the launch of the largest and most grand of wooden steamers, she was abandoned to break up in the seasonal storms with little more than a newspaper paragraph or two and this story to mark her passing. At present, the remains of the biggest wooden ore steamer ever constructed lay scattered around Watcher Reef, resting in an obscurity so great that not even recreational scuba divers think to look for her. The CRANAGE fell through the cracks in our maritime legacy and ended up a long, long way from that celebrated day of her launching. Now the pure blue waters of Georgian Bay cover her as completely as S.P. Cranage covered the circumstances of her end, and neither is willing to give up the secret of her loss.

Ice Follies

*J*anuary and early February of 1899 had seen bru-
tally cold weather across all of the Great Lakes. On
Lake Michigan, in particular, the temperatures had
dropped as low as the negative 30s and refused to move
higher. From the Wisconsin shore to the dunes of the coast
of Michigan, the northern half of the mighty lake had frozen
into a solid sheet of ice the likes of which had not been seen
in a quarter of a century. From shore out several miles, the
ice had cracked and been forced by the winds to fold over
upon itself, time and again, forming "wind-rows" that could
thwart even the best icebreaking vessels. In every port,
lakeboats rested—locked in a frozen hibernation. Only the
onset of spring's warmth would free the sleeping fleet to
once again haul their cargoes around the fresh water seas.
For the time being, however, the stinging winter wind could
do little more than play through the idle rigging and taunt
the closed shutters. Winter lay-up is as much a part of
Great Lakes navigation as the changing of the seasons—it
comes and goes every year and always will.

Until the down-turn in lakes commerce of the 1980s,
Lake Michigan had traditionally been the primary exception
to the winter shutdown of shipping. Year-round navigation
appears to have had its birth on Lake Michigan in the late
1800s as combination package and passenger steamers
constructed with the winter ice in mind, called "break-
bulk" carriers, began engaging in winter operations as early
as 1875. The term "break-bulk" was an old railroad

moniker meaning that all of the cargo had to be loaded and unloaded by hand. In the case of this class of vessel such a chore was accomplished through the use of side-ports and gangplanks. Wooden break-bulkers challenged the winter ice, but all-season navigation was the exception rather than the rule. Winter navigation of Lake Michigan became an apparent necessity when the Toledo Ann Arbor & North Michigan Railroad stretched a steel railed artery from the Ohio rail mecca of Toledo through Ann Arbor, Michigan and north—northwest to the natural port of Frankfort, Michigan, a distance of 291 miles as the crow flies. From Frankfort, the rail cars were placed aboard specially designed ferry boats and hauled 58 miles due west to the tiny Wisconsin town of Algoma, (then called Ahnapee) or 70 plus miles southwest to Manitowoc, but most prominently to the port of Kewaunee some 61 miles across the lake. The whole concept was the brain-child of railroad baron and politician James M. Ashley. Lake Michigan's car ferry service came into its own as Mr. Ashley's spanking new ANN ARBOR No.1 went across on her initial voyage of November 24, 1892. Constructed of oak, the big ferryboat had her stern cut open to allow her to back into a slip so that rail cars could be rolled directly aboard. On her car deck, railroad rails were placed side by side making her a floating rail yard. When the ANN ARBOR No.1 was designed, it was conceived that she would have to break winter ice in order to operate year-round. For that reason, her oak hull was sheathed on the bottom with heavy steel plates to fight off the plate-glass sharp edges of Lake Michigan's frozen surface.

Mr. Ashley's scheme circumvented the roundabout route to the flourishing northwestern states that ran along the southern tip of Lake Michigan and through the railroad spider web that was Chicago. This corner-cut not only slashed miles off the rail distance to the west, but most importantly cut dollars off the cost. Such cost effective undertakings were critical after the great financial panic of 1892, a recession so devastating that immigrants from Europe actually packed their bags and sailed back to the "old country." Ashley's scheme took on the appearance of becoming an immediate success in the middle of one of the worst economic down-turns in U.S. history. A month after ANN ARBOR No.1 went to work, her sister boat—appropriately named ANN ARBOR No.2—came breaking her way through the December ice from Toledo to Frankfort. Both boats worked successfully through the winter and the fuse was ignited for a Lake Michigan cross-lake cargo boom that would work year-round. Curiously, a year after he lit the fuse of the cross-lake commerce to come, Ashley's railroad foundation crumbled as the Toledo Ann Arbor & North Michigan went bankrupt in the depression. The need to transport freight and railroad cars across the wintry expanse of frozen water would not crumble, however, and became so great that the development of vessels that could do battle with the ice evolved. Soon steel hulled monsters were crushing the ice on their way to profits, joining the wooden hulled package break-bulk carriers which, of course, had their hulls sheathed with steel plate to give them an advantage in the frozen fracas. Certainly, nothing could slow these creations of man's industrial revolution as they challenged the winter in quest of the dollar.

Enter the winter of 1899 when the winds came calling from the arctic and pounced upon the lakes, putting mankind back in his proper place and demonstrating that the use of his machines against the Great Lakes winter was nothing more than an icy folly. Thick ice and blizzards tor-

Seen here as the WISCONSIN, this vessel would later be re-named NAOMI and would play a major role in the saga of the JOHN V. MORAN.

tured Lake Michigan then refused to release their grip on the port towns around the lake until late April and early May. Yet, even the likes of the unmerciful winter could not deter the vessel magnates from their lust for profit. Among these barons of fresh water commerce was W.G. Watson, manager of vessels for shipping czar E.G. Crosby. With the 1898 season drawing to a close for most of the Great Lakes fleet, the Crosby interests began to set their sights on the coming of winter navigation. Slim profits could be made if the weather held and if expenditures were cut close enough. With that thought in mind, Mr. Crosby purchased the 214 foot wooden break-bulker JOHN V. MORAN for $35,000. The boat would be pressed into service on Lake Michigan, and hopefully pick up the slack for her iron-hulled fleetmate, the WISCONSIN. Forced into dry-dock for extensive overhaul, the 218 foot WISCONSIN was a combination passenger and package freighter and had been doing battle with winter ice since 1881. Once off the blocks, the WISCONSIN would be renamed NAOMI and join the MORAN, as well as her fleetmates NYACK and BOYCE, in gathering a handy profit for Mr. Watson and the Crosby Line. Unknown to vesselman Watson, most of these boats would soon be players in an icy drama that would be acted out in the darkest of 1899's winter...

Over the side of the Crosby Line's wooden steamer BOYCE went clerk William Hannrehan and First Mate E.J. Humphrey. Rung by rung, each of the men made their way down the ladder to the frozen surface of Lake Michigan. Stepping onto the ice, both men struggled to gain footing among the rip-rap of shattered plate ice that surrounded their vessel, locking it tightly in a frozen vise. A short distance away, wheelsman Thomas O'Day was making a similar trek from over the side of the steamer NYACK. Converging together the three men set off to hike across the ice to the Michigan shore and the city of Muskegon six miles in the distance. It was just after 10 o'clock on Sunday morning the 19th day of February, 1899 and all around the three venturers the wind howled almost to the point of drowning out conversation. The sky was crystal clear and the low angled sun shone brightly in complete conflict to the sub-zero temperature. Looking into the wind caused the eyes to tear, so the three men pressed ahead with their heads bowed against the cold, looking up only occasionally to assure that they were still headed in approximately the

From over the rail of the steamer NYACK, wheelsman Thomas O'Day climbed to Lake Michigan's frozen surface. There he joined William Hannrehan and E.J. Humphrey in their trek to the shore and a report of having been unable to find the JOHN V. MORAN.

right direction. They had not gone far before a weak spot in the ice was stumbled upon, and after breaking through and being soaked the trio retreated back to their respective steamers.

Watching this whole scene through our periscope into the past, we cannot help but ask what would compel these three men to depart the warmth of their ice-trapped vessels and embark on a treacherous hike of over a half dozen miles of frozen lake to a distant shore? The answer resides in the departure of the BOYCE and NYACK from Milwaukee six days earlier. Both vessels had departed in search of one of their fleetmates—the JOHN V. MORAN.

Ten days earlier, Captain George L. Thompson of the powerful carferry MUSKEGON was driving his charge toward her namesake city. It was four o'clock on Friday evening and with Lake Michigan's frozen surface crushing beneath the big ferryboat's bow like a giant sheet of glass, the MUSKEGON was making slow but steady progress. Running about 15 miles off Grand Haven, Captain Thompson found rough going, but it appeared as if the conditions were nothing that the MUSKEGON could not handle. In the distance, several other boats appeared to be doing battle with the ice, occasionally belching a mass of black coal-smoke from their stacks indicating another stab at the frozen water. One particular boat, however, did not show any signs of activity. In fact, as the MUSKEGON drew closer, it became apparent that not only was the boat dead in the ice, but appeared in a sinking condition. Figuring fellow mariners were in distress, Captain Thompson ordered his boat full ahead and began a desperate crunch toward the stricken laker. As the MUSKEGON closed in the scene took on a renewed urgency. The luckless boat in the distance had her bow raised high out of the water and her stern sunk down to the guard rails. Haste was definitely in order.

For the better part of the next hour the MUSKEGON chewed her way to the rescue until Captain Thompson had driven her to within 50 feet of the sinking boat. Tooting the MUSKEGON's whistle and shouting through his megaphone brought none of the sinking boat's crew on deck. She simply sat there—sinking. The whole scene must have been rather spooky, a dead ship with no crew, slipping through a hole in the ice. About three miles away, Captain Thompson's binoculars magnified the familiar outline of the steamer NAOMI, and her track appeared to lead away from the derelict. Figuring that the NAOMI had probably picked up the castaways, Captain Thompson ordered the MUSKEGON under way once more and began breaking his way eastward. Putting his pen to the log, the well-meaning master dutifully noted the time, position and the name of the sinking laker... JOHN V. MORAN.

One of twins, the MORAN was born in the boatyard of famed Bay City shipbuilder Frank W. Wheeler. She was nearly an exact replica to the EBER WARD which had floated from Wheeler's West Bay City yard only a short time before. Listed as official number 76748, the JOHN V. MORAN measured 214 feet in length, 32 feet in beam and 22 feet in depth. Formerly known only as hull number 44, the steamer was given her name and launched on the 16th day of August, 1888. The boat was constructed with the hauling of both package and bulk freight in mind. For that reason she had three loading hatches as well as two twin access hatches on her deck, and two side-ports on each of her beams. Within her cavernous 1,350 gross ton hold, more than 50,000 bushels of grain could be carried. When package freight was the order, some 100 rail carloads of goods could be carted across her gangplanks and packed in her belly. The MORAN's deck houses were arranged in the same manner as the passenger vessels of the day with the exception of her middle, where it appeared that Wheeler had changed his mind and elected to build a bulk carrier, thus leaving the mid-deck clear. In fact, both the WARD and MORAN were built in an era when the design of a "classic" lakeboat was still evolving. The two lakers and their near sister ship, WILLIAM H. STEVENS, were simply three steps on the road to the classic laker. In 1888 when the EBER WARD and JOHN V. MORAN went into service they were the state of the art work-horses on the Great Lakes.

Breaking Lake Michigan's ice, the railroad car ferries SHENANGO No.2 (left) and SHENANGO No. 1 (right) were able to work year-round. In 1898, the SHENANGO No. 2 was re-named MUSKEGON and found herself steaming toward the helpless JOHN V. MORAN through the winter ice.

Now in the frozen grasp of the winter of 1899, she was little more than a vacant wreck. To find how she came to this sorry position, we need to wind our time machine back just a bit farther.

Lunch had just finished in cook Oswald's galley and the ship's porter, J. Kampout, was busily clearing the dishes as the MORAN began to break away from her dock at Milwaukee. With a hold chock full of package freight and a large quantity of barreled flour, all appeared to be in readiness for the steamer's departure. The total burden would be 1,250 tons, a hefty winter load, but as most of her officers knew, it was still 400 tons short of the maximum that she had carried in the past. Making his way up to the pilothouse, First Mate Robert McKay reported to Captain John McLeod that the last of the load was aboard and the thick oak sideport doors were closed. The temperature was hovering at two dozen degrees below zero, and down in the hold the closing of the side-ports brought little relief from the cold as deckhands Thomas Sheon, James O'Neal, John Shea, James Hall, William Gallagher, McManus, Smith, Clark, Shaw, and Poole shuffled about, putting the final securing touches to the load. Having resigned to be victims of the cold many hours before, the deck hands were in no apparent hurry to end their long toil. Even purser Haggerty was more concerned with his manifest than with his benumbed feet as he stood leaning over the paperwork with a coffee pot that had long before gone cold at his elbow. Soon the entire gang would retire to their warm cabins as the lookouts and wheelsmen took their places in the exposed cold. Only the vessel's lines remained to be handled and that was accomplished with the same resigned but steady pace as had been the load handling.

Surrounding the MORAN's hull, the harbor waters were a thick sheet of ice and breaking from the dock would be a chore. With the aid of a tug to crush the ice on her beam and bow, the MORAN wiggled from the dock. Thick iron plating sheathed the bottom of the steamer's hull in order to protect her oak timbers from the sharp edges of the frozen water. Apparently this was a recent addition to the vessel's structure, applied when she was purchased by the Crosby Line. In fact, many sources do not show the iron plating as a part of the boat and it is mentioned primarily in news accounts of the era. Captain McLeod proceeded

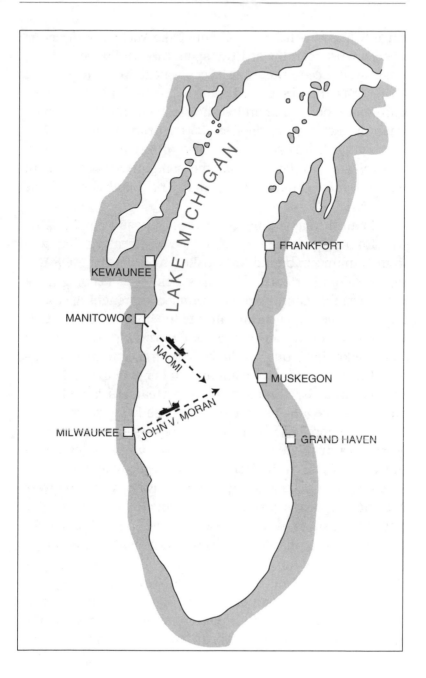

gingerly from the harbor and onto Lake Michigan, directing wheelsman Green toward the spots that appeared to be of least resistance in the ice. McLeod was about as new to the MORAN as the vessel was to the Crosby Line. For many seasons he had commanded the steamer OSCEOLA which was currently in dry-dock at Port Huron. Some $10,000 worth of cash was being expended to re-plank her bottom and replace her keel. Thus, the company's management had assigned Captain McLeod to the pilothouse of the MORAN.

About the same time as the MORAN was crunching her way from Milwaukee, the NAOMI was breaking her way from Manitowoc, bound for Muskegon. From the MORAN's rail, lookouts Herjuan and Lennis took turns keeping track of the ice and scanning the horizon for approaching vessels as Milwaukee was blending aft into the horizon. The NAOMI was sighted on a converging course, trailing a smudge of coal smoke that hung on the background. It appeared as if the MORAN would have company on her way to Muskegon. Angling onto the same course, the steamers joined company and began to make slow headway toward the Michigan shore. Although there is no record to say which vessel was in the lead the evidence seems to indicate that the MORAN was at the front. Down in the steamer's engine room, Chief Green and his second, Edward Egan, were keeping the boat's fore and aft compound steam engine under close supervision while oiler Clyde R. Boyce made his way among the undulating brass and polished steel on his lubricating schedule. Feeding the vessel's fires was a duty shared by John Taft and P.J. Foord. Their shovels spread the coal across the perpetual fires that heated her 12 foot by 12 foot Scotch boilers. Steam from these boilers was the life-blood that flowed through the entire boat and made her work. At 110 pounds of pressure, the steam not only spun her propeller at 84 rounds per minute, but was used for heating the boat. It may have been more than 20 degrees below zero, but in the MORAN's engine room the temperature was at a mid-summer high. One thing that a steamer has plenty of is heat, and down in the firehold of a wooden laker, where the works were surrounded by thick oak timbers, the heat was simply trapped. There was little knowledge or concern as to what went on with the frozen lake and the frigid wind outside—the coal simply continued to be shoveled, the steam pressure stayed up and the engine kept running as ordered from the pilothouse. The JOHN V. MORAN was at work.

As if 600 plow horses were harnessed to her bow, the MORAN smashed onward working hard at crossing Lake Michigan. In the boat's pilothouse wheelsman Haggerty and Ed Miller were looking to the change of shift as the clock ticked toward the end of Thursday and the lights of Muskegon glowed just beyond the horizon. It was about this time that burden of cargo, just 400 tons short of the vessel's maximum load, became very important. Although no one knows for sure, it is highly likely that the unusually thick ice, combined with a near maximum load, allowed the slabs of ice to ride up above the boat's iron sheathing. Soon the sharp blocks were able to bite into the MORAN's hull timbers, and perhaps even peel back some of the plates themselves. Exactly where the hull first gave way was never recorded, but in short order Lake Michigan came pouring in. While chunks of ice were shoved against the tender spots, the MORAN continued her way in the darkness. This turned the leak into a flood, and soon the bilges were overflowing and the waters coming up beneath the steel floor, grating in the engine works. When the pumps started, Second Engineer Eagan was dispatched to find the breech.

Shortly before midnight, it was determined that the MORAN was in a bad way and Captain McLeod ordered her engine stopped. The crew was mustered and the search for the flooding—and a potential stop-gap to save the boat— took on a new urgency. Decks began to groan as the timbers twisted and were forced together. The expiring laker contorted in what appeared to be her last moments afloat. Down in the engine room the water started to rise to the point where the boat's fires were threatened and the loss of steam seemed very near. The JOHN V. MORAN gave every indication of being about to sink, perhaps beneath the feet of her people. With the loss of steam in mind Captain McLeod started blowing a distress signal with what pressure remained for the whistle. To the rescue came the NAOMI, pulling alongside the settling MORAN at about midnight. It was readily apparent to all at the scene that the MORAN was rapidly sinking and Captain McLeod did not hesitate to give the abandon ship order. Gangplanks and ladders were hastily placed to bridge the gap between the two boats and the crew of the MORAN escaped to the NAOMI across them. Temperatures now were dipping toward 30 degrees below zero and the winds came swirling around the escaping vesselmen. Beneath the wobbly makeshift bridges, a jumble of shattered ice and bitter-cold water waited to devour anyone who might falter and tumble into its icy grasp. One by one the MORAN's frostbitten crew abandoned her to the lake as they made their way on hands and knees to the NAOMI. In less than 30 minutes, the floundering JOHN V. MORAN was on her own. With the thought of ice water contacting the red-hot boilers and the explosion that may result in mind, the NAOMI's master

The package freighter JOHN V. MORAN became a demonstration in the folly of man's machines against Lake Michigan's ice.

wasted little time in ordering his vessel moved away from the MORAN. The stiletto beam of the NAOMI's spotlight darted from the MORAN to the ice ahead as the boat smashed the way to a safe distance. There she stopped to await daylight and the next move.

Dawn illuminated the surface of Lake Michigan frozen solid as far as the eye could see. From the NAOMI's pilothouse an amazing sight was revealed by the daylight: there less than a mile away the half sunken MORAN squatted as if wrongly left behind by her crew. For some reason the boat, which had given every appearance of rapidly sinking, had stopped her slide to the bottom. Now she just sat there sadly beckoning her faithful crew to return for her and continue the battle with the ice. This was the feeling, but the reality was far different—the MORAN was still to be considered a sinking ship and everyone knew she could founder at any moment. Quickly a plan was conceived to return to the boat and attempt to take her in tow. Using the care of a surgeon, the NAOMI's master edged his boat up close to the MORAN. Like a frail draw-bridge over a mote of fractured ice, a long wooden-rung ladder was lowered to the rail of the stricken laker. With the bitter winter cold and the grim reaper perched on his shoulder, a single crewman scurried across the chasm between the vessels and dashed to the MORAN's prow. The boat seemed strangely quiet as he pulled at the lead line and brought aboard the towing hawser. There was an odd and frightening incline to the deck and a surrounding silence that brought a haste to his movements as he made fast the tow-line. Knowing full well that the boat could suddenly slide to the bottom and claim him as its only victim the daring lakeman did not even feel the bitter cold; he just made good the knot and then strode back to the ladder attempting to not give the appearance of terror to the throng of crewman watching from the NAOMI's rail. Again the ladder was crossed and this time the crewman put his foot back aboard the safety of the NAOMI. A shiver went down his spine, but it had little to do with the sub-zero temperature.

Breaking her way ahead of the MORAN, the NAOMI took up a towing posture. A crewman stood at the towing post, ax in hand, with orders to cut the hawser if the MORAN began to sink. There was the distinct possibility that if the holed steamer took a plunge, she would do significant damage to the NAOMI by pulling her tow-post out in the process. Pointing in the general direction of Muskegon, the two boats began their one way tug-of-war against the ice. Through the frozen hours of Friday morning and into the afternoon, the NAOMI struggled like an ant with a rock-candy. In the space of half a day less than half a dozen miles were made before the steamer's progress drew nil. By late Friday afternoon it was concluded that the best bet was to go aboard the MORAN and salvage what could be quickly transferred to the NAOMI and leave the luckless boat to her own ends. Again the NAOMI was eased close abeam the MORAN and ladders and planks were now put aboard. The gangways of both boats were opened and planks laid between. Like thieves raiding Lake Michigan's prize, the crewmen of the two boats hustled through the bitter cold relieving the sinking steamer of all that they could carry. This time the coming of darkness rather than the possibility of a sinking was all that stopped the efforts. For the third time in 24 hours, the NAOMI pulled away from the MORAN's beam; this time her sideports and doors were left open in the haste to remove the salvaged cargo.

Soon after the NAOMI left the MORAN to her fate, Captain Thompson and the MUSKEGON happened onto the scene. With the news of the MORAN's plight in their log-books the two rescue boats headed off, the MUSKEGON to her namesake port, and the NAOMI to the closer port of Grand Haven. On Saturday morning, February 11th, 1899, the car ferry MUSKEGON entered the port of the same name and crushed her way into her slip. Captain Thompson broke the news of the MORAN's trouble and the telegraph lines were soon alive with the story. No word came from the NAOMI, primarily because she had not yet made port. The rescue boat had managed to draw near Grand Haven when the ice trapped her. Now she simply sat a short distance out in the frozen lake held fast in its frozen grip. When it became clear that the NAOMI would be going nowhere for a while, the decision was made to send three men over the ice to give word of the distressed steamer. Completely unaware that the MUSKEGON had beaten them in with the news, the three crewmen made the bitter trek to the Grand Haven beach.

Word was flashed via the wire service to the Crosby Line office in Chicago and then to Milwaukee where First Mate E.J. Humphrey was dispatched to the steamer BOYCE on Sunday morning. The mission, as he relayed to the BOYCE's master, was to go out and find the MORAN. Once found, the stricken derelict was to be taken in tow and dragged to the nearest port. Together with the NYACK, the BOYCE was prepared for sailing. At this same time on the other side of Lake Michigan, Captain Thompson was preparing to get the MUSKEGON under way on her return passage across Lake Michigan. He had told those ashore that he would signal by whistle if he saw any sign of the MORAN. As the MUSKEGON eased from the slip, her screws churned up plates of ice, and with the speed of a snail she broke her way onto the lake. From the shore, the maritime community watched as the car ferry shrunk toward the distance. Hands were cupped to ears in hope of being the person who heard the distant whistle, while the MUSKEGON became just a smudge of smoke on the far off ice. No whistle was heard, the MUSKEGON simply vanished over the horizon leaving behind the boat watchers to scratch their heads and wonder about the fate of the JOHN V. MORAN.

Passing through the Milwaukee piers at 2:32 in the afternoon the following Monday, the NYACK and BOYCE had made only 35 miles before running into heavy ice. In the southern "pocket" of Lake Michigan there were some large areas of open water peppered by roving masses of ice. From just north of Milwaukee on up, the waters were frozen in a solid sheet from shore to shore. As long as the two vessels ran in the open, they could make good progress, but when one of the drifting islands of ice was encountered the story changed dramatically. The ice floes were largely made up of piles of windrow ice that would allow a vessel to plow into it and then simply move with the boat, effectively trapping it. Just as darkness set in the two Crosby vessels found one of the floating ice-traps and proceeded to attempt to fight their way through. After three hours bucking the windrows, both boats became firmly trapped for the night smack in the middle of Lake Michigan. By dawn on Tuesday the drifting ice had carried the two boats some 45 miles to the north, northeast, but still held them in its powerful squeeze. The search for their missing fleetmate, the MORAN, had now become side-tracked with the winds and ice-packs. On Wednesday morning the lookouts in both the NYACK and BOYCE's pilothouses sighted land at Little Point Sable where the ice-flow grounded and it began to look as if they might be stuck for a very long time.

Over the next several days, the dispensation of the JOHN V. MORAN became one of the small puzzles of the lake's maritime community. Considering that most of the battles of this icy war were taking place well out of the sight of land, the media of the day did the best that they could to cover the lakeboat ice follies. When eye witness information from the boats that did make port was made available, it was sent across the wire services. When rumors were spread around the frozen waterfronts, it was printed as news—anything else they made up. Ship to shore wireless radio was still two years into the future, (in fact—the first such use on the lakes was aboard the Pere Marquette car ferries to aid in winter navigation on Lake Michigan, thus eliminating the use of carrier pigeons), so those ashore had no other tools to use in doing their job. *The Detroit Free Press* from Wednesday, February 15, 1899 led off its maritime column with a story detailing the troubles of the Detroit River ferries. Apparently the cross-river movement of passenger rail cars between Detroit and Windsor had become so snarled by the ice that some of the passengers were becoming impatient and departed both the rail cars as well as the ferries to make the rest of the distance on foot. Not only was this an extremely hazardous venture, but it was driving the customs officers nuts. Other publications told of the Lake Erie car ferry SHENANGO No.1 which had been trapped in the ice at the foot of Long Point just off Clear Creek. Although she and her 15 crewmembers were safe and there were plenty of provisions aboard, she had been stuck for nearly three weeks. Ice around the boat was 15 feet thick and even the use of dynamite could not blast the boat free. Coincidentally, SHENANGO No.1 was the sister and exact twin to Captain Thompson's MUSKEGON which had come out as SHENANGO No.2. The No.1 would not get free until March which was a good indication of the conditions of ice on the lakes that season. Rounding out the *Free Press'* report was the following simple cut:

"Grand Haven, Mich., February 14.-(Special.)-The steamers NYACK and BOYCE are said to be off of this point with the wrecked steamer MORAN in tow. If so, the MORAN will be brought here, lightered, and brought into port. Ice fields are heavy as ever."

No doubt that at the Crosby offices, vessel manager W.G. Watson read this account and found hope in the words. He knew better than just about anyone that the MORAN alone, with all of the improvements that had been put into her, was now a $40,000 asset to the Crosby line. He knew also that there was not a dollar of insurance on the boat. It appeared as if all that he need do would be simply to wait for the BOYCE and NYACK to make port with the MORAN. What he did not know was that the article in the Free Press was complete fiction and the two rescue boats were at that moment stuck in the ice nearly 50 miles north of where the MORAN had last been seen—and they had not found a trace of the missing steamer. Around each vessel the ice had packed and folded, locking them tight and showing not a hint of loosening. Apparently Mr. Watson was going to have a lengthy wait for first-hand news of the laker.

Indeed it was nearly a week before the BOYCE and NYACK were near enough to civilization for someone to strike out across the frozen distance to bring back provisions, and give word of the results of their search for the MORAN. And so our story returns to where we began, six miles off shore of Muskegon where the BOYCE and NYACK sit trapped in the ice and steeped in sub-zero temperatures. After their first attempt to make dry land had failed Humphrey, Hannrehan and O'Day returned to their steamers swearing to try again once they had obtained dry clothes and what hot coffee remained. Just after noon that same Sunday the men set out once again. This time their hike had a more desperate tone—only a few hours of daylight remained and once darkness set in their steps would be in the ink-blackness of the open lake. There would be no way to see where the next step would take you. It could be solid ice or a yawning crack leading to the frigid depths of Lake Michigan. With a blistering wind threatening frostbite, the men trudged ahead, climbing an occasional snow drift and struggling over countless wind-rows of ice. As the sun sank slowly toward the horizon and the sky began to turn purple, the three pressed ahead toward the distant town of

Muskegon. Ashore, the residents of the port city had been alerted to the venture of the oncoming trio. Gathering on the beach, a large group of local folks started a bonfire to fight off the bitter cold and aid in guiding those three dark dots in the distance. At 5 o'clock that evening, with the sun having long set and the darkness falling as swiftly as the temperatures, the three plucky hikers stumbled onto dry land. With feet benumbed and faces frost-bitten, they uttered the news—the JOHN V. MORAN was nowhere to be found out on the frozen lake.

Not a living soul witnessed what became of the MORAN. When the report came from Muskegon that the BOYCE and NYACK had found no trace of the boat in their "search," Mr. Watson along with the rest of Crosby's management simply gave her up for lost. Considering that the "search" consisted largely of simply drifting with the winds locked in an ice-flow, the effort was considerably less than thorough. The fact is that no one knew exactly where or when the MORAN was claimed by Lake Michigan, she just went away beneath the ice with only the lake knowing her location and time of death. As of this writing she rests on the bottom in her esoteric grave, a monument of sorts to the folly of man's efforts to overcome the Great Lakes winters. In the MORAN's day, mankind believed that there was nothing that nature could bring that he could not build a machine to conquer. Such thinking was proven folly by the lakes time and again, but mankind has never learned the lesson. The silt coated hulk of the JOHN V. MORAN could teach volumes, that is... if only we could find her.

A Mooring of Family

*N*ovember screamed across all of the Great Lakes with its usual rage—as if to tell every mortal on or around the fresh water seas that this time of the year belonged to gales and gray seas. For nearly the whole month, the autumn storms had disrupted shipping schedules and played general havoc with the transportation of lake cargoes. The year was 1902 and by 10 o'clock on that ill-bred Sunday night, the 23rd day of the storm-raked month, most of the lake mariners were simply slugging their way through the ire that November was dishing out. Aboard the four-masted schooner-barge MABEL WILSON, the winds howled through the web of her rigging. Substantial amounts of Lake Erie were ripped from the crests of its waves and slung across the WILSON in the form of spray. A dense pile of coal heaped deep in the schooner-barge's belly weighed her down to the point where some of those waves took the casual liberty of washing aboard the boat and swirling among her hatches and deck clutter in an ice water annoyance.

From the WILSON's open-air helm, Captain J.E. Gotham had been keeping a sharp eye on the rolling lights at the opposite end of the schooner-barge's towing hawser. Ahead at the end of nearly a quarter mile of tow-line the steamer SILVANUS J. MACY was also pounding into November's temper. Much more than a simple tow line connected the two boats that ink-black night; in fact it was a

The MABEL WILSON was part of the Gotham family in as much as they lived and worked aboard her.

mooring of family that lashed the two lakers more tightly than any weaving of hemp could possibly provide.

In command of the MACY was Captain Myron W. Gotham, brother of the WILSON's master. Additionally, the steamer's master had signed aboard his two sons. Serving as the MACY's mate was M.A. Gotham and the duties of watchman were being performed by Lucius Gotham. All of the Gotham's were from the town of Richland Center, Wisconsin, and were currently under the employ of vessel magnate P.J. Ralph.

Shortly after the hour of 10 o'clock the WILSON's master heard the echoes of the MACY's steam whistle as it hooted five sharp blasts against the storm winds followed by four blasts. There was trouble and the WILSON was to take in her tow-line, which had, very apparently, gone slack after being released from the steamer. Now the schooner-barge would be left on her own against Lake Erie. It had taken more than a day for the two storm-tangled lakeboats to cover the 95 odd miles since their departure from the eastern end of the lake—a fraction of the distance that they should have run in that same time. Estimating his position to be about 30 miles west of Long Point, the WILSON's master ordered her anchor dropped and went about bringing the schooner-barge's head to the gale. The act of a storm-burdened steamer casting off her consort in the teeth of a gale had long been an accepted practice on the lakes, and would often lead to the survival of vessels when one or both would have been surely wrecked by an angry lake. Within moments of the order being shouted, the WILSON's crew went to work putting her giant stock anchors over the side. Although the crew of the schooner knew no different in 1902, this process was cumbersome under the best of conditions. A small hoist and boom, known as a cathead, was mounted on the schooner's forepeak. This, as well as sailor's elbow grease, would be used to drop the hooks of most schooners. A donkey boiler and steam powered windlass were mounted at the WILSON's bow and would take most of the work out of dropping her hooks. The big anchors, each weighing about a ton, needed to individually be lifted from the deck and swung over the side. The operation that was of great effort in the calm of a harbor, but in a raging gale the task was surely a desperate grapple. On the ice-coated deck this job must have seemed nearly impossible. Benumbed fingers fumbled the rigging while frozen feet slid across the deck planking and wave after wave of bitter-cold water burst over the crewmen, soaking them to the skin. Like circus performers in a frigid hurricane, the schooner's crew took to the cathead and steam windlass as the boat rolled madly in the sea-trough. The gale and towering seas smothered the splash as the anchors went over the side and toward Lake Erie's bottom. Rumblings of chain led to the slam and bang of the anchor grabbing the bottom of the lake as the chain paid out. Slowly the schooner-barge's stern swung as she weather-vaned into the wind. The combing seas now broke solidly over her prow, but she held fast to the bottom. Captain Gotham knew his boat could ride out the storm in this position...provided things did not intensify.

From the rail of the pitching WILSON her crew now turned their attention toward the MACY. Just why she had cast off the consort was not evident, but she did appear to be drifting in the distance. Apparently there was some sort of problem with the steamer yet there were no signals of distress, only the rocking of her dim lamps in the distance. Rendering aid to the steamer in any event would have been an impossibility from the WILSON. The seas were such that making the distance between the boats in the schooner's yawl would have been suicidal. Heaving anchor and sailing toward the steamer would have put the WILSON into the sea trough again which would have finished her. Captain Gotham could do little more than keep an eye on his brother's boat and hope for the best. Five hours passed as the winds wailed throughout the WILSON's wires and the seas smashed over the bow-rail with such repetitiousness that little attention was now paid to them. Captain Gotham estimated that his brother's boat was about three miles dis-tant—very little drift considering the winds. Odds were that the MACY, like the WILSON, had dropped her hooks and was riding out the storm tethered to the bottom. Dawn would tell the story, Captain Gotham reckoned. Perhaps the gale would then moderate enough to hoist the anchor,

The SILVANUS J. MACY sailed away on Lake Erie; what became of her will remain a mystery whose solution is known only to the lake.

set the storm sails and close the distance to his brother Myron's position. At three o'clock that morning, the lights of the MACY suddenly disappeared and Captain Gotham's concern for his brother brought a lump to his throat as if to choke him. Thoughts of logic defended the schooner's captain from the dread—snow squalls were dancing across the whole lake, Captain Gotham had seen it a thousand times, squalls so dense that they easily could blot out a steamer's lights. There could be a dozen other reasons why the lights had gone out, the concerned schooner master need only to think of them. Indeed, daylight could not come quick enough for him.

Buffalo, New York had been the port of departure for both the MACY and WILSON as they passed from the harbor's protected waters on Saturday afternoon November 22nd. Coal was the cargo that both boats had taken on as their burden: the MACY's bound for Kenosha, Wisconsin and the WILSON's bound a little down the coast for the port of Racine. This was a trip that the two vessels had made many times under the guidance of the brothers Gotham. Although the steamer and her consort were owned by P.J. Ralph, and the Gothams as well as the other crewmen were paid by that company, the boats were running under the flag of the Interlake Transportation Company. There is no record to be found of the fact, but the odds are that this was the last trip of the season for each vessel. Both boats carried an insurance rating of A2, and insurance coverage for vessels of the A2 rating expired on the last day of November. By the time the MACY and her schooner-barge completed the round trip, December would almost certainly be on the calendar page, so if management wanted additional trips it would be at their own risk. It is likely that P.J. Ralph would cut his liability and lay up both vessels as soon as their cargoes were unloaded.

There is little doubt that while the MACY and WILSON were loading the Gotham men took the opportunity to spend a bit of time together. This was a privilege that most lake mariners were not afforded in the early 1900s, as the very nature of the business kept them far from family members for most of the year. Unlike the lake mariners of today who have the convenience of scheduled vacations during the shipping season and vessels that are equipped with telephones, the turn of the century lakeman had to suffice with a postcard or letter mailed at the Soo or Detroit. The Gothams, on the other hand, were able to get together every time their two boats put their beams to the pier. Surely as they prepared to depart Buffalo the Gotham men did not say good-by to one another, just "talk to you on the other end."

As she cleared the Buffalo light, the MACY hauled her consort and their coal cargoes into an unsettled market. The rate for hauling coal had been fluctuating all month and causing no end of headaches to those who speculated such prices. The marketeers had been attempting to force the price between Buffalo and Duluth from 40 cents per ton to 50 cents per ton. They were unsuccessful and the steamer LANGHAM departed for the head of the lakes with a cargo of the fossil fuel at the 40 cent rate as no other vessel managers were willing to haul the propped up 50 cent coal. The price margin to Chicago was far better; after the push to 75 cents, it was dropped to 50 cents. Only then did the vessel barons make their formerly scarce boats available. Among the first lakers to head out with the half dollar coal were the MACY and WILSON.

Market speculation on the price of a ton of coal meant little to James Mack and Mark Hornby who, employed as firemen in the MACY's engineroom, spent their days and sometimes nights shoveling the stuff. Prices perhaps meant a bit more to Chief Engineer Walter Gregory and his second George Webb. After all—the vessel ran on such fuel and variations in price could cut or extend the boat's profits. Like the firemen, deckhands James Mahoney and John Hanolly as well as wheelsmen William H. Donovan and W.F. Giese, probably did not have the subject of coal prices on the top of their conversation list. As they sat in Mrs. Granger's galley teasing her son, who had come aboard as cabin boy, the crewmen were likely to have centered their discussion around this trip and the question of whether or not P.J. Ralph would elect to charge the MACY with additional trips after the insurance expiration date, as was sometimes the practice in the era of the oak hulled laker. If this were to be the last trip, as everyone wished, the crew would get their end of season bonus and be snug at home within days. However, if there was another trip or two, it would likely mean two weeks or more of very hard and very cold sailing. Certainly, the speculation across the galley table was of the season's end and when it would arrive.

Beating their way westward out of Buffalo, the two coal boats found the rude winds beginning to stiffen. Snow began to sweep ahead and gray seas marched toward the vessels of the Gotham captains in an infinite parade of white-caps. Slamming into the oak bow timbers of each boat the gray seas each burst into spray which was instantly frozen onto the MACY's prow like an icy mustache. The boat did not know—nor care—how many trips were ahead; she simply pressed on against the lake at Captain Gotham's command. Shortly, however, the winds grew to gale force and the little steamer was apparently giving it all that she had—and perhaps a bit more.

For the MACY herself this was the closing of her 21st season. Her hull came sliding down the ways at the Marine City boatyard of Morley and Hill in the summer of 1881. On July 29th of that same year her enrollment was issued at Detroit as official number 115784. Measuring 164 feet in length, the wooden steamer was of perfect dimension to work the docks, rivers and ports of her day. Her depth of 11 feet was just handy for maneuvering in the shallow lumbering ports where she was intended to make her career. Additionally, a beam of 31 feet across gave her the girth to carry profitable loads of assorted bulk cargoes when lumber was not the payload of choice. At birth, she sported the lines of a typical lumber hooker of her era. Planted on her deck were three elegant masts, each equipped with full rig

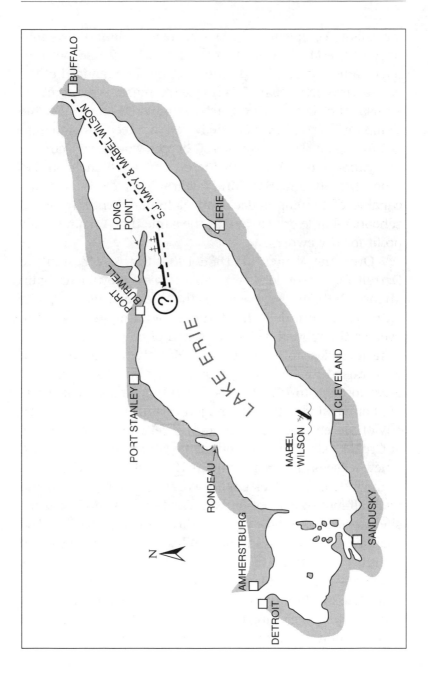

for sails to complement her steam power plant. Gross tonnage of the MACY was calculated at 548.42 and net tonnage came out at 474.93. She was, by the standard of the day, a very hefty boat. To propel this mass of oak timbers across the lakes, the Christie and Desotelle Engine Company of Detroit had delivered a steeple compound steam engine. The power of 450 horses would be produced as cylinders of 19 and 38 inches ran a 34 inch stroke. When the SILVANUS J. MACY started her career she was capable of hauling a deckload of lumber while towing a schooner-barge or two, and at the same time turning a tidy profit for her owners.

Over the winter of 1886-1887 the MACY went to Detroit for a rebuild. It was about this time that Captain Myron Gotham was wed to the steamer. It is likely, although unrecorded, that Captain Gotham was aboard to oversee the rebuild which consisted of converting the boat from a hooker to a well-decker. Her sides and spar-deck were raised to the level of her fo'c'sle thus increasing her gross tonnage to 752.56 tons and at the same time increasing her earning potential. The job was finished on the 24th day of March, 1887 and the MACY returned to the chores of Great Lakes maritime commerce with a new master and a new lease on life. Sometime in 1894, she was re-boilered at the Detroit Dry Dock engine works, giving her a nine and one half foot by 13 foot firebox. For the next three seasons she worked the lakes as a three masted well-decked steamer, until mid June of 1897 when she was again in Detroit, this time to have her two after-most spars removed—probably to clear her deck from the clutter of rigging that would obstruct the newer unloading equipment that was just beginning to appear around the lake. She left carrying only her forward mast and the storm sail that it was to support. Such was her appearance in November of 1902 as she worked her way across Lake Erie in the company of the MABEL WILSON.

Bay City, Michigan was the place and 1866 was the year when the MABEL WILSON's planks were assembled. Like so many of her era, the WILSON slid down the ways at the F.W. Wheeler yard. It was the 16th day of September and unlike her contemporaries, the schooner was a four-masted monster. Her oak hull stretched 242 feet two inches in length and her cavernous hull was calculated to be of 1224 gross tonnage. It seemed to take a considerable time to walk across her deck which stretched 39 feet two inches from rail to rail, and once at her side the view was 16 feet two inches straight down. Along her deck those four masts reached toward the sky and would support the sails that the boat would use to grab the wind, and wing her across the Great Lakes. By 1866 standards, the WILSON was a giant, and 36 years later—when others of oak construction surpassed her—the boat was still considered to be a hefty laker.

A gray dawn illuminated the WILSON on Monday the 24th of November, 1902. With the first hints of daylight, Captain Gotham began squinting toward the horizon in search of his kin and the MACY. Binoculars were put to the task, but no matter how hard the schooner-barge's skipper looked, there was nothing in view but the churning lake. There was no waiting steamer at anchor in the distance, but the gale was still blowing hard and the visibility could easily have been obscured to only a few miles. Additionally, there was the possibility that the steamer had drifted over the horizon or gotten under way and run for shelter. As for the WILSON herself, Captain Gotham elected to keep the boat riding safely at anchor until he was absolutely sure that the storm let up. There was no sign of substantial flooding and her hooks appeared to be holding. The schooner-barge was simply riding well and there was no need to change the situation.

At two o'clock on Tuesday morning the winds had shifted and died to the point where Captain Gotham felt it safe to up-anchor and set the WILSON's canvas. Cold and ice powdered the blustery air as the schooner-barge's retired canvas was called back to active duty. The long lost pop and flap sound of sail catching the wind surrounded the WILSON once more as her crew scrambled among the standing rigging. Setting sail was a task that they had not performed in a while, but the operation was also one that once learned is not forgotten. The crew manning the windlass and cat began hauling aboard the hooks as the WILSON grabbed the wind and gained way. For a full day Captain Gotham worked his way toward the Detroit River, all the while holding out the hope that his brother and nephews had found shelter from the gale.

Across all of the Great Lakes the weekend gale had played havoc with the mariners, but what would become the most remembered event occurred up on Lake Superior. When the massive storm front started to cross the region it hit Superior first, and made a legend as it passed on November 20th and 21st. Sailing into forever, the steel three-island steamer BANNOCKBURN was lost with all hands. For years to come there would be yarns and tales woven around the "vanished" steamer. It was said that no trace of the vessel was ever found, but the facts are that a good deal of flotsam was left behind. There was also the tale of an oar found wrapped in canvas with the letters B-A-N-N-O-C-K-B-U-R-N carved in it, and to make sure that the carved letters could be read they were highlighted in blood.

This nonsense is blatant fiction when seen in today's hind-sight, but in the era of the steamer's loss, the story swept from ear to ear as fact. Most prominently there were the reported sightings of the BANNOCKBURN long after she had foundered. The vessel was said to be unique in her construction—one of a kind whose outline in the distance was unmistakable. So, when the silhouette of the lost vessel was spotted in the hazy distance, the lakemen said that they had seen the "lost dutchman" of the lakes... they had glimpsed the ghost ship BANNOCKBURN. In fact the steamer ROSEMOUNT was a twin to the BANNOCKBURN and ran the lakes along the same routes in the same era for the same fleet. We can easily imagine a lake mariner spotting the ROSEMOUNT in the distance and then dashing to the galley claiming the fame of having seen the lost dutchman of the lakes, the existence of the lost vessel's twin being conveniently overlooked—of course. As of this writing, the BANNOCKBURN, like so many other boats that have foundered in the vast depths of Lake Superior, remains missing. One day, perhaps soon, technology as well as the curiosity of the Great Lakes maritime historians will catch up to the deep-water resting place of the BAN-NOCKBURN. To Captain Gotham, aboard the WILSON, the BANNOCKBURN's loss was not even news yet, as real fear for the steamer's well being would not begin to spill over for another full day. His thoughts were of his brother and what Lake Erie might have done.

Early Wednesday morning, November 26th, 1902, the schooner-barge MABEL WILSON anchored off Bar Point. Later in the day a passing steamer took the storm-beaten coal boat in tow to the port of Amherstburg, Ontario. Captain Gotham wasted no time in going ashore to inquire as to the whereabouts of the MACY. He found that the vessel had not reported into any port, and worst of all, a large area of wreckage had been sighted floating off Long Point— exactly the area where the MACY's lights had gone out. As soon as the report that the WILSON was at anchor five miles below Amherstburg reached the desk of Mr. H.C. Ralph, he headed to that city. Representing the P.J. Ralph firm, H.C. was on his way to interview Captain Gotham as to the details of the missing steamer. Their meeting lasted only a short time before Mr. Ralph came out and announced that there was no hope remaining for the missing steamer and her crew.

Dawn on Friday saw the tug FLORENCE taking the same tow line that the ill-fated MACY had let go five days before, and pulling the WILSON upbound once more. An atmosphere of sorrow so thick that it smothered the clamor of the working day hung over the boat. H.C. Ralph would deliver his coal before the first day of December and the closing of the A2 insurance rate, but only one of the four Gotham men would return to Richland Center, Wisconsin— ever. The tug and schooner passed Detroit that morning just in time for another weekend gale to strike. Almost as if the WILSON brought destruction with her passing, another four boats—the D.F. ROSE and her three consorts—were wrecked during that Saturday and Sunday as the star-crossed WILSON shared Lake Huron with them. More significant to this story, however, was the fact that as this storm reached Lake Erie, it swept the last traces of the MACY's wreckage from the surface and churned away most of the attention that had been given to the event.

Just exactly what happened to the MACY will forever be known only to those who were lost with her. At the time there was speculation that her steering equipment had failed, or that she had experienced some other type of mechanical breakdown. All of this was indeed nothing more than conjecture as the real answers had gone to the bottom of Lake Erie with the MACY. To the rest of us, the exact circumstances of the vessel's loss are a mystery that we cannot solve and which had been played out behind the blackness of that stormy shroud in 1902.

On December 2nd, 1902, the Bay City *Times Press* hit the waterfront where many mariners had already laid-up their vessels for the season. Still, those who made their careers on the inland seas would invest the pennies needed to obtain a copy of the paper and immediately then turn to the column labeled "Marine News." There the headlines would first spout "Boats In Bad Luck," and tell of the woes of the steamer D.F. ROSE and her consorts on Lake Huron. Next down the page bold letters stated flatly "Given Up For Lost" with the accompanying article giving scant details of the soon to be infamous disappearance of the steel steamer BANNOCKBURN on Lake Superior. The third and final head would read "Season's Losses." "Over $1,500,000 on vessels and their cargoes," read the kicker below the headline. "Chicago, Dec. 1." the article began, "All of the less desirable insurance risks, or A2 class of boats closed their season yesterday..." Indeed they were almost right, all but one of the A2 rated vessels had closed their season the previous day. Missing from the fleet, however would be the SILVANUS J. MACY. When she took her crew to the bottom of Lake Erie without a cry, she carried an insurance rating of A2, and thus ended the season seven days early. Perhaps she simply no longer wished to be classed among the "less desirable" and decided to retire ahead of the rest. It was, after all, an undeserved moniker for a once proud and always reliable laker to be tagged with simply due to her age. Tellingly, the MACY's loss is mentioned nowhere on the page. In just one week's time, the tragic loss of a hard-working steamer and her entire crew had been completely overshadowed by the everyday clamor of Great Lakes maritime commerce.

There was no search effort ever conducted for the missing SILVANUS J. MACY or her crew. It seems as if those ashore simply took it in stride that an overdue laker and her crew of 13 had been swallowed by Lake Erie and there was no point in making a search effort. The MACY and her crew had simply been written off. In pondering these events, it is important to put the autumn shipping season of 1902 in perspective. At the time of the MACY's loss, bodies from the steamer C.B. LOCKWOOD, which foundered in October, were still washing ashore. In fact, across all of the lakes wreckage and an occasional body could be found mixed with the autumn seas. So, there is little wonder that the MACY's loss was so easily written off. On March 31, 1903, the MACY's final enrollment was endorsed "Vessel Lost" as it was surrendered at Detroit and the boat and her crew were on the way to being forgotten. Forgotten that is, to everyone but Captain J.E. Gotham, who lost his brother and nephews—and to you, who have read this story.

Four seasons after the MACY's loss and approximately 80 miles south southwest of the steamer's unmarked grave, the MABEL WILSON met her end. Having taken on a cargo of iron ore at Escanaba, the schooner-barge was towed down the lakes by the wooden steamer C.W. ELPHICKE. Standing in command of the schooner-barge, as in 1902, was Captain J.E. Gotham. On May 28th, 1906—both boats were off the port of Cleveland where the WILSON's load was consigned. With a signal between the steamer and consort, the towing hawser was cast off and the WILSON set free of the ELPHICKE and picked up by the tug LUTZ for the tow into the unloading dock. The seas were running high , and just a mile and a half west of the harbor, the star-crossed schooner-barge took a heavy one over her nose. Immediately she began to fill at the bow and sink. All but one of her crew escaped to the tug and the steamer WILLIAM KENNEDY, which happened to be near by. Captain Gotham and First Mate Gunnison ended up in the marine hospital while the WILSON ended up on Lake Erie's bottom. And so ended the career of another of P.J. Ralph's lakers. The MABEL WILSON rests today with her bones in the sand just off the Cleveland breakwater, connected only by the invisible mooring of the family Gotham to the missing SILVANUS J. MACY somewhere out there across the expanse of Lake Erie.

Which Boat Are Ya Waitin' On?

*A*s the tug FLORENCE pulled the mournful schooner-barge MABEL WILSON up the Detroit River on Friday the 28th day of November, 1902, just four days after the MACY's wreck, a Great Lakes perplexity in the making followed directly behind. Steaming upbound practically in the wake of the tug and schooner came the wooden lumber hooker H.E. RUNNELS, and attached to her heels in tow was the schooner-barge CELTIC. When those aboard the WILSON looked aft at the RUNNELS and CELTIC, they had no idea that they were casting eyes upon a tragedy and mystery whose questions, like those of the MACY, would never be answered. Ahead lay Lake St. Clair, the St. Clair River, Lake Huron, a building gale and the vortex of time—all of which would do their best to scribe a line in the puzzle to come.

The sky over the St. Clair River had been blue for only a short while on Friday and by the time that the RUNNELS pulled the CELTIC into the lower portion of the waterway the heavens had turned gray and sullen. One by one the RUNNELS blew passing signals to a roll-call of historic wooden-, as well as steel-hulled lakers that passed her downbound. Classic vessels such as the JOHN OWEN, which would disappear with all hands on Lake Superior 17 years later, appeared ahead and slipped silently past. There also came the PARNELL, PECK and PUEBLO, followed by the SAXON and her whaleback consort—all in a parade of

Seen here receiving new planking in winter lay-up, the H.E. RUNNELS towed the schooner CELTIC onto Lake Huron, then lost her forever.

what was the finest of the lake shipbuilder's art. Soon passing signals were blown for the GRIFFIN and after her the ELIZA STRONG who was pulling a string of schooner-barges. History in motion would find the STRONG a sunken wreck in the shallows off of Lexington, Michigan in the year 1915. In total, another two dozen lakers would pass the RUNNELS and CELTIC before the two boats would shove their way onto the choppy waters of Lake Huron. This was a typical passage for the year 1902, but one that any modern boat-nut would just love to have been able to venture back and watch from the rail of the RUNNELS. What no one aboard either the RUNNELS or her consort CELTIC knew was that, like some of the vessels that were passing, they too would soon become entries in the annals of Great Lakes shipwreck history.

Cargoes of coal had been loaded aboard both the RUNNELS and CELTIC at the port of Buffalo, New York and were consigned to Sault Saint Marie. Much like the cargo of the barge WILSON, the burdens of the RUNNELS and CELTIC were meant for the winter stockpile at the Soo, a small addition to a store that hopefully would be large enough to keep the town warm until the first laker came calling the following spring. In charge of the movement of the CELTIC's load was Captain H. Jefferies of Detroit. A respected master of vessels, Captain Jefferies was also responsible for the seven crewmembers aboard the schooner-barge, including Margaret Quirk, the ship's cook. It was with no small sense of resignation that Captain Jefferies felt the wind freshen and listened to its familiar moan in the rigging as the CELTIC followed the steamer faithfully up the thumb of Michigan. The very last days of November were never friendly toward the wooden lakers and December normally posed the same attitude.

Like so many vessels of the era of oak-hulled lakers, the CELTIC was built on the Saginaw River at the port of Bay City. The year was 1890 and when launched the CELTIC had the rigging of a three masted schooner. Measuring just 190 feet in length, 13 feet in depth and 34 feet across her beam, the schooner was one of the more modest vessels to come from the ways of the James Davidson yard. In a time when Davidson was turning out wooden steamers longer than 200 feet with capacities greater than 1000 net tons, the CELTIC was produced with a meager net tonnage of 680. Certainly there was no great fanfare of celebration as hull number 39 slid into the water; she was simply another schooner coming from the Mecca of white oak lakers. Assigned official number 126662, the CELTIC sailed off to work with what appeared to be a bright career to come. What only we, who have the advantage of viewing these events through the tunnel of history can know, is that the CELTIC's first seasons on the lakes were actually the declining years of sail powered vessels. By the time the CELTIC had seen the start of her second decade, her masts and most of her wind-power rigging had been cut down and she had been pressed into making a living as a barge at the end of a towing hawser. It was not the kind of duty that went well with her fine schooner appearance, but it was a toil that would turn a slender profit.

Records concerning the events of the CELTIC and RUNNELS on those last days of November, 1902 are scarce in the extreme. What was to come involved no duties for the Life-saving Service, so no reports were made. No appearances near lighthouses were made, so no logs give the event mention. And most importantly, no witnesses were left to make an account of the end. The probability is that as the RUNNELS and CELTIC cleared the lee of Michigan's thumb, the true force of the gale set upon them. Blowing from the southwest, the winds were from just the right direction to not only deliver punishing seas built along the length of Saginaw Bay, but also rob the vessels on the open lake of any reasonable shelter. Pulling upbound for DeTour, the CELTIC and RUNNELS were taking a loathsome quartering sea on their heels. Captain Jefferies would have ordered the forward sail raised to help the pair along, and seas would rise up and board the boats over their stern rails.

For what must have seemed like endless hours, the two lakeboats worked northward toward DeTour and the

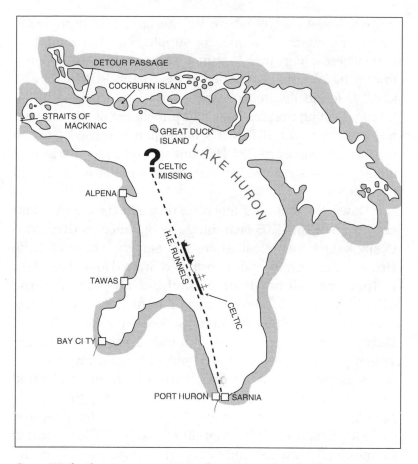

Soo. With the snow spitting from the clouds the pair were locked in a frigid sphere of isolation where Lake Huron was free to torment them at its pleasure. Feeling their way through the expanse between the Straits of Mackinac and Great Duck Island—using only their compass—the storm-tossed lakers had hopes of coming out somewhere near DeTour's passage into the Saint Marys River. While part of the dilemma to come was the direct result of sailing blindly, the fact of the matter was that the master of the RUNNELS did not know exactly where he was and had been using "mariner's instinct" alone to supplement his compass. Somewhere along this "instinct seaway" the thick hemp towing hawser that stretched between the RUNNELS and CELTIC found its limit of stress and parted like so much thread. Feeling that his boat had pulled free of her consort, the captain of the RUNNELS immediately turned back to look for the wayward CELTIC, but the schooner-barge had already been swallowed in the snow squalls as it drifted into the gale.

Dawn the following morning revealed the captain and crew of the RUNNELS searching the distance as they frantically sailed their boat along the eastern shore of Lake Huron. The search was conducted from Duck Island to DeTour, with all hands at the rail but not a trace of the CELTIC was found. On the first day of December, a discouraged RUNNELS and crew sulked into the village of DeTour and reported the missing schooner-barge. Telegraph messages were sent out and word given to the down-bound lakers to keep a sharp lookout for the drifting CELTIC. Time passed, however, and among the steady parade of upbounders, none had word of sighting the CELTIC. Eventually, the captain of the RUNNELS decided to move up to the Soo and deliver his cargo. One by one he watched the upbound boats pass always keeping the hope that one may have word of the schooner-barge CELTIC. To this day no upbounder has ever brought word of the CELTIC or the eight souls aboard her to the Soo; she is still missing.

Just what happened to the CELTIC, as well as when and where the event took place, is a mystery whose solution is known only to those aboard her. At least one source reports that wreckage thought to be from the missing schooner-barge washed up on the southeast point of Cockburn Island, but the fact remained that the vessel took her cargo and crew and drifted off never to return from the storm. Much the same as the SILVANUS J. MACY, just a few days earlier, the CELTIC was simply written off by her owners and obliterated from memory in the passage of time. Today, even the names of those aboard seem to be as lost as the coal cargo that she carried. Perhaps the next time that you, the reader of this brief account, are visiting the Soo and find yourself perched on the lock-side observation platform waiting for the next boat to pass, you may take a moment to wait for the CELTIC. Then when some other visitor approaches you and asks "Which boat are ya' waitin' on?," you can say, "The CELTIC—she was due in on the first day of December, 1902 and she's still out there somewhere."

Footnotes to the Storm

*W*hen autumn came calling on Lake Superior in 1905 it did so with historically disastrous results. Two major storms made war on the lakeboats and their crews using wind and wave as the weapons. The November blow ravaged the lake wrecking the steel steamers MONKSHAVEN and LAFAYETTE, the scow-barge GEORGE HERBERT, schooner-barge AMBOY, the steel ore barge MADEIRA and swallowing with only a trace left behind the steamer IRA H. OWEN and her crew of 19. From the 27th of November into the 29th, the storm pillaged some 30 vessels on the lake as well as in the ports, the most famed of all being the 450 foot Pittsburgh Steamship oreboat MATAAFA. In an attempt to run for the shelter of the Duluth harbor, the MATAAFA was tossed by a big wave and slammed head-on into the north pierhead of the Duluth ship canal. She was then spun around and settled in the shallows in full view of the local residents. As the Duluthians looked on, the waves washed over the wreck and turned her and nine of her 24 crewmen to ice. Volumes have been written about that November 1905 storm, and legend grown around the ships and men who found themselves tangled within it.

Nearly three months earlier, the first days of September opened the autumn sailing struggle with an early season gale of its own that would come in second only to the November storm. Disastrous losses of the steel-hulled oreboat SEVONA and the oak-hulled steamer IOSCO with her schooner-barge consort OLIVE JEANETTE have captured most of the attention of the authors and historians when considering the September 1905 blow. Among the disastrous losses were mixed the numerous tales of lakers and people who were put in peril in the storm but later overlooked by the writers and historians. In fact with 43 mariners losing their lives to Lake Superior, other events in the gale are easily written off as a murex footnote to the storm. To Captain Thomas Stevenson, Second Mate N.P. Tufeson, watchman John Lindquist and Captain Charles Hahn the first Saturday and Sunday of September 1905 was far more than a footnote—it was frightening reality.

Friday, September first, found the staunch 436 foot steamer FRANK W. GILCHRIST pushing her way up Lake Michigan bound for Duluth and a cargo of ore. At that same time the whaleback steamer SAMUEL MATHER was poised to start her loading at that same port, while the package steamer NORTH WIND pushed toward the head of the lakes. Over the next 48 hours, Lake Superior would turn into a giant blender of anxiety and some 50 vessels and their mariners would become the garnish.

Lake Superior was in a summer mood as the sun set over the western horizon ahead of the Mutual Transit Company's package freighter NORTH WIND. In fact, the vessel had experienced late summer sailing weather all of the way up from Buffalo. Making his evening appearance in the freighter's pilothouse, Captain Stevenson tapped at the barometer and gave a casual look across her deck cargo. It was indeed a fine Friday evening and the NORTH WIND was shoving toward Duluth—right on course. Figuring that he should make the Duluth ship canal just around midnight Saturday, Captain Stevenson was looking ahead to a pleasant passage all of the way to the head of the lakes.

For a few days, it was said that the FRANK W. GILCHRIST was lost with all hands. The rumor was based on a bucket washed ashore.

Since her launch in 1888, the steel-hulled NORTH WIND had been hauling assorted package items in and out of nearly every port on the Great Lakes. Born as hull number 19 at the Globe Iron Works in Cleveland, the steamer entered into an era of giant package vessels. In fact, at just six inches over 312 feet in length, she was outsized by several vessels already in the package trade. Such vessels were used to project the service of the major railroad lines to the west, and with the big railroad dollars came a boom in the construction of these carriers. On the builder's ways and scheduled for completion in 1888 were a surprising number of sisters to the NORTH WIND, among them being the CORONA, NORTHERN QUEEN, NORTHERN LIGHT,

NORTHERN KING and CORSICA. Each of these vessels were to be constructed with 40 feet of beam and 24 and one half feet in depth—it was a banner year for package freighters as well as for the Globe Iron Works. Through the remaining years of the 1800s, the prosperous times for the package freighters continued and the momentum pressed into the early 1900s. By September of 1905, the NORTH WIND had been going about the toil of package freight, hauling with casual anonymity, for nearly two decades.

As the NORTH WIND churned a wake in the direction of Duluth, Captain Stevenson played his keen gaze of inspection across the boat's deckload as he made his way forward after finishing dinner. The lashing across the deck-cargo of pipe appeared secure in every respect. This was the easy part of the cargo to inspect; below decks was a medley of cargo the likes of which could easily stock a modern day mall. Some 350 tons of merchandise—ranging from clothing to pianos—was crammed within the hold. Like most package freighters, the NORTH WIND's hold was divided into two levels, with a "tween deck" that in many of the breed could be removed to facilitate the loading of bulk cargoes—such as grain. In order for Captain Stevenson to inspect that portion of the cargo, he would have to crawl around in the hold like a mouse—not exactly worth the effort at this point. Approaching the forward cabins, it became apparent that there would be little to raise concern—Lake Superior stretched ahead as flat as glass into the hazy distance and the barometer read high and gave no indication of change. Indeed this passage would be as routine for Captain Stevenson as was his supper.

The profile of the NORTH WIND was typical for a steel laker born in the later 1800s. Her cabins were arranged in the standard fore and aft configuration with her forward cabins plopped right on the spar deck and aft of her forward hatch. Three masts and a single tall smoke stack, all with elegant rakes, completed the vessel's outline. By lakeboat standards at the beginning of the 1900s, the NORTH WIND and her sisters were efficient as well as pleasant to look at—an exception to the rule. From the steamer's pilothouse, it is doubtful that Captain Stevenson gave much consideration to the boat's aesthetics. His mind was more likely to dwell on the paperwork and housekeeping items that every master needs to get in order prior to a boat's arrival in port. As Friday evening passed into Saturday morning, the steamer NORTH WIND pressed ahead as if on an endless watery treadmill. Some may have considered the trip to Duluth to be a dull routine, and the crew of the NORTH WIND knew that soon the twin ports would appear ahead and the process of unloading would begin. Lake Superior, however, had other ideas about what to do with the mariner's routine on this particular Saturday.

Most old-timers who had sailed Superior for many years knew that she had a thunderous temper, but it took a while to build the lake up to a rage. Normally a dead swell would lead to a building of wind accompanied by a falling barometric pressure. The "old-tars" also knew well that the big lake had no end to her bag of tricks, and the autumn sailing season was just the time to pull them out. Late on Friday evening, trouble started at the far western end of the lake. With no warning, a booming wind exploded out of the northeast and the seas rose up as if to throw every vessel from the lake. Captain Stevenson, like many other masters on the big lake, found himself going from protracted monotony to struggle with the storm. The entire day Saturday brought nothing but winds in excess of 40 miles per hour.

Seen here in the Mutual Transit Companies colors, the NORTH WIND sails quiet waters. That situation would change in the autumn of 1905, when her namesake came calling.

Spume from the winds ripping the crests from the waves mixed with driving rain squalls and Lake Superior came aboard to swirl among the deck cargo of the NORTH WIND. Marching the width of the lake, the seas attacked the package freighter at her stern quarter, rolling the boat in a manner that Captain Stevenson, like all mariners, despised. This sudden tantrum had caught every vessel master off guard, and now showed no sign at all of easing up. Boarding at her stern the seas rolled right up the NORTH WIND's deck and burst at her forward deck houses. With endless patience, the mighty fresh water sea seemed to toy with the steamer; the boat needed only to show a single sign of weakness and Superior would take her away forever.

Daylight on Saturday expired and Lake Superior continued to rage. Winds were sustained at over 40 miles per
hour and reported as high as 50 miles per hour at Duluth
and 60 miles per hour at Ashland. Surprisingly, during the
day some vessels had finished loading and sailed directly
out into the tempest. Among these was the whaleback
steamer SAMUEL MATHER, which had taken aboard a full
load of ore at Duluth. Whalebacks were a breed unique to
the lakes and were designed by Alexander McDougall with
heavy weather in mind. Looking much like a surfaced sub-
marine and running the seas in the manner of a floating
log, with rounded decks and a cigar shaped bow and stern,
the whaleback's design welcomed the waves aboard so that
their weight would stabilize the vessel. As the MATHER
stuck her snout into the open seas off the Duluth ship
canal, her crew included Second Mate N.P. Tufeson and
watchman John Lindquist. When the boat was driven back
by the storm later in the day, it would be missing one of
these crewmen. With the storm winds blowing fresh from
the northwest, the MATHER's master elected to run the
north shore route to buy a little bit of the lee of the land so
as to shield his boat from the storm.

Riding low in the water, as she was designed, the
MATHER received little shelter from the north shore and
each wave nearly totally submerged the whaleback. Just off
Knife Island, less than three hours out of Duluth, a problem developed concerning the boat's hawse-pipes. The
hawse-pipes commonly are the tube through which the
anchor chains pass into the boat's hull. On a whaleback,
the deck houses were set atop cylindrical turrets, and the
forward turret had two hawse-pipes facing forward. Exactly
what the problem was with the MATHER's hawse-pipes is
not recorded, but in the heavy seas the forward turret

would have taken the brunt of the abuse. It is not hard to imagine what a little damage in this area could lead to. There is the possibility that anchor chain, which was strung in the open prior to the hawse-pipe on this class of boat, loosened and with the wave action started to demolish the forward area. Second Mate Tufeson was dispatched by the MATHER's captain to go forward and get the situation under control. He took John Lindquist with him, and the two mariners started working their way toward the bow. Waves waist deep and more crashed aboard, the wind screamed past their ears, but they made it forward and went to work. The situation must have been nearly impossible, with the fully loaded whaleback offering only a few feet of freeboard in calm waterways. In the gale, the full force of the waves met the struggling crewmen. As each wave rose up ahead, Tufeson would spot it coming. "Hold on!" he would shout against the wind as both men were deluged. From the MATHER's pilothouse all eyes were fixed upon the two struggling figures at the bow. Then, one enormous comber grew ahead and the big whaleback jammed her snout directly into it. Caught between tons of plowing steamboat and a wall of ice water the two crewmen were completely helpless. A moment later the whaleback's snout emerged from the other side of the wave. Visible at the bow now was only a single man, draped over a derrick, like a stringless puppet. The other crewman was gone.

Nearly half a day after she had steamed out of the Duluth ship canal, the whaleback SAMUEL MATHER returned through those same piers. Having the gale at her heels, the black billows of coal smoke ripped from her stack and spread across the canal as the MATHER pounded through the passageway and into the confines of the harbor. Suffering from bad cuts on his head and face, Mate

So battered was the whaleback SAMUEL MATHER that she was forced back to Duluth.

Tufeson was in need of medical attention, and with her hawse-pipes damaged, the whaleback was no match for Lake Superior in its current mood. Worst of all, the steamer was now one crewman short. Having washed overboard, John Lindquist was out there, somewhere, forever a resident of the lake's cold depths. In the brutal storm there was no chance to search or attempt a rescue, the luckless watchman was simply swallowed by the churning lake and became a footnote in the storm.

Just after midnight Saturday, the glow of Duluth became visible through the spray spattered pilothouse windows of the NORTH WIND. Clearing the blur of sleep depravation from his eyes, Captain Stevenson drew some sense of relief from the fact that he would be off Lake Superior in just a few hours and safely inside the Duluth harbor. At 3:15 that morning, the pitching and rolling package freighter was lined up with the narrow ship canal. Gauging the winds, Captain Stevenson called directions to his wheelsman. At 3:25 a.m. the NORTH WIND's bow entered the pier-heads of the famed harbor entrance, and at that same time the storm seemed to peak. Entering the concrete channel and navigating through it is a task in good weather, but as the NORTH WIND attempted entry at the height of this tremendous gale, the task became impossible. As if Lake Superior did not want to let the vessel escape untouched, it reached out and suddenly overpowered the boat's steering gear. Tossed like a child's bathtub toy, the steamer slammed into the south pierhead. Impacting just forward of amidships, the laker's hull broke open like a giant steel hard-boiled egg. In the cargo hold plates bent inward as if made of clay and water shot through the cracks and sprayed among the cargo like a fire hose gone mad. Up in the pilothouse everyone fought to maintain their footing as the NORTH WIND was ground against the pier. Shuddering moments after the boat found the wall, she rebounded and rolled to starboard and then took an immediate list to port as if to founder right on the spot.

Captain Stevenson knew instinctively just what he had to do—he had to get his boat out of the ship canal and into protected shallow water and he had to do it right now. Ordering full ahead on the boat's engine, Stevenson took hold of the whistle-pull and started blowing signals for tugs as the NORTH WIND limped the rest of the way through the canal. Ever alert, the captains of the tugs EXCELSIOR and HELM responded to the crippled package freighter. In short order, the lines were made secure and the NORTH WIND was pulled toward the Northern Pacific slip at Lake Avenue. The boat barely made the slip entrance before she settled to the bottom in 26 feet of water with a hard port list. In the pilothouse Captain Stevenson hung his head in disgust, but if Lake Superior was going to sink your boat—it was probably best that it should happen in the Lake Avenue slip.

Through most of Sunday the storm blew itself out. At a number of points on the south shore the evidence of disaster was cast up. Flotsam from the soon to be famous wrecks of the IOSCO and OLIVE JEANETTE came onto the beach at Keweenaw Bay. Among the Apostle Islands the wreckage of the SEVONA as well as the PRETORIA found the beaches. All of these boats were total losses. Apparently every beach-comber on the southwestern shore seemed able to find evidence of a lost lakeboat. At Houghton a basket marked "Gilchrist" washed ashore and the word quickly spread that the big steamer FRANK W. GILCHRIST had come to grief. About the time that the rumor of the GILCHRIST's demise really started to gain momentum, the big steamer steamed casually into Duluth without a wire out of place. Her Captain looked astonished when the dockside folks started asking about his boat's harrowing passage across Lake Superior. The fact was that the GILCHRIST had locked through the Soo as the storm was blowing itself out and experienced little more than a choppy ride to Duluth. Most of Captain Hahn's problems were experienced on Lake Michigan where the north, northeast winds created seas such as he had never seen. When asked about the bucket, the good captain simply stated that he could not imagine where it had come from. In checking the recorded vessel movements, we find that the FRANK GILCHRIST was the only laker bearing the "Gilchrist"

99

moniker on Superior that stormy weekend, and she did not enter the lake until late Sunday. The odds are that the basket washed off another "Gilchrist" earlier in the season and was simply tossed ashore by the lake in her unending effort to puzzle us. It worked.

Notably, one contemporary source attributes the basket incident to the "J.C. GILCHRIST." However, a careful examination of the vessel movements of that weekend shows a "GILCHRIST" passing up at Detroit at 3 a.m. on September second, "JOSEPH GILCHRIST" upbound at the Soo at 2 p.m. on the forth and "J.C. GILCHRIST" arriving at Duluth on the sixth. The gale ended 24 hours before this boat reached Lake Superior. To many people this small event may seem like an insignificant footnote to the storm, but decades after it washed up on that Houghton beach, that simple basket continues to have the ability to confuse us.

As the storm abated and Lake Superior calmed down, the pieces of the shattered shipping business began to settle back into place. With the regularity of common practice the toll was taken of which boats had survived and which had not. By mid-week the tally listed the IOSCO and OLIVE JEANETTE in the most infamous category of "Gone Missing with all hands," assuring that their tales would be told over and over again in Great Lakes lore. The SEVONA and PRE-TORIA both went into the "wrecked" column, with each boat losing almost half of her crew to the angry lake. In the footnotes category, John Lindquist was gone forever, Captain Hahn was left explaining the implications of a simple basket and Captain Thomas Stevenson was supervising the removal of water-soaked cargo from the listing deck of his half-sunken boat at the Lake Avenue slip. It had been a terrible start to an autumn sailing season that would soon get worse—the great November storm was yet to come.

For several days tons of water-spoiled goods were hauled out of the cargo hold of the steamer NORTH WIND. Captain Joseph Kidd, a well known local wrecker, had been sent for as soon as the steamer settled in the slip. The elder Kidd was elsewhere, however, so the task of evaluating the damaged NORTH WIND was taken up by his son, Robert. Dawning hard-hat and diving suit, the younger Kidd was lowered over the side to examine the damage done by the canal pier. The water in the slip was as murky as an ink well. Tracing by touch alone the wreck-diver outlined a massive crease in the boat's side. It was indeed a bad wound and would require dry-docking, but as soon as the cargo was removed the hole could be tarpaulined and the hold pumped out. The repair would be expensive, at least one contemporary source lists the total damages in the $100,000 range, but the NORTH WIND would sail again.

By Thursday, September 7th, 1905 the package freighter was ready for her move to the dry-dock and well on her way to becoming a footnote to the storm. Today accounts of both of the autumn storms of 1905 are written and re-written but the disastrous losses of major vessels often overshadows the many other boats and people who found themselves entangled in the storms. These become the footnotes in history. If anyone had asked captains Stevenson and Hahn as well as John Lindquist they would have all surely preferred not to be a part of this history at all, let alone a footnote.

Three Button Coat

*F*ishermen normally start their workday several hours before the sun peeks over the horizon—a schedule which, with a good catch, normally allows the toil to end about mid afternoon. Such was the case for the crew of the fishing tug ANGLER on the fine summer afternoon of the second day of June, 1893. After having netted a nice haul of Lake Huron's bounty, the tug's crew were heading back for their home port of Alpena, Michigan, beneath a bright blue sky laced with a few powder puff white clouds. The afternoon's weather was a far cry from the pea soup fog and pre dawn damp shivering cold in which the ANGLER's crew had started their workday. About 11 miles southeast of Thunder Bay Island, the tug's crew spotted a few objects bobbing on the surface a short distance ahead. Steering directly into what became a field of wreckage, the stunned crew of the ANGLER began to pull aboard every piece that was within reach. By the time that the little fishing tug started back for Alpena her crew had brought aboard a red galley table cloth, a white cabin door, two window sashes that were blue on one side and white on the other and an old black walnut table with one leaf showing a repair using a piece of pine. Also plucked from the lake was a coffee boiler, a sounding lead and line and a few lamps, some with four globes and some with three. The most heart wrenching item pulled onto the tug, however, was a three buttoned pea coat.

As the crew of the ANGLER gathered around, the tug's captain began to search the sopping wet coat that had just been pulled from the lake. Pocket by pocket the callused hands of the career fisherman probed the coat until his burly fingers extracted a soaked sheet of paper. With as much care as he could manage the captain peeled open the smudged letter. "My dear brother..." was how the letter began and after a brief text it concluded being signed "Joe Davy of 213 Cherry Street, Green Bay, Wisconsin..." and was dated March 20, 1893. As the fishing tug made a bee line for Alpena with its recovered flotsam aboard the thought came to mind that over in the city of Green Bay, someone's dear brother, Joe Davy, was in for some very bad news as his kin's vessel had apparently gone to Lake Huron's depths leaving only a three buttoned coat behind.

When the ANGLER reached Alpena, the word of its discovery spread quickly and in short order the tug RALPH went charging onto the lake to further the recovery efforts. Lake Huron did not cheat the RALPH, as the lake gave up 18 feet of a shattered deck-house and roof that appeared to have been mauled by a ship's giant propeller. Also recovered were a number of buckets and other odds and ends common to every lakeboat. It was quite apparent that at least one proud vessel had come to a sudden and violent end about 10 miles off of Thunder Bay Island.

The story of what happened off Thunder Bay Island that Friday morning really began several days before. As the month of May drew to a close, four very different lakeboats were busy working at different jobs at opposite ends of the Great Lakes. Headed up lower Lake Michigan with a belly full of pig iron and the wind at her heels came the two-masted schooner ST. LAWRENCE. Bound for the eastern lakes, the 144 foot schooner had her sails set "wing and

The laker CORSICA was just going about her work on a fog-bound Lake Huron when she encountered a phantom schooner.

wing," meaning that one sail was set out over the port side and the other set over the starboard so as to catch the most of the tail breeze. It would be slow going for the heavily burdened wind grabber, but her master figured to be off the Mackinaw Light by noon on Thursday, June first and, with favorable weather, well down Lake Huron by that same time the following day.

Up on Lake Superior the 312 foot steel steamer CORSICA, of the Globe Iron works fleet, was taking the last of her full capacity of ore and making hasty preparations to depart for the Soo. Captain Cummings would surely have the CORSICA's cargo in Ashtabula by Saturday considering that the gales of spring and fall were now months away. Constructed in 1888 at the owner's yard, the CORSICA was considered as being the state of the art and a goliath of her day. By the summer of 1893 she was still in command of such stature but would soon be overtaken by the sweeping growth of lake vessels brought about by the industrial revolution. Much like her sister ship, the NORTH WIND, her lines were the trendy configuration of the era with her pilot-house and Texas cabins mounted on her spar deck aft of the number one hatch. It was an elegant design that would vanish with the coming of the Hulett unloaders in the first decade of the 1900s because the configuration of the vessels interfered with the movement of the unloaders.

As the CORSICA snailed away from the loading piers her steward, a fellow whose last name was Davy, gave little attention to the departure. Entering the warm confines of the CORSICA's galley, steward Davy had no need for his woolen three button pea coat. After all, the weather on the upper lakes would soon warm as it already had on the lower lakes. Davy's coat was at that moment securely pegged up in his cabin waiting to again protect him from the bite of the Great Lakes when the weather turned foul.

Shortly after the CORSICA had departed the ore dock on Lake Superior and in the darkness of Wednesday evening, the last day of May, more than 600 miles away the mighty tug CHAMPION came to a near stop just outside of the St. Clair River on open Lake Huron. Trailing behind the tug, a string of four schooners began to release the towing hawsers that had attached them to the CHAMPION's stern. All the way from Detroit the tug had huffed against the swift currents to deliver the schooners onto the open lake. This type of charter was commonplace in the era of wind powered lakers and was by far the most efficient way to move the big sailing vessels through the connecting waterways of the Great Lakes. The CHAMPION, in fact, had been performing this task since 1868; after all, this was the work for which the hefty tug had been constructed. Spreading their canvas to the southerly breeze, the schooners SELKIRK, ELIZA, GERLACH, CORSICAN and SENATOR BLOOD took to their own and headed into the ink black summer night. Of the CHAMPION's tow, the CORSICAN and SELKIRK would soon play parts in the occurrence off of Thunder Bay Island.

Hauling pulpwood from St. Ignace to Cleveland had been the CORSICAN's most recent contract. At the rate of two dollars a cord the schooner's deck would be piled high with the glamourless cargo that fed the paper mills. On this trip, however, her contract was to haul coal up to Cheboygan. Apparently Captain Bernier, an opportunist like all schooner captains, had gotten wind of a coal load that just happened to be going his way. In the previous weeks, coal charters had become scarce and this was a chance to pick up a few extra dollars while on the way upbound to fulfill his pulpwood contract. He was certain that Captain S.B. Grummond, the CORSICAN's owner, would not object to the extra time spent in unloading the schooner at Cheboygan when the cash paid for the cargo came across his desk. Both the CORSICAN and the tug CHAMPION were in the brotherhood of the Grummond's vast Detroit-based fleet and there were extra salutes between the two as the tug let go and the CORSICAN headed off on her way.

SENATOR BLOOD was bound from Sandusky, Ohio to the village of De Tour on the mouth of the Saint Marys River. Also sporting a hold stuffed with coal the schooner was being paid 40 cents a ton to haul it up the lake. Odds are good that this rate was the same that the CORSICAN had attached to her cargo. On the SENATOR BLOOD's return, she was to put into Cheboygan and haul lumber back down. The SELKIRK was Lake Michigan bound, but there is no record of her cargo. It is a good bet that she too may have been hauling coal, as it was only on rare occasion that schooner captains ran their boats empty. Likewise, the GERLACH went on her way without any notation being made of her cargo or destination. All of these lakers readily melted into the scores of vessels that were moving along the courses that all seemed to converge off Thunder Bay Island. It took only the formation of a thick summer fog to turn these individual boats into a brotherhood of jeopardy.

The lakeboats worked in a rainy summer day all of Thursday. But it was a warm rain that came in the form of occasional showers and was easily tolerated under a sailor's oilskins. By nightfall the rain had stopped, yet the thick clouds blocked out the moon and stars. With the darkness came a slow drop in temperature, and as the moisture-saturated air grew cooler, the air molecules slowed their movement and drew closer together. When the air mass compressed it could no longer suspend the water vapor that it did when it was warm, and as a result the daytime's moisture condensed out into a pea soup fog. From Whitefish Bay to northern Lake Michigan, through the Straits of Mackinac and down as far as Port Huron, the central Great Lakes were consumed by the cottony mist. In spite of the fog, these conditions were accompanied by a steady northeast wind that no self respecting schooner master could resist. Through the muddle the schooners pressed ahead with sails filled and with only a few dim lamps and hand pumped fog horns to mark their presence.

Earlier that same evening, around dinner time, Captain Cummings had directed the steamer CORSICA past the village of De Tour and ordered her pointed on the downbound course for Port Huron. Ringing the brass chadburn to "Ahead full," the master waited for a ring back from the engine room. For a long moment Captain Cummings stood sensing his boat beneath his shoes. When the CORSICA had taken on her normal loaded wiggle the exhausted master left the pilothouse to the mate and strolled aft for some of cook Davy's hot supper. Captain Cummings had been at his post since the boat passed Whitefish Point, and the ever crowded passage down the Saint Marys River and through the Soo locks had made for a very long day. A leisurely dinner in Davy's galley followed by a quiet period in the captain's cabin doing light paper work was surely in order.

It seemed as if Captain Cummings had just closed his eyes and drifted off to sleep when there came a knocking at his door. The watchman had come down from the pilot house to wake the CORSICA's captain and inform him that the boat was running into fog. As he reached the wheelhouse the master found his boat moving into thickening patches of the pea soup fog. Following regulations, Captain Cummings ordered the speed checked to half and the whistle to blow the standard fog signal. By midnight, Mate Johnson had appeared in the pilothouse to relieve Captain Cummings who was by now hollow eyed from lack of sleep. At this time the CORSICA was coming up to a point that her master reckoned to be about 225 degrees and a dozen miles off Middle Island. It was time for the course change that would bring the steamer angling across Saginaw Bay, and some time the next morning have her off Sand Beach where the next turn would head her directly for Port Huron.

Once Captain Cummings had satisfied himself that the CORSICA, which was now slogging along at just over five miles per hour, was established on her new course, he retired once again to his cabin. Mate Johnson was now in command and told to summon the frazzled master if anything unusual occurred.

Blindly the CORSICA felt her way through the fog. Atop the pilothouse the watchman, wheelsman and mate attempted to act as the steamer's eyes and ears from her open air bridge. 1893 was a half century before World War II and that lifesaving device called radar; it was the senses of the mariners that probed the murky distance in search of concealed hazards. It was Mate Johnson's mariner's sense that drew his attention over the CORSICA's starboard side. From the mist, a dim red lamp suddenly materialized and just as the opposing vessel's amber masthead lantern appeared, the bowsprit of a schooner raked across the steamer's bow rail and was ripped away with the noise of a breaking tree. Before the startled eyes of the steamer's crew, the schooner just kept coming and slammed into the CORSICA 20 feet from the steamer's stern.

A violent shock rocked the steamer and the mate instinctively grabbed the chadburn and wrenched the device to "Reverse." From the pilothouse roof, the three crewmen watched in stunned horror as the schooner twisted from the hole that she had made in the steel plates of the CORSICA. Then, with the sound of tortured oak planks and the shouts of distant voices, the schooner and steamer were separated by their own inertia. A moment later the wounded wind grabber vanished back into the fog with her bow crushed and her sails filled with the fresh wind like a sailing poltergeist. It was half past three in the morning.

All around the central lakes, other vessels were set into peril by the dense fog. One half hour before the CORSICA was struck by the schooner from out of the fog, the tug WINSLOW of the Saginaw Bay Towing Association was bound from Bay City to the northeastern shore of Georgian Bay to pick up a raft of logs. Unfortunately, shortly after the tug entered Georgian Bay, someone decided to put Club Island in the way. In fact, the tug's captain had success-fully navigated the shoal and island studded entrance to the bay while nearly blinded by the fog. He then made his turn toward the northeast headed for French River. (A newspaper account of the time indicated her destination as Spanish River, but that would put her in the North Channel on a course 70 miles west of Club Island. This was appar-ently a misprint as a course drawn from the entrance of the bay to French River comes within a point or two of Club Island.) In the muddle of fog, the tug's master misjudged his turn and plowed into the island. The whole incident must have been highly embarrassing to Ben Boutell, the tug's new owner. Mr. Boutell had purchased the WINSLOW the previous winter from the brotherhood of the S.B. Grummond fleet, and during the lay up months he had expanded her cabins all the way aft to provide luxurious guest quarters. On that foggy night in June of 1893, not only was Mr. Boutell aboard the tug as it was driven onto Club Island, but he had brought along former congressman S.O. Fisher as his guest.

Elsewhere around the lakes, a fleet of boats were at anchor at the Soo where the locks had been closed by the fog. Such an event is common today, but nearly unheard of in the bustle of the 1890s. For more than 10 hours the Soo traffic was snarled, giving a good indication of the density of the weather. At Partridge Point on the Saint Marys River, the IRON KING had lost her way and run ashore with her consort standing nearby. On upper Lake Huron near Cheboygan, the schooner MOSHER slammed ashore while running under full sail in the blinding mist. Farther south in the St. Clair River, the steamer SIBERIA had attempted to negotiate the southeast bend during the befuddlement and found herself aground. In all, the fog was taking its share of the lakeboats while being aided by the winds.

In the hours that followed the discovery of the floating wreckage off Alpena, the news of the discovery became as wide spread and confusing as the fog that had caused the collision. There was only speculation as to what vessels had been lost, primarily because the wreckage had yet to yield any positive identity to the victims. For nearly a whole day the rumors ran rabid until the report came down from the tiny town of Ossineke, Michigan, about a dozen miles south of Alpena, of a beached steel whale of the lakes.

The morning sun illuminated the outline of a large steamer brooding ashore in the shallows off Ossineke. Local residents had quickly gathered on the sandy beach, squinting into the misty distance at the outline of the big lakeboat. At first it appeared as if the oreboat had lost her way in the fog and run ashore providing a good day's excitement for the folks of the tiny town. With the sound of the lapping waves of the nearly calm lake in the background, a small yawl became visible between the crowd and the distant beleaguered giant. Slowly the tiny craft drew near the sandy beach as the men aboard pulled at the oars. As the keel of the yawl skidded onto the beach, First Mate Johnson of the CORSICA stepped ashore. The boat that rested in the distance was his. The CORSICA had been beached to prevent her sinking and Captain Cummings had dispatched the boat's yawl to summon help from

Alpena. Within that same day the CORSICA was patched and towed to Alpena where temporary repairs were undertaken so as to allow the boat to continue on to Ashtabula and unload. With the discovery of the CORSICA, however, the confusing mystery of wreckage found off Thunder Bay Island only deepened. It was apparent that the flotsam was that of the schooner that had struck the CORSICA, but what schooner was that? Scores of sailing vessels were milling about in the fog that night on northern Lake Huron, any one of which could now be resting on the bottom somewhere east of Thunder Bay Island.

Prime candidates for the list of possible victims were quickly narrowed down to the SELKIRK, ELIZA, GERLACH, CORSICAN, SENATOR BLOOD and most likely the ST. LAWRENCE. The light of suspicion focused on the ST. LAWRENCE due to the reports of the CORSICA's crew stating flatly that the schooner that struck them was showing a red lamp. Considering that the CORSICA was on the downbound track and that the schooner struck her on the starboard side, the luckless wind grabber was apparently also a downbounder. Reportedly the ST. LAWRENCE had passed downbound through the Straits of Mackinac within the right time frame to meet the CORSICA. Four days after the collision, the ST. LAWRENCE had yet to report at Port Huron, so many considered her to be the phantom schooner.

At half past five o'clock on Saturday June 3rd, 1893 a day and a half after the collision, the SELKIRK was logged as passing upbound through the Straits of Mackinac. Likewise the ELIZA, GERLACH and SENATOR BLOOD all reported at their destinations. As the days passed, only two schooners remained agonizingly overdue, the upbound CORSICAN and the ST. LAWRENCE. Meanwhile, 24 hours after the SELKIRK was reported safely passing Mackinaw, repairs to the CORSICA had been completed and she was preparing to set out for Ashtabula. At the Alpena shipyard of Gilchrist and Fletcher the big steamer's steel hull plates had been drilled so that planks could be bolted to her hull covering the gashes that the phantom schooner had inflicted. Oakum was packed into the seams between the planks in an effort to keep the lake out and the wounded oreboat was considered bandaged. Gushing leaks still penetrated the patch, but the steamer's pumps were now able to keep up. If the pumps kept working, the CORSICA would easily make the lower lakes.

As a minor footnote to the CORSICA's career, just two years after she met with the phantom schooner she would collide with and sink another laker. The year would be 1895 and the month, September and the vessel would be the ROBERT L. FRYER. This time the event would take place on Hay Lake near the Soo and the damage would be to the CORSICA's port bow. Both boats would shortly be returned to service with only embarrassment to burden them. At the moment, all of that was in the unseen future for the CORSICA's crew as they were far more concerned with getting out of Alpena and down the lake.

Unknown to the crew of the wounded CORSICA, the mystery of the phantom schooner was being solved by the tug ANGLER at about the same time as the patched oreboat cleared Thunder Bay. While gathering wreckage for the third day in a row the little fishing tug came upon an overturned yawl that had been once attached to a schooner's stern. Scrolled across the stern of the recovered lifeboat was the name "CORSICAN," which solved the puzzle of the day, but more than a century later leaves us with an interesting question. If the CORSICAN was upbound, how is it that she struck the CORSICA on the starboard side while showing her red light?

An answer to this question could be in the weather that caused the accident. Certainly only those who went to the bottom with the CORSICAN knew what actually happened in the fog that night, but it does not take a wild stretch of the imagination to visualize the chain of events. Clipping through the dense fog ahead of a brisk wind, Captain Bernier, using his clock and taffrail log, hoped to cut close enough to Thunder Bay Island to see the light through the fog and make his turn toward a more westerly course. At the appointed time, however, there was not a trace of the island. Perhaps his navigation was off, or his timing was wrong or the light was out, or the fog was just too thick, but for whatever reason, the good captain wanted no part of the island's rocks and elected to turn toward the open lake. After running a few miles east he could turn and haul toward Cheboygan once more with much more room between him and the Michigan shore. On his run southeast, the captain blindly slammed his boat into the slow running bulk of the CORSICA. The schooner's wooden bow was shattered as the two boats drifted apart as the fog lowered between them like a final curtain. A torrent of Lake Huron burst the schooner's oak bulkheads as the mass of her coal cargo took her to the depths like a sack of rocks. There was little time to escape and those with a mind to leap for their lives were pulled down by the suction of the foundering schooner. Captain Bernier would have been better off had he run onto Thunder Bay Island.

This is simply a guess as to the way the two lakers collided; there are probably many reasons why the schooner and steamer with nearly the same names came together that night. In looking back through a century we find that not even a listing of the names of the lost crew remains, so facts regarding the CORSICAN's loss are scarce indeed.

Spooling back through 100 years of microfilm, we can solve one apparent puzzle in the CORSICAN's loss. Since the steamer CORSICA and her cook, Mr. Davy, survived to work the lakes for many more years... what about the finding of his floating three button coat and the drenched letter discovered by the fishing tug? How did the coat of the crewmember of the boat that survived end up among the floating wreckage of the vessel that was lost? The puzzle is easily solved by scouring the newsprint of the time. Moments after the ill fated schooner ripped clear of the CORSICA, Mate Johnson rang the general alarm and set the whistle to blowing. The steel steamer was taking water quickly and certainly looked as if she were about to go to the bottom. As Captain Cummings was making his decision to attempt to beach his boat, the crew were ordered to ready the lifeboats. Figuring that he was in for a protracted period in a lifeboat, steward Davy dashed back into his cabin and snatched his trusty three button coat from its peg. With coat in hand he made his way to the deck-house roof to aid in the dispatch of the lifeboats. In that process, the coat was fumbled from his hands and fell into the fog-shrouded blackness of the lake.

The finding of Davy's coat among the flotsam of the schooner CORSICAN does yield one important clue. Considering that the wreckage was probably stripped from the schooner as she plunged and that Davy lost his coat in the haste of preparing the lifeboats, we can conclude that the CORSICAN sank very near where the two boats struck and perhaps immediately after the collision. Shortly after the coat went over the side, Captain Cummings ordered the CORSICA full ahead in a desperate charge to beach his sinking oreboat. This left the three button coat behind to mark the spot where the steamer stopped relative to the wreckage of the schooner.

To this day the schooner CORSICAN and her crew remain one of the minor tales in Lake Huron's list of missing vessels. In fact, nearly everything that can be said about the wreck has been presented here. The general area of the loss is in one of the deeper portions of the lake, and as far as is known publicly, her bones have yet to be found, or if discovered have been unreported. Like so many lakeboats and lake mariners, the CORSICAN and her crew were soon lost a second time—in the clutter of history's passing events. After all, of what significance is the fate of a diminutive schooner and crew in the shadows of world wars, economic upheavals and the other disasters of modern humanity.

While his boat was undergoing repairs in Alpena, it is doubtless that Davy caught wind of the story of his trusty coat being recovered with the schooner's wreckage. The foreboding discovery of the three button coat and the soaked letter from steward Davy's dear brother was a major part of the early accounts of the mystery surrounding the phantom schooner's loss. Reclamation of his property would definitely have been in order and the odds are good that while the CORSICA was perched in a Cleveland dry dock receiving permanent repairs, Davy's trusty three button coat was hung in its rightful place in his cabin... still just a little bit damp from its soaking in Lake Huron and waiting for the next coming of winter.

Matchsticks

*I*t was through their friendship with Chief Engineer Philip Trottier that 21 year old Marcel Messenau, 23 year old Henry Seguin and 26 year old Theodore LeRoy found themselves aboard the steamer ROBERVAL. All were from the Canadian town of Hull, just north of Quebec City and in 1916 a personal reference from a vessel's chief was as good as being signed aboard the boat. A job aboard the Canadian steamer meant a bit of certainly in some very uncertain times for the three young men from Hull. The Canadian economy was still suffering the effects of a two year recession and the "war to end all wars" had drawn in the Dominion and her citizens. Indeed a berth aboard a laker meant much more than a place to sleep and a steady paycheck; it meant security amid insecure times. Both Messenau and Seguin would work in the ROBERVAL's engine room under the supervision of Chief Trottier while LeRoy was given the position of deckhand. Coincidentally, young Henry Seguin would find himself standing watches with Second Engineer Ovila Seguin, who was from the town of Hull as well, but oddly was no relation at all to Henry.

Also serving aboard the boat at the courtesy of one of her officers was 30 year old Delia Parent of Ottawa. Miss Parent was a good friend of the family of Captain Peter Eligh, the ROBERVAL's master. Yet unmarried at the age of 30, Delia was no doubt considered a spinster by 1916 standards and probably suffered from the inevitable pressures of her lady kin folk. Shipping out aboard the steamer could

Working a brief career on the St. Lawrence River, the steamer ROBERVAL was rarely captured by lakes photographers. This drawing is taken from one such photo.

—Author's concept

have been the result of her relatives attempting to shove her from the nest in hopes that she might at long last find a good fella, or her own attempt to simply escape the cackles of the surrounding hens. The job aboard the laker would certainly unshackle Miss Parent from the forces that were likely pulling her in many directions, as well as providing the spinster with a fair wage. Only Captain Eligh and Delia knew for sure why she took charge of the ROBERVAL's galley in mid July of 1916, but like the others of the crew, the lakeboat soon became her home. All of the crew were French Canadian, so English was the foreign language aboard the steamer, which is quite common on the lakers that work the St. Lawrence. ROBERVAL was indeed a French speaking vessel on a fresh water sea.

From the ROBERVAL's galley, the sharp sounds of clinking dishware echoed into the companionway as the unshackled spinster saw to the washing of the last of the lunch dishes. It was Monday, the 25th of September, 1916, and the chilly breezes of autumn were cavorting in and out of the ROBERVAL's open windows. The boat was currently moored to the lumber dock at the town of Cape Vincent, where the St. Lawrence River meets Lake Ontario. Being stacked aboard the ROBERVAL were the last planks of her cargo, 248,000 board feet of lumber, with the placement of the timbers being supervised by 66 year old Mate Joseph Parisien. Boards of fragrant spruce measuring one inch by six inches and having lengths between eight and thirteen feet were to be the vessel's cargo. As the last planks came aboard, Captain Eligh made his way from his cabin to the ROBERVAL's pilothouse—in due time the pattern of departure would begin. Down in the steamer's engine room, Chief Trottier also prepared for getting under way. This activity was part of a routine that all of those aboard the ROBERVAL had run through many times before.

Hauling lumber from Cape Vincent to the Diamond Match Company at Oswego, New York was the ROBERVAL's current livelihood. The neatly stacked boards that were arranged upon her deck were consigned to be cut into countless match sticks that would light innumerable lamps, candles and fireplaces. It is interesting to think of how those who would use the matches would never give a thought to their origin, but those nondescript sticks were the means by which the ROBERVAL's people made their living.

Under the watchful eye of Captain Eligh, deckhand LeRoy brought aboard the steamer's lines as the dock workers released them. Strolling into the pilothouse, the captain yanked back the whistle pull, signaling the boat's departure with a single short toot of her steam whistle. Then he casually moved to the chadburn and rang the ROBERVAL ahead. Wheelsman Edward Legault stood leaning on the wheel awaiting the skipper's first order. With the haste of a turtle, ROBERVAL pushed free of the dock just after one o'clock in the afternoon. Astern of Captain Eligh's lumber-laden boat, the steamer GLEN ALLEN was also letting go of the pier, carrying a like cargo of spruce for matchsticks. In an unofficial game of "follow the leader," the two steamers cleared the cape and started on a course for Oswego.

A fresh wind out of the south, southwest was blowing across Lake Ontario and gusting toward 30 miles per hour. Ahead of the autumn winds came a sizable chop in the lake's surface, more in fact than Captain Eligh was comfortable with. About 16 miles out of the St. Lawrence River, the ROBERVAL and GLEN ALLEN passed Galloo Island off the port side and shortly thereafter Captain Eligh ordered wheelsman Legault to bring the boat onto a course that was south southeast. His intention was to hug up a bit closer to the eastern shore, apparently believing that the winds were going to swing more out of the east. His boat would take to rolling, but if his guess was correct, the ROBERVAL would find herself running in the lee of land when the gale came up. Onboard the GLEN ALLEN, Captain A.Y. Clark had apparently decided that the winds and seas were already a bit too fresh for his boat as he remained on the due south course for Oswego. This heading would bring the GLEN ALLEN's head to the seas and hopefully keep her from rolling so much. The master's concern was primarily with the deck load of spruce that was stacked nearly as high as the steamer's pilothouse. Any kind of rolling action or

At first, Captain Clark of the steamer GLEN ALLEN thought that his fears over the safety of the ROBERVAL were exaggerated. Later he found that his mariner's instincts were all too correct.

boarding seas could easily dislodge the dunnage, causing the load to slide over the side, or worse. While Monday afternoon stretched on, the two matchstick boats angled away from one another plodding along at about six and one half miles per hour.

Shortly after the ROBERVAL departed from the beaten path to Oswego, the winds did indeed shift... but to the west. Although huffing a fairly stiff blow, this autumn tantrum was nothing near what Lake Ontario could conjure up if she wanted. To Captain Clark, the GLEN ALLEN's tossing was uncomfortable, but by no means threatening. Shortly after the sun had sunk behind the western horizon, the sky turned from an autumnal sapphire blue and faded toward the blackness that can only be found on the open lakes. Both Captain Clark and First Mate P.H. Brieult saw the last of the sunlight glint off the ROBERVAL's deckload of white lumber some eight miles off the GLEN ALLEN's beam.

"Her bow looks high." Captain Clark pondered aloud as he watched the ROBERVAL being consumed by the dusk.

"That's because of where her ballast compartments are built," Brieult answered casually. "She was made for the saltwater trade you know."

Out of habit, both men had glanced at the pilothouse clock and noted that it read five minutes past six o'clock.

For the next two and one half hours, the GLEN ALLEN rolled through the waves as Captain Clark guided on the Oswego light. At half past eight o'clock in the evening, the GLEN ALLEN plowed into the Oswego River and eased up to the dock at the end of West Seneca street. Having busied himself with the chores of tying up his boat and getting the process of unloading arranged, neither Captain Clark or Mate Brieult had noticed the ROBERVAL's arrival. When the thought occurred to him, however, Captain Clark stepped to the pilothouse window and scanned the waterfront. Across the river at the East Seneca street dock were the lights of another vessel that had just arrived. Now that the GLEN ALLEN was secure, her skipper decided to go ashore and across the river to go aboard the ROBERVAL and see how his good friend Captain Eligh had weathered the crossing.

As Captain Clark neared the east side of the river he realized that the vessel lights he had been looking at were not those of the ROBERVAL. Hunched there at the east side dock was the 123 foot steamer JESKA that had been Oswego bound behind the GLEN ALLEN. Captain Clark felt the gnawing of concern growing in the pit of his stomach and decided to head straight over to the Coast Guard station. The guardsman on duty stated flatly that the only boats to enter the Oswego River that evening had been the GLEN ALLEN and JESKA; the ROBERVAL had never made port.

Shortly after Captain Clark had expressed his concerns at the Oswego Coast Guard station, Captain Clemens, the station commander, was alerted and quickly mustered all hands to their action stations. Eyes were trained on the distance of the dark lake as each of the guardsmen strained for any sign of the ROBERVAL. Feeling a bit like an alarmist, Captain Clark tried over and over again to assure the station personnel that the ROBERVAL was a staunch boat and should easily be able to weather this minor blow. Perhaps she had experienced engine troubles or had pulled into Mexico Bay and dropped her hooks to wait for better weather. Once alerted, however, the guardsmen were not so easily put off. It was their job to rescue mariners in distress, and they very much enjoyed their work. As Captain Clark sheepishly made his way back to the GLEN ALLEN, he left the station crew scouring the sackcloth black emptiness of Lake Ontario. There was not a light, or a flare or any other sign of life in the void.

The ROBERVAL herself was an unassuming, but unique vessel. Measuring a meager 128 feet in length, 24 feet in beam and only eight feet in depth, she was a midget among her steel hulled kin. With all of her cabins stacked aft and a single mast and kingpost boom arrangement mounted just forward of amidships, she had all of the appearance of a coastal saltwater tramp. In fact, the saltwater trade was how the 278 ton steamer had started her career after she was launched at Toronto in 1907. Exactly when Captain Eligh and Captain Hall, the ROBERVAL's owners, decided to bring her back to the Great Lakes is not recorded, but for a number of years previous to 1916 the little tramp had been hauling lumber to Oswego from Ottawa and Cape Vincent and then returning with coal. It was an easily overlooked trade, but it made for a steady income and in the 1916 season it kept the ROBERVAL from being drafted into World War I service and out of the periscopes of the German U boats.

Monday expired and Tuesday began, and there was still not a hint of the overdue ROBERVAL. The hour of midnight passed, and then the hour of one, and only the moaning of the winds was heard. Captain Clemens had alerted by telephone the other stations along the Lake Ontario shore in case the ROBERVAL had experienced some kind of mechanical problem and could be drifting just out of sight of the Oswego station. As the clock struck the hour of two, the fate of the ROBERVAL was about be unfolded in front of the startled eyes of the onlooking guardsmen. Through the darkness at the mouth of the river, the dim image of a single battered lifeboat with three shivering occupants rowing toward deliverance began to materialize like a ghost. At the beckon of a vigilant guardsmen, the yawl eased ashore, nearly flooded, with its bow stove in. Three exhausted mariners, Chief Trottier, Engineer Ovila Seguin and wheelsman Legault, were helped from the lifeboat. At first all three were simply too beaten by the lake to talk beyond utterances in broken French. But after being treated to hot drinks and dry blankets, they told the station crew the story of how they alone had survived the end of the ROBERVAL.

Quartering on the ROBERVAL's bow, the waves had set the steamer to rolling heavily in a cork screw motion when the winds shifted. At about half past five o'clock Monday evening, Lake Ontario decided to lash out at the matchstick boat and raised a rogue wave that held the steamer's fate in hand. Having put off supper until the ROBERVAL got into calmer waters, Delia Parent was attempting to sleep in her cabin when the lake came calling and slammed into the starboard side. The unexpected sea blasted out the galley windows and rampaged through the spinster's dining room like a dozen loose fire hoses. Carrying a tangle of table linens and dishware, the wave did not stop at the galley, but instead cascaded down the companionway and surged into the engine room. A blinding cloud of filthy steam was formed as the icy lake water contacted the hot engine works. Crashing into the ROBERVAL's starboard side, the wave put her sharply over onto her port beam. The sudden roll was apparently more than the boat's deckload could take, as the timbers that were stacked on the port side broke loose of their fastenings and slid off into the lake with an agonizing rumble. Slowly the ROBERVAL righted herself only to roll back to starboard. The next wave smashed into her now tender deck load and plucked most of what was on that side away. Now the doors and gangways were set upon by the lake, and a flood of water threatened to sink the steamer like an old bath tub.

Since it had immediately become clear that something was very wrong with the boat, the members of her crew headed for the open deck. Along with the others of the engine crew, Henry Seguin dashed topside to see what was the matter and paused, bewildered for a moment, at the port rail. Unfortunately, just as he reached the open deck, the stern of the ROBERVAL began to sink severely and the remaining planks of her deckload slid aft. As if shot from a sling, one of the boards rocketed from the top of the pile and struck the fireman squarely in the back of the head, sending him overboard in the same stroke. At this same time, eight miles away, Captain Clark was pondering the ROBERVAL's bow-high appearance from the GLEN ALLEN without a hint of the other steamer's plight.

Fighting their way up the now inclined deck of the sinking ROBERVAL, Chief Trottier and Ovila Seguin made for the lifeboats. The steel deck was wet and slick and their struggle to reach the yawls was a nightmare, to say the least. Meanwhile, Captain Eligh saw Delia Parent clinging to the steamer's rail, frozen in panic. He ordered wheelsman Legault to pry her loose and get her into a lifeboat. Legault had been through two previous shipwrecks and was certainly up to that task. No sooner had the wheelsman brought the panicked cook to the rail than the ROBERVAL lurched in a death throe. Chief Trottier was tossed bodily into the lifeboat that he had been struggling to launch and Delia Parent was washed overboard on the port side. Captain Eligh was standing among the lumber at this same time and slid over the side as the remainder of the spruce cascaded overboard. Somehow the second engineer, wheelsman and chief managed to free the starboard boat. The steamer was by now sunken to the point where the waves were licking at the still-davited yawl. Even though each lumber-studded wave threatened to smite them the three crewmen soon found themselves liberated from the ROBERVAL among a seething jumble of lumber. The lake was not about to let them escape unscratched, as floating timbers had caved in the bow of the yawl and the water was seeping in freely. Darkness, the hull of the ROBERVAL and a sea of spruce separated the lifeboat from Captain Eligh and Delia Parent. In fact only First Mate Joseph Parisien was near enough to be taken aboard the

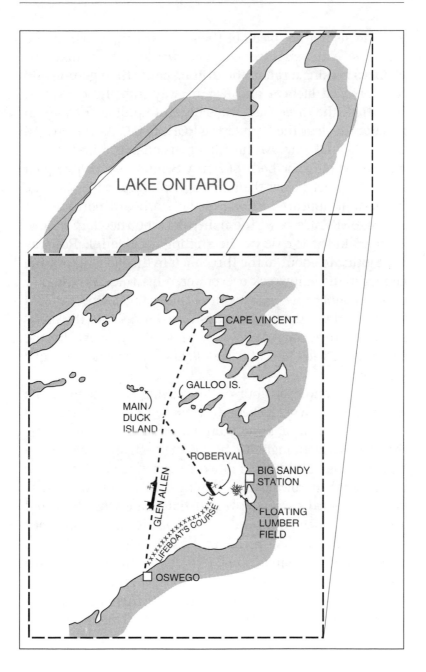

yawl. Resisting the pleas of those aboard the yawl, the 66 year old mate shouted that he would rather take his chances making a raft of the drifting cargo than getting into the damaged lifeboat and swam away into the darkness. With that, the three castaways began to pull at the oars in an effort to clear the foundering ROBERVAL. As they rowed away, they all saw two horrifying visions. The first horror was the sight of the body of Henry Seguin as it drifted past about five feet below their lifeboat. More terrible was the image that appeared in one of the starboard portholes at the ROBERVAL's bow: the ashen face of Theodore LeRoy. Trapped in the fo'c'sle by the shifting deckload, LeRoy was attempting to shout to the three men in the lifeboat, but the clamor of the shipwreck overpowered his voice. As the bow of the steamer rose higher out of the water, LeRoy shouted in vain and the three castaways rowed away into the darkness. To this day, LeRoy remains at his post in the ROBERVAL's fo'c'sle, 200 feet below the surface of Lake Ontario.

For a couple of hours after leaving the scene of the wreck, the survivors pulled at the oars, heading blindly into the lake. Navigating strictly on instinct they headed in the direction they thought to be Oswego—fighting against a blow that had just beaten down a steel steamer. They took turns between rowing and bailing. With each wave that washed aboard came the threat that Lake Ontario would swallow the lifeboat as it did the ROBERVAL. Finally they sighted what they all recognized as the Oswego light and their benumbed hands were renewed in the effort to row and bail. With hope as their only warmth, the three rowed for their lives and reached safety with their last drop of strength. Their trip had covered just over 15 miles—against the wind.

Immediately after the ROBERVAL's survivors were taken ashore by the Oswego Coast Guardsmen, Captain Clemens ordered the station's motor lifeboat launched in an effort to locate anyone else who might be remaining out on the lake. Meanwhile, the castaways were taken to the Diamond Match Company's dock and put aboard the GLEN ALLEN. Through the miserable night the guardsmen searched in their open boat, but not a token of the unfortunate steamer was found. At dawn, after having covered nearly 60 miles, they returned for breakfast and then went out once more.

Tuesday's newspapers from Oswego to Duluth carried headlines in their marine news sections such as "Lake Steamer Lost; Six Die," "Six Drown As Ship Sinks" and "Six Perish In Lake Gale" followed by a confused account of what supposedly had happened. Regardless of the accuracy of the stories, this was the biggest marine disaster since the loss of the S.R. KIRBY on Lake Superior in May. The maritime readers soaked up the news like a sponge. However, the story of the ROBERVAL continued to unfold out on Lake Ontario.

On the surface of Mexico Bay, the seas had died with the winds by Tuesday afternoon. From the Big Sandy Coast Guard Station, acting Captain S.E. Nobles and his crew had been searching for signs of the disaster all day and hadn't found a twig. At half past four in the afternoon, however, Captain Nobles noticed a sizable flock of sea gulls and kingfishers circling in the sky far out on the lake. Knowing that these scavengers were attracted to floating dead things, the commanding guardsmen ordered his patrol boat headed for the sea birds. Within a half hour, the guardsmen spotted a large mass of floating lumber and as they drew closer, four bodies floating atop a makeshift raft of gathered planks became visible. Then, to the amazement of the searchers, the bodies atop the raft began to wave and beckon; they were alive! As the motor lifeboat worked through the mass of spruce planks, the seabirds headed off toward land and shortly thereafter Captain Eligh, Mate Parisien, fireman Messenau and cook Delia Parent were plucked from the lake and headed toward dry land.

At the Big Sandy Station over a hot meal, Captain Eligh told his side of the ROBERVAL's saga. When the captain slid over the side of the foundering steamer he clutched a couple of planks with the hope that they would buoy him up. After he landed in the lake, he was only a few feet from where Delia had gone in, and he saw her go under. As she surfaced, Captain Eligh reached out and pulled her to him, telling the floundering cook to hold on to him while he attempted to gather enough boards to make a raft. A short distance away, the first mate was engaged in a similar struggle to make a raft of his own when he noticed the captain and cook. Paddling over, he joined forces with them in a battle against the lake as time after time they gathered enough spruce to keep them up, only to have the waves wash them apart. After several exhausting hours, they had managed to gather enough timbers to get atop and hold together. Through the night the castaways were kept busy and awake, holding their raft together.

Nearly a mile away, fireman Messenau was having a grapple of his own with Lake Ontario as he attempted to form one raft after another. Finally, he spotted a floating water cask that had been stripped from the roof of the ROBERVAL when she sank. Swimming over, he pulled himself onto the cask and found that it supported him quite handily. For a long while he drifted slumped over the barrel. In the distance he could see the amber glow of the lights of Oswego on the horizon. With all of the optimism of his youth, the 21 year old found a handy plank and started to paddle toward the city that was more than 16 miles away. If the weather held, he just might make the Oswego River—in a month or two!

Back on Captain Eligh's raft, Mate Parisien found two life jackets floating among the rubble. Giving one to Miss Parent, he offered the other to Captain Eligh who told him to keep it for himself. What the captain did want, however, was the emergency light that was attached to one of the jackets and was intended to be used in just this kind of situation. Supposedly the small electric light was activated by pulling a ring on the side, but when Captain Eligh tugged on the ring nothing happened. Over and over the frustrated master pulled at that accursed ring, but the lamp refused to light. Finally in a fit of rage the shipwrecked captain threw the light as far away as he could. Bouncing onto some of the floating lumber in the distance the little lamp lit up brightly. The sight of the tiny lamp shining in the distance provoked snickers from all aboard the raft and continued to do so as it slowly drifted farther and farther away—mocking them all the while.

Daybreak revealed that the raft's occupants were out of sight of land but not far from the plucky fireman who had finally abandoned his floating cask and made a raft of planks and was still paddling for Oswego. When Messenau spotted his shipmates and their raft, he promptly changed his course, and upon reaching them combined his raft with theirs. Through the rest of the day Captain Eligh kept everyone's spirits high by quipping with his sarcastic wit about his fancy new raft command, their distance from shore and their impending rescue. Deep in his heart, however, the 66 year old master of vessels worried over the fate of his good friend, Chief Trottier.

With the appearance of the Coast Guard boat from Big Sandy, the ordeal of the ROBERVAL came to a close. Of her crew of nine only two, Henry Seguin and Theodore LeRoy, did not come off Lake Ontario alive. Considering that both were aboard at the favor of Chief Trottier, there is little doubt that he felt a special pang of guilt when he was reunited with the rest of the survivors. At noon on Wednesday, the automobile from Big Sandy with the four castaways aboard arrived at John S. Parsons' ship chandlery. On the sidewalk in front of Parsons' store the group rejoiced and reviewed their own tales of the wreck. Relieved belly laughs mixed with the cackle that only survivors from the lake's grip can produce. Every detail of the worst marine disaster on the lakes in months was boisterously exchanged for everyone to hear. But, much to the disappointment of the gathered crowd of local onlookers, the excited narratives were all in French.

Bohemian

Sometime, (no one knows exactly when), during the sultry month of July, 1880, an anonymous writer strolled casually into the offices of the *Bay City Evening Press*. Seeking publisher E.T. Bennett, the vagabond reporter shuffled his way through the stuffy office clutter. Every window in the building was propped open and meager ceiling fans stirred the muggy vacuum of the steamy day. Although there is no written account of the events that transpired, it is highly likely that the bohemian journalist was in town from Buffalo to cover the Bay City rowing regatta. Since the rowing events had ended, the reporter was looking for a passage home, the best means of which being via water. Ever resourceful, the writer had decided to combine travel with work by doing a story on his trip to Buffalo and then attempting to free-lance the piece to a local paper. Regardless of the deal that was agreed upon in the offices of the *Evening Press* that day, the reporter made his trip to Buffalo, wrote his story, submitted the piece to the paper and saw it printed on the 12th day of August, 1880. In doing this he left us a fascinating first-hand look into the past that has slept fading away in the Bay City *Evening Press* for over a century. Unfortunately, in the hand type-setting and hasty proofreading of the era, some of the minor facts and details were either left out or misprinted. With these items corrected "on the side," the actual 1880 article is presented here—spelling corrections having been made to avoid having to make the notation "(sic)" with great repetition.

BAY CITY TO BUFFALO
Notes of a trip on a Lumber Barge
Correspondence of *The Evening Press*

"BUFFALO, Aug. 9.—A trip from Bay City to Buffalo by water is certainly no uncommon occurrence, yet I feel satisfied that a majority of THE PRESS readers have not enjoyed the pleasure, and a word in regard to it may be of interest.

"Your correspondent, through the kindness of Capt. Peter Cummings, of the barge S. CLEMENT; was given quarters on that comfortable craft Tuesday, July 29, and that evening the boat departed for Buffalo in tow of the propeller BELLE P. CROSS, accompanied by the barges LITTLE JAKE, BREDEN and JOURNEY-MAN."

It is at this point in the correspondent's account that the mixmaster of time and the reporting of the day combine to begin to slice the setting of the story into a bit of a puzzle. First, the 29th day of July, 1880 was a Thursday, not a "Tuesday" as published. On that Thursday the "Arrivals and Clearances" section of the *Bay City Evening Press* lists the BELLE P. CROSS as departing for Tonawanda, New York with 250,000 board-feet of lumber aboard. Additionally, the barges JOHN BREDEN and JOURNEYMAN are listed as clearing for that same port with 370,000 feet and 300,000 feet respectively. But, there is no listing for the LITTLE JAKE, or the S. CLEMENT. Now, there are several possibilities here—first of all the unlisted vessels may have been simply overlooked by the ship reporter, which often happened in this era. There is also the possibility that one or both of the boats may have loaded up-river at Saginaw and then were tugged to "the anchorage" near Bay City to await a steamer going their way. In this case, the reporters would have omitted them because their shipments had nothing to do with the local market. Lastly, the CLEMENT is listed as being in and loading at Bay City on the 13th. Although it is highly unlikely. Captain Cummings may have elected to stay in port awaiting a good price on a tow, or what he considered to be better rates on his cargo, which he found on the 29th. Lumber rates had started out the month of July at $2.50, but dropped to $2.25 the day before the CLEMENT's arrival on the 11th and stagnated there until the 28th when it was speculated that they would go back up to $2.50. They did indeed go up to that price on the 29th which was most likely the true day of the CLEMENT's departure with the nomad reporter aboard. With these facts in mind we can continue to peek through our window to the past...

"The sun had faded in the west long before the can buoy, marking the channel, was reached, leaving all that could be wished, a fair wind and pleasant weather."

"When morning dawned it found the tow off Port Austin reef, and in a few hours Point aux Barques was reached, the propeller pointing toward Port Huron. When rounding the point I could not refrain from thinking of the many, especially those of the life-saving crew, who have lost their lives at this dangerous place, while braving the wind and waves, and of the number of families that have been bereaved and broken up by the loss of dear ones at this point of the lake."

Aside from having a propensity for writing run-on sentences, the journalist was paying homage to the worst disaster to overtake the U.S. Life-saving service on the lakes. Just 15 months before the CROSS pulled the CLEMENT and her guest past Point aux Barques, the entire crew of the Point aux Barques life-saving station, with the exception of the captain, was wiped out by Lake Huron. The tragic loss occurred on the 23rd day of April, 1879 as the crew attempted rescue of the scow-schooner J.H. MAGRUDER. In all, six brave storm warriors perished in the waves off the tip of Michigan's thumb. These, of course, were not the first nor would they be the last persons lost off Point aux Barques; even in modern times it is a fresh water graveyard. If the traveling journalist was unaware of the ways of this place, no doubt those aboard the CLEMENT informed him of the many terror stories that the mariners knew off-hand concerning Point aux Barques. For those who know the tales, even a fine summer day can be haunted by the bitter memories that hover around those waters. As he watched the tree-lined distance beyond the waves slip by, it is likely that the bohemian writer took new consideration toward the lake and the people who lived and died on it.

> *"When fairly pointed down Lake Huron, a head wind or a "fair wind for jibs," as the sailors call it, sprang up, impeding our progress to some extent. The west shore could be plainly seen, and the numerous towns and villages scattered along the coast showed plainly that man had long before invaded this section of the state and left his mark. Sand Beach Harbor attracts the attention of the stranger as he passes. Captain Cummings assured me that this harbor was one of the best on the lakes, and expressed the wish*

that there were more of them at other points, for said he, "A person on the lakes can't just exactly tell at what moment he may be compelled to make use of them." At 9:30 p.m. the light at Port Huron could be discerned at intervals, but when the CROSS passed that burgh, its residents save one were wrapped in slumber. This particular one was a newspaper man, at his post reporting the vessel passages, so that the interested public in different cities might know by their next paper what had passed up and down.

"At day-break we had passed the rapids and were wheeling around the crooks and bends of the St. Clair, frightening ducks and divers here and there, and at 8 a.m. were floating upon the blue and placid bosom of Lake St. Clair. A propeller and tow bound up were passed now and then and at 11 a.m. the tall steeples and spires of the city of the straits, (Detroit), loomed up ahead. Hog Island—Belle Isle as it is now known—greets the eye as Detroit is neared. The isle looked exceedingly beautiful as we passed, with its huge oaks in their dark green foliage, shady walks and comfortable settings. A merry crowd were landing at its wharf from the steamer GARLAND and I wished to be among them for a moment, but the wish died away as the more attractive features arose ahead. Michigan's metropolis from the river front is an interesting sight. Her avenues and thoroughfares show signs of thrift and business as the casual observer glides by. The river bank in the outskirts of the city affords handsome sites for private residences but I am of the opinion that the bank on the Canadian side is more beautiful and appropriate for this purpose.

"The CROSS came to and landed at Detroit to coal, and making use of the opportunity I took a stroll up town, but soon learning that the ordinance prohibiting the blowing of whistles at the wharves is strictly enforced I afterward remained in close proximity to the craft which was to bear me to Buffalo. In a number of cases, when barge captains and sailors are ignorant of the existence of this ordinance, they have been left on the shore while waiting for the signal, which they failed to hear and proceeded to Buffalo by rail to overtake the craft which had suddenly forsaken them.

"The CROSS was soon on her course again. The notorious limekiln crossing was passed before 6 p.m., and a dredge was seen at work removing the blasted stone from the point, which, at times gives so much trouble to heavily laden crafts. Considerable care must be taken here by propellers with tows to keep the right course or on the rocky bottom they will surely go. At sundown the tow had entered Lake Erie and was nearer her destination than ever. This sheet of water which is so often boisterous and much more so than the remainder of the lakes was as quiet as the day of its birth on this occasion. Sunday passed with land out of sight. The sunset of that evening was grand and will long be remembered by those who witnessed it. Would that I were able to describe it. A stiff breeze had sprung up during Sunday night from the west which sent the CROSS and tow on at a rapid rate and Buffalo was reached three hours earlier than was expected. As Buffalo was neared, a small schooner lying about a mile south of the entrance to the harbor, was flying a signal of distress, but no one in port seemed to notice it and in a short time it was taken down. Entering Buffalo Creek I was somewhat amazed at the liveliness exhibited in marine matters. Everything seemed to be on the move—pushing ahead as it were to secure the last available dollar. The huge *elevators and storehouses were busy hoisting grains from lake craft, or discharging it into canal boats to be shipped to New York or intermediate points on the "raging canal." Everything has a lively appearance and the stranger is favorably impressed with the western metropolis of New York."*

It is the writer's unabashed promotion of Buffalo that leads one to conclude that the bohemian journalist may have been local to that area. In the pre-1900s, rivalries between towns as well as those across towns were common. In an odd sort of way the printing of an article that ran down the local community in favor of a distant town showing up in the local paper probably added to the fun.

"As the CLEMENT neared her dock she was met by a gang of longshoremen who pounced upon her cargo and commenced unloading before the lines had been made fast to the wharf. The stevedores at Buffalo receive 30 cents an hour for their labor and are eager to procure that amount. They are not as independent as those in Bay City, who don't care whether or not they work for 40 cents.

"Capt. Cummings, unlike a majority of lake captains, does not use harsh or improper language in addressing his crew, and for that reason the sailors on the CLEMENT speak highly of the boat and its merry commander. Capt. Cummings is reckoned as one of the best masters on the lakes, and well may he be. He was born and bred on the water, so to speak, having sailed since he was a mere youth. He made the trip exceedingly pleasant for me, by pointing out the different places of interest and answering the many questions I propounded to him during my four days on the water."

In tow of the BELLE P. CROSS, the bohemian reporter was given a tour of the lakes aboard the schooner S. CLEMENT.

The reporter's opinion of Captain Cummings was high praise indeed, and the good captain remained master of the CLEMENT for two more seasons. Local records show that he assumed command of the schooner-barge "FANNIE NEIL" at the start of navigation in 1883 ending six seasons on the CLEMENT. After that we sort of lose track of him, but the chances are good that his name will pop up once again among the adventures of the Great Lakes.

As with most newspaper pieces of this ilk and this era, the article simply ends at this point. What was printed as a simple side-light used to fill space in a local Bay City newspaper more than a century ago has been our time-machine providing an intriguing glimpse into the everyday events of the forgotten past. As the essay runs out, our look through the keyhole of time is abruptly terminated leaving us without so much as the writer's name—it is by-lined simply...

"BOHEMIAN"

The Fang of Mud Lake

*T*ypical for late September was the weather that hung over Sault Saint Marie as the wooden lake-boat MONTEAGLE cleared the locks and headed down the St. Marys River. It was noon on the 19th day of the month, 1909, and the annual autumn grain rush was just beginning. A few stray birds pecked at grains of sprouting wheat that had been lodged in the seams of the steamer's worn oak deck planking and seemed to pay no attention at all to First Mate Thomas L. Van Dusen as he made his way toward the pilothouse from the galley. Stuffed in the steamer's hold beneath the hollow thumps of the mate's footsteps was a cache of 51,700 bushels of the seed grain, more than the pecking pigeons on the MONTEAGLE's deck could imagine in their wildest bird dreams. Just five days earlier, nearly to the minute, the big wooden laker had passed upbound headed for Duluth. She spent only a few hours under the elevator's chutes, departing through the ship canal's long piers on the 17th with the grain in her belly. Now, with the ore laden tin-staker ZENITH CITY keeping her company and the locks fading astern, all aboard the MONTEAGLE were in the mood for a casual passage to the lower lakes.

Scaling the ladder to the pilothouse roof, Mate Van Dusen joined the MONTEAGLE's captain, S.M. Murphy, as well as the vessel's wheelsman standing on the open air bridge. All three men stood watch as the steamer's bow was pointed down the West Neebish Channel and she funneled

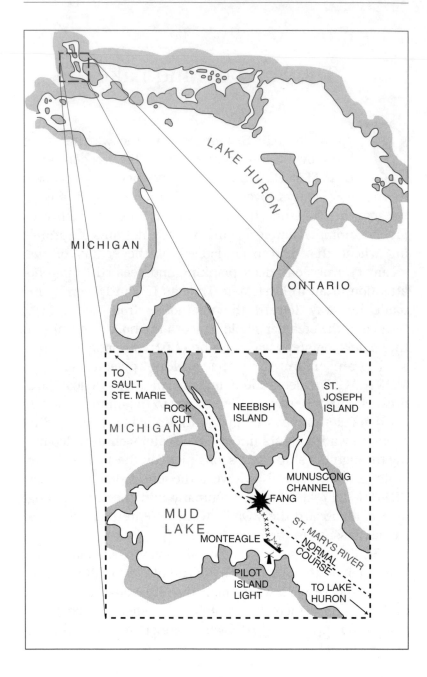

A fine career was put on "hold" when the MONTEAGLE met the Fang of Mud Lake.

toward the narrowing confines of the Rock Cut. The Rock Cut passage between Neebish Island and the mainland of Michigan's Upper Peninsula had been completed just over a year before the MONTEAGLE slid into it, and was specifically constructed to relieve the bottleneck of traffic through the Munuscong Channel to the east side of the island. Now, upbound lakers used the east channel and downbounders used the Rock Cut, thus eliminating the potential for collision between two way traffic in the bottleneck and the blockades that had been caused when vessels came to grief in the confines of a single narrow passage on the east side of Neebish Island.

With no fuss at all the MONTEAGLE eased silently through the rip rap stone confines of the cut and headed onto the relative expanse of Mud Lake. Now, with the very worst of the St. Marys River behind him, Captain Murphy felt at ease enough to leave the boat in the charge of the mate and take a few moments to go below decks. Mate Van Dusen was a thoroughly capable mariner and knew each turn and landmark along the St. Marys well enough to navigate them in the black of night while beset by fog or snow, so he would have little problem at nearly four o'clock on this September afternoon. After giving the standard small talk of command exchange, the captain made his way down the ladder and left the MONTEAGLE in charge of Van Dusen.

Sailing with the swift current the grain laden steamer was making about eight miles per hour as she approached the Mud Lake beacon. A black buoy that was not marking the channel caught the mate's attention and he gave the order to pass starboard of it. Then, without warning, Van Dusen saw the distant treeline moving to the right beyond the MONTEAGLE's steering pole at an uncomfortable clip. For some reason the steamer was taking a sheer to the port side.

"Steady up to port," the mate ordered calmly as he noticed the steamer's drift. The deviation, however, only intensified. Thinking that the helmsman had gotten the order backward, Van Dusen shouted, "Port!" toward the flustered wheelsman who was by now wrestling with the MONTEAGLE's big wooden wheel.

"Something's the matter with the wheel!" the boat's helm handler grunted back as he continued his grapple with the steering apparatus. A moment later, as Van Dusen reached out to join the struggle, the steering gear freed and the MONTEAGLE began to haul back toward her course. That moment of relief was short lived, because no sooner had she come back under control than there came an agonizing crunch and a dull shock that nearly tossed the crew from their feet. At the channel's edge and submerged a few feet below the surface, a stone crib had been waiting to snag the first vessel to stray from the downbound course. Apparently the MONTEAGLE had drifted far enough for the stone fang to bite into her port bow.

The shock of the impact brought Captain Murphy bounding back up to the bridge. By the time the frantic master reached the pilothouse roof, the MONTEAGLE was already taking on a sinking posture. Shouting down the speaking tube to the chief, Captain Murphy ordered the pumps started in the hope that the boat's touch with the crib had only opened a few seams. Even with the syphons running, however, the MONTEAGLE continued to lower her head and list to port. The oak laker was obviously badly wounded and now only drastic action would keep her from sinking. Captain Murphy decided to beach his boat and rang for "ahead full." With that the floundering MONTEA-GLE slogged ahead and stuck her bow into the shallows just above the Pilot Island light. Slowly she settled onto the river bottom with the groans of a beached sea monster. Now at least there would be time to summon assistance from the Soo, patch the shattered bow timbers, lighter the cargo and pump the water from the hull. Thereafter, the boat could probably go on with her work with only a few day's delay.

MONTEAGLE was not the first vessel to be bitten by the fang of Mud Lake. In fact she was the fifth laker damaged there since the opening of the Rock Cut. Previously the hidden obstruction had snared the lighthouse tender AMARANTH, as well as the revenue cutter MACKINAW and the 263 foot wooden oreboat ALFRED MITCHELL. All of these managed to escape with only wounded pride. For the big 405 foot whaleback steamer JOHN ERICSSON, however, it was a different story. Running with the deep draft that was the nature of the whalebacks, loaded or unloaded, the ERICSSON was bitten firmly by the fang crib. It was only after a lengthy toil by two tugs that the big whaleback was released, probably sporting a hefty and expensive need for repairs. Now the MONTEAGLE had the ill favored distinction of being the latest victim.

Since the third day of May, 1884 the MONTEAGLE had been hauling cargos across the Great Lakes. On that festive Saturday the freshly painted hull of the spanking new MONTEAGLE met fresh water for the first time at the Buffalo, New York shipyard of Robert Mills & Company. By the standards of her day the steamer was a modern monster in every respect. She sported the lines of an oreboat of the future with her pilothouse perched atop a fully raised fo'c'sle and her spar deck cleared all the way aft to the coal bunkers with the exception of a single "dog house" that was planted amidships. Such a cleared deck would facilitate the unobstructed loading and unloading of the MONTEAGLE by shoreside equipment. Her engine crew quarters were placed aft, which gave her the overall look of what was to become the standard laker.

An iron sheathed boiler house was lodged aft of the MONTEAGLE's coal bunkers and separate from the after quarters. This was a real leap into the future and was supposed to cut down the risk of fire caused by the boat's own steamworks as well as give the owners a significant break on their insurance. This was just one of the MONTEAGLE's features that was highly similar to the steamer configurations that later became the trademark of Bay City, Michigan's wooden shipbuilding czar James Davidson. It was later applied to the largest wooden steamers ever constructed on the lakes, vessels that would sail well into the next century. In fact, every line of Davidson's monster oak steamers smacked of the MONTEAGLE's earlier design. This striking similarity of vessel design between two shipyards that were several states apart is quite remarkable and a bit puzzling. Breeds of lakeboats have always been as easy to distinguish from one another as breeds of dogs. Granted that in the 1800s there were many mutts, but the Davidson boats were purebreds. Somehow it seems as if the line may have had some of its genesis in Buffalo with the construction of the MONTEAGLE. The puzzle is, how did the design migrate from Buffalo to Bay City? Had Mr. Davidson "borrowed" parts of this design, or had some anonymous nomadic engineer joined the Davidson staff having migrated from the employ of the Robert Mills yard? Such are the trivial ponderings that true lakeboat buffs dwell on more than a century after the fact. Here it will suffice to say that the MONTEAGLE was a true prototype of wooden lakeboats to come.

Power to move the MONTEAGLE was provided by a fore and aft compound steam engine with 23 and 48 inch diameter cylinders on a 42 inch stroke. Constructed by the Frontier Iron Works at Buffalo, the power plant was provided steam from two fire box heated boilers measuring nine and one half feet by 16 feet. In all the engine gave the MONTEAGLE some 600 indicated horsepower and a loaded speed of just under 10 miles per hour.

At 222 feet in overall length and 35 feet across her beam, plus a depth of 19 and one half feet, the new steamer must have seemed like the most monstrous thing that ever floated from the Mills yard. Surely the MONTEAGLE drew the attention of the workers and management of the Union Dry Dock Company that was located directly across the river from the steamer's birthplace. Normally the Mills yard concentrated on repairs and refits of wooden vessels, but this futuristic giant could be cause for concern among Robert Mills' competitors. Surely she made the side-wheelers and package steamers that had been produced across Buffalo Creek at the Union Dry Dock Yards seem antiquated. As it turned out, however, there would be no real competition from Robert Mills, as over the years that followed the MONTEAGLE's launching, his boatyard would turn out barely enough steamers to count on one hand. Still, the odds are good that when the MONTEAGLE entered enrollment on June 10th 1884, and steamed proudly onto Lake Erie, the ends of more than a few cigars were nervously chewed at the Union Dry Dock Company.

Settling in 16 feet of water on that gray Sunday afternoon, a quarter of a century after her birth, the MONTEAGLE was now safe from sinking and in wait of assistance from Sault Saint Marie. A drenching cold rain fell that night, the unceasing kind that is common to the Soo in September. With the Saint Marys River filling her hold nearly to the hatch tops and invading all of her lower spaces, the fires in her boiler room were promptly snuffed. With them went the steam that heated her cabins. Being of the hearty breed from which the mariners of wooden lakers are born, her crew elected to remain aboard—heat or not. Through the night the rain pelted the steamer's windows and cabins in a depressing noise that seemed as if it would never go away. The MONTEAGLE's crew members did what they could to pass the indifferent hours while keeping as comfortable as possible around the galley's woodburning stove and the coffee pot that steamed atop it.

By dawn, the lighter RELIANCE arrived from the Soo and was moored alongside the stricken MONTEAGLE. The plan was to lighter nearly all of the steamer's burden of grain, place a temporary patch over her wound and take her to DeTour for more permanent repairs. Through nearly all of the day Monday, the RELIANCE's clam-shell bucket was lowered repeatedly into the MONTEAGLE's hold, taking immense bites of the luckless steamer's soaking grain and dumping it into the lighter's own hold. With the rain having let up, the work went at a very steady pace indeed and by late afternoon the MONTEAGLE was well on the way to being afloat again. The only hitch was that the 152 foot RELIANCE was only able to take 10,000 bushels into her hold, just under one quarter of the MONTEAGLE's cargo, before darkness brought the process to a stop. The lighter would have to return the following morning for another day of unloading. Once more, about 10,000 bushels were removed from the MONTEAGLE's cargo hold. This just about topped off the lighter's hold capacity; now it appeared as if the RELIANCE was going to need some lightering herself. Word was sent out to Marquette in request of a convenient vessel to take aboard the discarded grain. Although the entire content of the MONTEAGLE's hold had not been taken off, it was enough relief to get the steamer floating, and provide access to her ruptured bow planking. With all of the haste that could be mustered, the steamer's crew set to work at making temporary repairs to their vessel.

As darkness set upon the Saint Marys River that Tuesday evening, the MONTEAGLE's crew were hard at work using every means thinkable to cast the remaining water from her hull. As the hands on her pilothouse clock pointed toward the hour of 11 o'clock, the boat's chief was sloshing his way around the still partially flooded engine-room in an effort to get the machinery back in working order. It had been a long few days for all of the steamer's people. Sleep had been hard to come by within the unheated cabins and now all hands were in a marathon effort to get their boat sailing once more.

Under these circumstances it is easy to envision that galley stove was stoked just a bit too high, or unattended for just a bit too long. Perhaps one too many oil lamps were placed in an obscure nook of the boat's inner hull for needed light and left unattended or some exhausted crewmember drifted off to sleep with lit smoking material— whatever the reason, just before midnight, the MONTEAGLE's after quarters were found to be ablaze. Within minutes the flames were running ceilings and consuming fixtures in a way that no arsonist could imagine. In less than an hour, the situation was hopeless. Gathering what few possessions they could snatch, the boat's crew went over the rail and made their escape in the MONTEAGLE's deck yawl.

With the flames consuming the steamer's upper structure, she was fast lightened and soon went adrift as a free-floating requiem of flame to a hardworking lakeboat. Swept downstream she was consumed to the waterline and finally sank while the river put out the flames. Curiously, Captain Murphy was very closed mouthed about the details of the end of his command. His only public statement was, "When I awoke the boat was on fire in the after end... as to the cause I know nothing." One would think that when a master has his boat burned from underneath him, he would certainly waste no breath on his crew to find out what happened. Indeed, from the time they rowed to the Pilot Island lightkeeper's house for shelter, until the logging tug RUSSELL STEVENSON dropped them off at the Soo at two o'clock the following afternoon, there was plenty of time for such a discussion. No matter, the whole crew were promptly paid the wages that they were due and sent off without another word. Was there really just some unknown flame that caused the steamer's end, or were the circumstances just so embarrassing that Captain Murphy wished them consumed with the boat? The exact cause of the MONTEAGLE's burning remains a mystery to this day.

On Thursday, September 23rd, 1909 the Cleveland Cliffs steamer CHOCKTAW plodded into the upper Saint Marys River and locked down at noon. Bound from Marquette, the monitor-styled laker was there to relieve the RELIANCE of the soggy grain that she held for lost MONTEAGLE. Through the day the RELIANCE's clam-shell again scooped the spoiling grain and this time transferred it into the CHOCKTAW. Clearing the Soo the following day, the CHOCKTAW headed for Milwaukee to deliver her soaked burden to a distillery. Meanwhile, at the lock wall Otto Gibbs, a crewman aboard the oreboat WILLIAM LIVINGSTON, had managed to get his hands on a bottle of a distillery product for himself. As the boat made her way through the locks, Gibbs proceeded to "make things lively" and at one moment was walking along the edge of the lock wall. At that point one of the lockmen spotted a gun protruding from the drunken sailor's pocket. Figuring that hard liquor and hand guns do not mix, the lockman slickly removed the weapon from Gibbs' possession and shuffled him back aboard the LIVINGSTON. The vessel's captain would have no drunken antics aboard his boat and ordered the mate and several burly dockhands to put the drunken sailor in his bunk and make sure that he stayed there. As the LIVINGSTON cleared the Soo and steamed past the spot on Mud Lake where the insurance underwriters were dragging the water in quest of the MONTEAGLE's remains, Gibbs was in his bunk. As to what method was used to keep him there, no record was made, but he was in his bunk and would not make things lively aboard the LIV-INGSTON in the near future—that was for sure.

With the passage of time, the MONTEAGLE faded from the memories of most of the Great Lakes maritime population—much like the anxiety of Robert Mills' competitors at the Union Dry Dock Company when the boat was launched. The insurance underwriters claimed to have found the vessel's hulk in 40 feet of water directly west of the Mud Lake beacon, and announced their intentions to dredge the remainder of the grain out of her and sell it to a distillery as well. In the months that followed the MONTEAGLE's end, across the nation many an elbow would be bent to hoist a potent glass of spirits—a portion of whose contents having been distilled from the salvaged cargo of the MONTEAGLE. Perhaps among the crowd would be Otto Gibbs, looking to "make things lively" in another place and time. Without knowing it, the happy drinkers were making a silent toast to the fang of Mud Lake and the vessels that it had bitten.

Today the actual location of the MONTEAGLE's remains seem to be, like the cause of her burning, another of the small riddles in the thick binder that is the Great Lakes mystery file. Although her location was supposedly published, modern divers who went looking for her at that location found nothing. Up to the time of this writing, the swift currents of the Saint Marys River have kept the long lost steamer's grave a closely guarded secret and made quite a perplexity for local scuba divers. Like so many other little mysteries on the lakes, this one will be left for you to ponder.

Just What Became of Them?

Daylight had started to brighten the low lapping waves of Lake Huron as the number one lifeboat from the steamer PHILADELPHIA, crowded with 22 survivors, pushed from the fog-bank and rasped onto the sand and rocks. It was dawn on the seventh day of November, 1893, and no sooner had the overburdened yawlboat skidded her bow onto the beach than several burly crewmen went over the side and proceeded to grapple the craft onto dry land. As fast as his feet were planted on the beach, Captain A.E. Huff turned to squint back toward the fog-shrouded lake in search of the image of the number two boat. A moment later he was joined by Captain A.J. McDonald, who himself was scouring the muddle with his eyes, both of these cast-away captains having shared the same lifeboat.

"How far behind us do you suppose they were?" would have probably been the first question.

"Not too far; maybe they'll come in down the beach there."

"Get some of the boys to walk on down the shore that way, and on up there a bit in case they come along farther up."

Shouts were cast into the fog and soaked up like water into a cottonball. The seconds turned into a minute.

"They ought to be here by now." More shouts were sent toward the gray lake in a harmony of concern as the sur-

Two lifeboats from the PHILADELPHIA set out for shore; what happened along the way is a mystery to this day.

vivors fanned out along the beach, each in hope of being the first to sight the tardy lifeboat.

"Don't fret too much," Captain Huff murmured, "Hunt's a good man, if anyone can handle that yawl he can." Both of the vessel masters began to pace the beach. Minutes stretched into an hour.

"I just don't know what could have become of them," was the question that was repeated over and over as the cold morning protracted. That question has hung over Point aux Barques as that hour turned into a century, and the shouts into the fog were never answered. The occupants of the PHILADELPHIA's number two lifeboat never emerged from the silent fog. No cries for help were ever heard, nor were the sounds of disaster—those who were in the number one boat were simply left to pace the cold beach until all hope was given up. Just what did happen to yawl boat number two and its two dozen occupants out in the fog of Lake Huron that November morning has become one of the truly unsolvable mysteries of Great Lakes maritime record.

The pieces of this puzzle were started into place two days before captains Huff and McDonald were to find themselves pacing the foggy beach of Point aux Barques. On Sunday evening, November 5th, 1893, the 1678-ton steel steamer ALBANY pushed passively from under the lights of Chicago and into the open blackness of Lake Michigan. In command was Captain A.J. McDonald and aboard were some 17,000 bushels of corn and 75,000 bushels of oats. Additionally First Mate George F. Drury had supervised the loading of a "roll-on" cargo of 250 barrels of flour to round out the payload. Buffalo, New York would be the ALBANY's port of destination. At about the same time as the ALBANY went plodding up Lake Michigan, the PHILADELPHIA departed Buffalo with a pile of coal in her hold as well as a tween-decks cargo of iron stoves and other assorted goods. In command of this Duluth bound vessel and cargo was Captain Huff who, just like his counterpart on Lake Michigan, had no idea that their boats were already on a collision course.

Just nine seasons old, the ALBANY was running under the house flag of the Western Transportation Company. The displacement of her iron hull was a whopping 1,917 tons and she was representative of a rather confused era in lakes shipbuilding. Her lines were similar to wooden vessels of the day and she had side-ports for the roll-on cargo and series of three deck-houses topping her hull. Twin stacks were complemented by three elegantly raked masts. Captain Huff's command, on the other hand, was of 1867 vintage. Constructed by vesselman David Bell at Buffalo, the steel hulled PHILADELPHIA measured a respectable

1,486 tons in displacement. Like the ALBANY, the PHILADELPHIA had been born with the lines of her wooden-hulled contemporaries with a similar deck-house arrangement. In contrast to her counterpart, however, the PHILADELPHIA sported only a single spar and a single stack. As testimony to her fine construction, even though she was in her 26th season the sturdy laker carried a value of $80,000 and an insurance rating of A1/2. Certainly, both boats were well suited for whatever the Great Lakes could dish out.

As Monday evening turned into Tuesday morning, the PHILADELPHIA steamed silently from the confines of the St. Clair River and plowed onto the expanse of Lake Huron. The calm seas that met the laker's bluff bow were a marked contrast to early November's normal disposition and the night's canopy seemed filled with stars. It had been a long day's passage up the Detroit and St. Clair Rivers, and Captain Huff found himself rubbing the blur from his vision as he relinquished the pilothouse duties to First Mate Hunt. With his dog at his heels, the exhausted master managed to find the way to his cabin. There had been too many vessels to pass and too many turns to make on the way up and now the captain's bunk would be as welcome a relief as the open waters ahead. With a resigned flop, Captain Huff "hit the hay" and at his bedside his faithful pooch curled up and fell asleep with a heavy dog-sigh. Aft, in the Chief engineer's quarters, a second dog was dozing while keeping a keen ear to the steamer's every hum. Between the captain's dog and the chief's dog, it would be difficult to conclude which pup had established command on the vessel or whose turf was where, but there is no doubt... they knew.

PHOTO COURTESY OF MILWAUKEE PUBLIC LIBRARY MARINE COLLECTION

A proud and powerful steamer, the ALBANY rests today on the bottom of Lake Huron.

Far ahead of the upbound PHILADELPHIA on open Lake Huron, the ALBANY was pushing downbound. In command of her pilothouse was First Mate David Conners who was often on watch with lookout Robert Breckel or his counterparts William Sherry and S. McMutrie. Wheeling of the ALBANY was shared between William McPherson and Dan McLeod—one of whom, tonight was guiding the boat on her compass alone into the ink-black distance ahead. As the steamer made greater progress toward lower Lake Huron, banks of thick fog were encountered. Each new patch of the muddle grew thicker as the boat took longer and longer to pass through. As the mist turned into a cotton-thick blanket, the boat's lookout took an exposed position on the vessel's bow. His sharp ear, as well as those of the pilothouse crew, made for the ALBANY's only early warning system. The boat's whistle was sounded at regular intervals, this signal normally being three blasts each minute on the Great Lakes. In return, the ears at her pilot-house listened intently as the toots of the whistle rolled off into the distance.

Shortly after two o'clock that muddled morning, the pilothouse crew of the ALBANY could hear the whistle of a vessel directly ahead. As receptive ears endeavored to catch the next series of whistle blasts so as to determine the direction and distance to the boat sounding the signals— the PHILADELPHIA loomed from the fog and answered the question. Instinctively the ALBANY's wheelsman spun the boat's wheel hard to port in a vain effort to avoid the on-coming steamer. It was too late. Before anyone could do more, the PHILADELPHIA struck the ALBANY amidships on the port side. Cutting the boat nearly in half, the bow of the PHILADELPHIA crashed ahead as if to pass clean through. The watch at the pilothouse said that they had been hit just forward of the number two gangway abaft of the cabin doors. As if about to roll over with the force of the impact, the luckless ALBANY rocked and then crunched back onto the nose of her assailant. For a long lingering instant the two vessels poised as if waiting for some higher power to orchestrate the next move.

In her effort to avoid the collision the PHILADELPHIA's engines had been ordered full astern and shortly after the impact the two boats were drawn apart from one another. Although not immediately sinking, the ALBANY was now certainly not the place for her crew. Sensing that the boat he had just ran into was in far worse condition than his own vessel, Captain Huff directed the PHILADELPHIA run up along side the ALBANY to facilitate an escape for the crew. Being of a like mind, Captain McDonald wasted no time in giving the order for the crew to evacuate to the PHILADELPHIA. The ALBANY herself, however, was not abandoned. Rather her crew put a line on her nose and the wounded steamer was taken in tow of the PHILADELPHIA. It was reckoned that the shallows off the tip of Michigan's thumb were just seven miles distant and if the wounded ALBANY would stay afloat for just another hour, both might be beached. It was a good plan, sound in intention, but short on time.

Some of those on the PHILADELPHIA that night said that the pull toward the shallows lasted a half hour, others said it was more like 45 minutes. Whatever the time, the results were the same—the ALBANY suddenly began to founder at the end of the towing hawser. The decision to cut his boat loose was an easy one for Captain McDonald, and Captain Huff agreed; with the swing of an ax, the compromised steamer was sacrificed to Lake Huron. Now the charge to save the PHILADELPHIA was on. At full steam the broken-nosed package freighter was running for her life. The objective was still the same, beach the boat, but the urgency was greatly increased. Now, upwards of 45 people were depending on the PHILADELPHIA to make shoal waters. The muddle of the fog combined with the night and the confusion of the collision left Captain Huff with his instincts alone to find the beach. His was a blind race against the lake, and it was off to a bad start. Apparently, the good captain had his bearings a bit off—believing that land was due south. Once he was free of the sinking ALBANY he could make better headway toward survival.

What Captain Huff could not know was that a turn to the southwest would cut his trip in half. This point soon became moot, as the forward bulkhead on the PHILADEL-PHIA began to moan and fail. Perhaps it was the pressure of the water under full headway, or maybe the damage inflicted in the collision—no matter, the PHILADELPHIA,

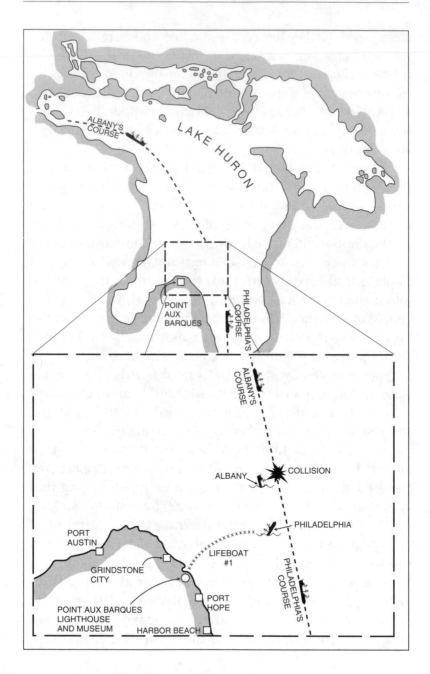

like her victim, was now about to sink. With the steamer still under full steam, but giving every outward indication that she was about to take a nose-dive, Captain Huff gave the order to take to the lifeboats. Both yawls were put over and lowered. In boat number one went Captain McDonald along with first Mate George F. Drury, second engineer David Connors, fireman William Brown, Jonathan Reed, Phil Bloddel, oiler J. McPartlan, wheelsman Dan McLeod, William McPherson, lookouts Robert Breckel and William Sherry, cook Herritage and deck hands Charles Stanton, John Watson, J. Parkinson and G. Selden, all of the ALBANY. These castaways were under the charge of PHILADELPHIA crewmembers, Samuel Hunt, William Brown, William Fitzgerald, James Flynn, P.A. Wilson and Captain A.E. Huff. With all aboard, the number one lifeboat was lowered, released and pushed clear of the sinking laker and made for the shore.

Between the darkness and the fog there was no way for those aboard the number one boat to see what was happening over at the number two lifeboat station. Hidden in the befuddlement, First Mate Hunt was supervising the launch of the number two boat. Aboard it were the ALBANY's Chief, S.B. Muirhead, Second Engineer Jason Molly, Second Mate Thomas Pearce, watchman Jacobe Price, waiter S. McMutrie, porter William Sturrah, as well as deckhands Frank Ketcham and Albert Holm. Of the PHILADELPHIA's crew, Second Engineer Jerry Morran, Second Mate A. Hanna, wheelsmen W. Gibbs and C. Linguist, lookouts C. Rowen and R. Renshaw, watchman C. Williams, firemen James Labelle and John Paint, first cook George Reidermaster, second cook George Wise, porter J. Conners and at least one deck hand whose name was never recorded. So crowded was the boat now that there was room for only one more man, Chief Leggitt, and no space remained for his dog. Both mascots of the steamer PHILADELPHIA had to be left aboard. As the two lifeboats pulled away the howls of the stranded pets echoed painfully in the distance like the cries of impending doom.

According to those on the scene, as each of the lifeboats made their escape, the PHILADELPHIA was left at "full ahead" on her engines. By this time a slight wind had come up and the yawls were steered so as to keep into the wind. As a result the steamer and the castaways were quickly separated. From the black distance soon came a shattering rumble and crashing sounds as the PHILADEL-PHIA was heard to go to her end and to the bottom of Lake Huron. From boat number one, Captain Huff shouted a hail into the sackcloth distance, and from the fog-shrouded night a voice answered from boat number two. They too had heard the steamer as it made its plunge. For the next 10 minutes assorted hails were tossed into the night and answered by those aboard boat number two, and with the resignation of those now unemployed the shipwrecked crew pulled for land. There was probably some satisfaction that everyone had successfully escaped the sinking steamers, but still there was the feeling of having lost your job and your home in one night.

Sometime around half past seven o'clock that morning, the folks in boat number one saw the flashes of the Point aux Barques lighthouse. Guiding on that alone, they soon ran smack onto the Michigan shore. Once safely on dry land, the people in boat number one fanned out along the fog-bound beach. It was figured that boat number two was a bit down-wind and would slide ashore shortly after boat one. Now their hails into the fog were no longer answered. The calm waiting soon turned to frantic searching—something was wrong, very wrong. Alarmed, the crew hiked to the Point aux Barques lifesaving station where Captain Ferris immediately dispatched the station's boat in search of the missing crew. Additionally, the steamer CITY OF CONCORD was engaged to join in the search. While the occupants of lifeboat number one split their time between combing the beach and waiting at the lifesaving station, the searchers criss-crossed the foggy distance out of view of those ashore.

Not long after the search had started, the lifesavers found themselves rowing into a field of floating wreckage. Shortly thereafter they pulled directly into the mystery that would hang over the lake forevermore. There, on the edge of the wreckage field, was a body; and soon another and another. All were clad in lifebelts. The CITY OF CONCORD was soon making the same terrible finds. It was discovered that lifeboat number two had capsized with its hull stove in—nearly to the point of being halved. In all, 11 bodies were found and recovered. When the forlorn lifesavers rolled the shattered yawl over in order to tow it in, they found another body. After gathering their sad harvest, the searchers returned to Point aux Barques and the question spread through the Great Lakes maritime community—just what had become of the passengers of lifeboat number two?

On the following morning, Captain Huff and the ALBANY's First Mate, George Drury, traveled to Tawas City where a hearing board was assembled. There followed a few days with far less than the normal amount of finger-pointing. Meanwhile, the remainder of the castaways headed for Buffalo. On Wednesday morning, Captain Ferris left the lifesaving station once more, in search of the sunken steamers. Sticking straight up out of Lake Huron eight feet high—like a signpost of catastrophe—was the black mast-tip of the PHILADELPHIA. Calculating his position as being six miles northeast of the station, the good captain returned to report his findings. There would be no additional persons of either boat to return from the lake and the hails of concern, like the questions of what happened to that lifeboat, would never be answered.

Today, more than 100 years after the collision between the ALBANY and the PHILADELPHIA, anyone can drive the state road 25 route that circumnavigates Michigan's thumb. Without regard to where you start, be it Bay City or Port Huron, the trip will pass through the lake-shore towns and villages that were once the seeds planted by the Great Lakes maritime industry more than a century ago. Now they are pleasant little fishing and vacation spots in the fair weather months and hibernating habitats of solitude in the winter. Places such as Sebewaing, Lexington, Port Crescent and Port Hope dot the shoreline with little reflection of their maritime past. As the road reaches nearly the tip of the thumb, a slight deviation will bring the visitor to the Point aux Barques lighthouse park. The visitor will find that the light is somewhat mis-named because it is several miles south and east of Point aux Barques itself. Although the lifesaving station has been moved to Huron City as part of a collective display of historic local buildings, the lighthouse remains and at its base is a small museum. Collecting a bit of dust in one corner of the museum are bits and pieces of assorted wrecks that have been removed by divers in the days before the bottom lands were protected by the state. Looking closely, one indifferent wooden piece which appears to be part of a doorjamb can be found to wear the label "PHILADELPHIA." Exiting the lighthouse museum, one can walk down to the rocks and sand of the beach exactly where lifeboat number one came ashore in

1893. The lapping waves seem to hold tightly the secret of lifeboat number two while wandering feet crunch on the beach. Gazing out toward the shimmering blue of Lake Huron, the visitor can ask the question, "Just what became of them?"

No one other than the passengers of lifeboat number two will ever know the answer to the question. There were several theories put forward as to what became of boat number two, none of which could explain the loss. The first was that the steamer PHILADELPHIA itself, abandoned under full steam, somehow rammed and sank the yawl. Those in boat number one, however, said firmly that they could clearly hear the steamer founder and that the people in boat number two answered voice hails for 10 minutes thereafter. So much for that solution. The next theory was that a passing steamer inadvertently ran down the lifeboat. But would not the passing steamer have been blowing fog signals? And even if not signaling, a collision such as that would have caused a great deal of racket—surely those in the nearby number one boat would have heard something. Maybe a passing schooner ran down the yawl and having sails up was unable to stop or turn back. But no schooner reported a collision, and the winds were reported as light from off shore, so the odds are that they were not hit by a sailing vessel. Finally there was the far-fetched contention that the CITY OF CONCORD ran down the yawl while searching for it. But, the CITY OF CONCORD was dispatched long after the yawl was considered missing.

No explanation for the loss of the PHILADELPHIA's number two lifeboat and its people will be presented here. The wrecks of the ALBANY and PHILADELPHIA rest on the bottom about three miles apart with the ALBANY nearly due north of her assailant. The question as to why two dozen people in a life boat who should have reached shore, did not, was left hanging over Point aux Barques, but has faded from memory by the passing of more than a century. It is up to those who learn of this story to stand on the beach at the base of the lighthouse and ask toward the lake, "What ever became of them?" in order to keep the memory of those aboard lifeboat number two alive. When you do, do not expect an answer to come back from the indigo distance—Lake Huron has kept that to herself for more than 100 years.

Threads of Happenstance

*W*ith the peck of each finger the keys of Mrs. H.R. Mills' typewriter sounded a clacking that echoed through the cozy silence of her winter-bound home. Upon a single, legal-sized sheet of paper the hammer-head keys slammed out the words of Mrs. Mills' thoughtful message to a beset stranger many miles away. With just a few typos the letter read...

Iroquois Island, White Fish Bay, Michigan.
Brimley, R.F.D.#1.
Dec. 9, 1919.
Captain W. R. Neal,
Bay City, Mich.

My dear Captain Neal:—

Under separate cover I am sending you the glasses and a small flash light that were found on the main land across from this island shortly after the wreckage of the MYRON came ashore on the island and mainland.

The other evening when speaking of the pilot house, I remarked to my husband that I would like to have it brought across from the mainland and set out here near the island bay so that I could have it fixed up for a summer house. It was then that I learned from him that you had expressed a wish for it. In the event that you may wish it sent to you next year, we will have it brought across to the island after the ice forms; if it is found possible to move it at that time and will preserve it for you. When I learned of your expressed wish concerning the pilot house, I told him that very likely you would like to have the glasses and flash light and that I would send them to you. We have had them apart and cleaned them as well as we could, though when found they were filled with sand and water. We trust they reach you in safety.

During the terrible storm of those few days little did we dream of the tragedy that was being enacted such a few miles from us, and my first exclamation the morning we discovered the lumber and wreckage on our shores was "Oh I hope the men are all safe." Though I like living near the water I am always fearful of its pitiless power, especially at this season of the year.

My husband and I want to congratulate you upon your restoration to your family, and we sympathize fully with the great happiness that we know is yours and theirs over the reunion.

With the very best of wishes for your complete recovery from the effects of the terrible exposure you underwent, we remain,

> *Very sincerely yours,*
> *Mrs. H.R. Mills."*

For some reason, the community of the Great Lakes maritime industry has an odd habit of connecting people, vessels and events. This was especially true in the era of wooden lakeboats—a time which came to a sudden, but

Captain Walter Neal was the only survivor of the MYRON wreck.

rotting end with the 1929 stock market crash and the massive economic depression that followed. In the years that preceded the end of the white oak lakers, there had been a steady decline in their numbers and as the 1919 season drew to a close only a few wooden lakers were still making a good profit. Beginning on the night of November 22, 1919, the threads of Great Lakes happenstance were, again, about to begin to be woven between several vessels and people who made their living among the aging oak fleet.

Through the storm-raked night of the 22nd and into the stinging cold morning of the 23rd day of what is traditionally the most foul month of lakes navigation, a benumbed Captain Walter R. Neal had clung to the roof of the floating pilothouse of his former charge—the wooden lumber hooker MYRON. Keeping the frost-bitten master alive had been a fire that burned within him, a flame of anger. Through the long frozen hours he had kept himself

This piece of the MYRON's stern gives one the idea of the size of the vessel, as well as the violence of the wreck and power of the lake.

awake and alive by his ire, not toward the Lake Superior gale that had just pounded his vessel to the bottom, but toward the captains of the two steel oreboats that had left him and his crew for dead on an angry Whitefish Bay. He had to stay alive—if only to be sure that they paid for what they had done, for surely if the lake were to claim Captain Neal, the truth would never be told. So, with his hands robbed of feeling and his clothing frozen to his body the frost-bitten captain let the icy waves wash over him as he burned in his heart. The enraged skipper had no way of knowing that he would turn out to be the only survivor of one of the most infamous shipwrecks in Whitefish Bay history and that he was already firmly ensnared by the threads of Great Lakes happenstance.

Warned to be on the lookout for the floating bodies of the MYRON's crew, Captain W.C. Jordan of the steamer

W.C. FRANZ was keeping a sharp watch out of his pilot-house windows. Upbound out of the Soo and headed to Fort William, the 366 foot steel oreboat was beating her way into the chop of Whitefish Bay and would soon be in the area of the previous afternoon's wreck. In the distance, the first indication of the expected flotsam soon appeared as a bobbing white speck or two on the white-capped horizon. Focusing his binoculars on the distant objects, Captain Jordan was astonished to see the image of a man sprawled atop the pilothouse of the lost MYRON, magnified in his view. It was just about noon by the time Captain Jordan managed to maneuver close to the distressed castaway. The solid hull of FRANZ was blocking the waves and wind as Captain Neal was plucked from a frigid doom after nearly 20 hours. With all of the heat and comfort that the FRANZ's accommodations could muster, Walter Neal began his recovery as the steamer pushed on toward the head of the lakes.

No sooner had the FRANZ made her lines secure beneath the waiting grain chutes at Fort William than a telegram was being dispatched from Captain Neal. From the main office of the Phoenix Block Postal Telegraph-Cable Company at 719 Washington Avenue in Bay City, this message of salvation was promptly dispatched to the wife of Captain Neal:

70 DE C $3 Collect 5 15p
Fort William Ont Nov 25
Mrs Walter Neal
403 South Erie Ave ayCity (sic) Mich.

Rescued Sunday noon by steamer W C Franz after twenty hours bath in Lake Superior. I am on board

*Franz at Fort William either you or Williams meet me
at Soo on the way down will wire time later doing fine
answer quick.*

W R Neal.

Only the date was wrong on Captain Neal's message as
it was received by his wife. The day was in fact Monday the
24th rather than the 25th as the hasty telegraph operator
had transcribed. Mrs Neal, in turn, wasted little time in dic-
tating her response which arrived at the Canadian Pacific
Railway's office at Fort William:

*83 WN W 25
Bay City Mich Nov 24th 1919
Capt Walter R Neal.
Str W.C.Franz. Fortwilliam (sic)*

*Our prayers have been answered Mother and I will
meet you at the Soo on way down let us know when
you will be there.*

W.J. Neal.
1905

Such was the end of a most exhausting chapter in the
sailing career of Captain Walter Neal. It was an event that
would be well written of and extensively yarned over the
years. All of that would mean little to the careworn lakeman
as he was reunited with his spouse and made the pilgrimage back to his home on Erie Avenue.

Many months would be taken up in Captain Neal's
complete recovery from his frozen ordeal. It would take far
less time for the master to recover enough to tell his story

fervently and often to the people in power in the Great Lakes maritime community.

He had brought the MYRON out of Munising, Michigan with a full load of lumber and towing the schooner-barge MIZTEC which had a similar load aboard. Both lakers were running under the house flag of the O.W. Blodgett lumber company, the last of the "big" lumber fleets on the lakes. Shortly after their departure, Lake Superior pounced upon them with a classic November gale, complete with thick snow and arctic temperatures. Wallowing in the storm the 194 foot MYRON and her consort were making little progress toward Whitefish Point as the storm began to get the better of them. Through the blizzard, Captain Kenneth McRae, master of the steel oreboat ADRIATIC of the Interlake Steamship Company, had spotted the Blodgett boats. It was clear that both steamer and consort were suffering, so McRae ordered his boat headed over to their aid. Easing the 440 foot ADRIATIC's hull as close as he dared to the beset lumber boats, Captain McRae did his best to offer some lee from the storm. Despite the Interlake boat's hovering near by, the situation onboard the MYRON steadily went to pieces. Leaking severely and with only 700 horse power in her steam engine, the wooden steamer was making little headway with the MIZTEC attached to her heels. So Captain Neal made the best decision that he could at that time—he ordered the schooner-barge cut lose.

Just before dusk the intruding lake got to the MYRON's fires and snuffed out her steam. Together captains Neal and McRae had brought the two boats barely into Whitefish Bay, but had reached the traditional shelter too late. Twice Captain McRae had attempted to reach the floundering Blodgett boat as they came around the point and twice the big steel steamer had been slammed into the sandy bottom when between the waves. This was more, much more, than a laker of any size could be exposed to without being damaged. The ADRIATIC's master could not afford to stray from the channel again; he could do nothing more than stand off as the MYRON foundered. As darkness began to set in, Captain Neal ordered the crew to the lifeboats. The MYRON was rapidly filling and the end was now in sight. As the crew went over the side, Captain Neal had no way of knowing what the ADRIATIC's master had already put his giant steel boat through, and saw only the frustrating sight of the lights of the massive steamer standing far off the doomed lumber hooker. When the MYRON finally plunged to the bottom, Captain Neal was in the pilothouse and the ADRI-ATIC appeared to be pulling away.

Shortly after the MYRON went down, Captain Neal managed to claw to the lake's surface and found his way to the top of what had been the boat's pilothouse. The ADRI-ATIC was gone, but the lights of another steamer were pressing down upon the scene. Apparently, Captain Lawrence Francis had been watching the Blodgett boat's difficulty from the pilothouse of the 540 foot oreboat H.P. McINTOSH and was now drawing up on the site of the wreck. The boat came within about 15 feet of the drifting Captain Neal, and Captain Francis called out to the ship-wrecked master that he would send a boat back for him. Then, without further explanation, big steel lakeboat sim-ply churned off into the night. Surely a line could have been easily thrown to the shipwrecked Captain, but there was no such offer. The fire to survive, the fire of anger within Captain Neal had been stoked.

Drifting with only her storm sail, the MIZTEC did not go unpunished by the storm. Her deck-load was swept over the side and she was generally pummeled by the tempest.

Accused of failing to render assistance, Captain Francis of the II.P. McINTOSH (seen here in later years as the EDWARD S. KINDRICK) had his master's certificate revoked for life.

She did, however, survive, giving warrant to Captain Neal's decision to cut her loose. When the tug IOWA came huffing into the Soo with the MIZTEC attached to her towing hawser, there was no real surprise in the Great Lakes maritime community. The act of cutting a barge lose in a gale often saved the consort. Likewise there was little surprise when both Captain Francis and McRae had their Master's certificates revoked for life by the U.S. marine inspector's office in Marquette for failing to render assistance to mariners in distress. A harsh sentence, at least for Captain McRae. Some sources say that his revocation was overturned in later years, others say that both were eventually overturned and others say that they were never over-turned—as of this writing, no records have been uncovered to detail the end results. For all three captains, the strings of happenstance had not tangled them together in a good manner as the 1919 season expired.

By the spring fit-outs of 1921, Captain Neal had long since recovered to the point where he was ready to ship out once again. Unfortunately, the Blodgetts had lost two of their schooner-barges, the GOSHAWK and MARY WOOL-SON the previous year, so they had an abundance of qual-ified officers this season. The best that the company could do for Captain Neal was to offer a job as mate on the steamer ZILLAH. Such an offer was just fine with Walter Neal; after all, it has long been a tradition on the lakes that when circumstances dictate, mariners that are qualified as captains will sign aboard as mates. As he made his way to the foot of the Third Street bridge, where the ZILLAH laid up each winter along with the other Blodgett boats, he had the same mixed feelings as any other experienced master who has to go to work as mate. There was probably the itch of playing second fiddle to one of his peers, offset by the relief of not being burdened by the awesome responsibili-ties of command. In many ways, it must have felt good just to go back to work.

Fitting out the ZILLAH did not take long, considering that the boat was beginning her 31st season. The wooden lumber hooker was well broken in. Her birth took place on March 31st, 1890 at the West Bay City yard of shipbuilder F.W. Wheeler, located very near where she now spent her winter lay ups. As hull number 67 she was originally chris-tened EDWARD SMITH and given an official number of 136106. The steamer's rig, construction and dimensions of 201 feet by 37 feet and a depth of 13 feet were all typical

Seen here towing two unidentified Blodgett schooner-barges, the ZILLAH outlasted most of her kin.

for an oak lumber hooker of her era. She ran as the SMITH for a decade, being re-named ZILLAH in 1900. By the time Walter Neal came aboard, the little steamer's timbers had their sharp edges worn round, but she still earned her way in the hard working world of lakeboats.

Like tall trees in a lakeboat forest, the masts of schooner-barges MARION W. PAGE, BRIGHTIE, MIZTEC, J.L. CRANE, PESHTIGO and MINGOE jutted toward the sky along the crowded banks of the Saginaw River where the ZILLAH was getting up steam. Also preparing to start their seasons were the wooden steamers P.J. RALPH, CHARLES M. BRADLEY, and W.H. SAWYER. Elsewhere along the West Bay City waterfront many other oak lakers were waking from winter's hibernation. Down at the Davidson yard the steamers SHENANDOAH and SACRA-

MENTO were likely fitting out along with the schooner-barges GRANADA, GARRETT SMITH, GRAMPIAN, MATAN-ZAS and MONTEZUMA. Additionally the little lumber hooker MIAMI was in the season-opening process and aboard her were the three men of the Heilbronn family. Twin brothers George and Charles, as well as George's son Calvin, all of Saginaw, made their living aboard the same boat. Indeed, West Bay City was the Mecca of the wooden lakeboat, even in the declining era of such vessels. In this atmosphere Walter Neal felt quite at home, but as he boarded the elderly oak deck of the ZILLAH, he had no way of knowing the ways in which the strings of happenstance were binding some of the vessels and men on the river and how they would cross paths in the future.

Winter seemed to be unwilling to release its grip on the upper lakes as dawn struggled to break on Friday the 13th day of May 1921. Without a twinge of fear for what many people considered a traditional day of bad luck, Walter Neal was bringing the ZILLAH up the Saint Marys River toward the Soo locks. As the steamer drew near Mission Point, Mate Neal surrendered the pilothouse to the captain and made his way down on deck to play his proper role. Supervising the line handling and tending to the management of the ZILLAH's two barge tow was the job of the mate at this point in the trip and Walter Neal could perform this duty in his sleep if need be. Trailing behind the huffing ZIL-LAH were the schooner-barges MIZTEC and PESHTIGO, both, of course, members of the Blodgett fleet. Like her towing steamer, the MIZTEC was loaded with a cargo of bulk salt bound for Duluth. The PESHTIGO, however, was running empty and according to the trip sheet hanging in the ZILLAH's pilothouse, was scheduled to be dropped off just outside of the port of Munising, Michigan. All around the three boats, the sky boiled in a brooding gray stew of clouds that appeared much more like the weather of late fall than that of mid May.

Once all three boats were secured in the lock, Captain Campbell, the PESHTIGO's master, greeted L.E. Harris as he came aboard over the schooner-barge's rail. Mr. Harris was a government employee at the American locks and was looking for a passage to Munising. Even today the modern blacktop road that leads to Munising from the Soo through the tree-lined wilderness of Michigan's upper peninsula makes for a long trip, so in 1921 the best and fastest way to get to the secluded village was by catching the next lake-boat bound that way. Captain Campbell led the lockman down the PESHTIGO's long wooden deck toward the after quarters and galley where he would be made at home for the relatively short duration of his trip to Munising.

Launched as a three masted sailing vessel in 1889, the PESHTIGO eventually had her middle spar, or mainmast, removed to better facilitate the deck-loading of lumber and thereafter she was compelled to earn her way being towed behind a steamer. Measuring 210 feet in length with a 34 foot beam and a 12 foot depth, the PESHTIGO was not far from being just ordinary. To Captain Campbell, however, she was his command as well as his home for the season. As he extended his vessel's hospitality to the traveling lock-man, the captain may have mentioned that his brother, Robert Campbell was over on the MIZTEC serving as mate; doubtless there was more than a towing hawser binding the two Blodgett boats together.

Indeed, across the way Robert was dutifully tending to the process of getting the MIZTEC through the lock. The whole process was being conducted under the casual command of Captain Pederson who, like his counterpart on the

PESHTIGO, was one of the vanishing breed of schooner-barge masters. Also aboard the MIZTEC were Bay City residents Eric Johnson and Louis Florance serving as deckhands. Additionally there was John Disher and, as often seemed the case in the world of wooden lakers, a man whose name was never recorded. As the MIZTEC was tied up at Port Huron, Captain Pederson found his vessel in need of a deckhand and the man without a name came along in need of a job. Even though it was the 1920s, it was still a time when a vagabond sailor could find berth on a "walk-up" basis. Rounding off the crew roster was Captain Pederson's wife Florence who served as the MIZTEC's cook. Surely the presence of his spouse made the long shipping season less lonely for the boat's master, not to mention adding to the family income.

After passing through the locks with the normal amount of groans and creaks that all of the old wooden boats were prone to make, the three Blodgett lakers headed into the widening upper Saint Marys. With the additional sea-room, the towing hawser was let out until the three boat convoy stretched nearly a quarter mile. Now the Blodgett vessels pounded toward Whitefish Point and what was surely going to be an indignant Lake Superior.

Exactly what possessed the ZILLAH's skipper to sail out from under the shelter of Whitefish Point in the prevailing weather conditions we may only speculate upon. The odds are that like so many masters of his breed, the ZILLAH's captain simply had little regard for weather. There was work to be done and hiding in shelter every time that the sky turned foul was no way for boats to earn a living. Such was probably the mind-set of the crews of all three of the wooden vessels as they entered the open lake resigned to the fact that they were going to have a rough go across

Superior. What the lake served up, however, was far more than a bit of angry spring weather—it was a freakish spring storm of near hurricane force. Heavy snow came with blizzard strength as the temperature plummeted and the winds began to scream. A towering sea developed with the crests of the whitecaps being ripped away by the wind and shot at the boats as freezing spray. Before long, ice began to build on the wooden trio as they pitched and rolled in a struggle just to stay on course.

With only 785 horsepower at her disposal, the fatigued ZILLAH found her over-the-bottom speed frittered away by the storm until it was all that the steamer do just to keep her head to the seas. After hours of struggle the ZILLAH's pilothouse crew estimated that they had made less than 10 miles since rounding Whitefish Point. The closest shelter would be another 40 miles into the gale at the port of Grand Marais and the very real possibility began to form that none of the boats would take the pounding that far. Considering that—the 70 miles needed to make Munising was now an insurmountable distance. Dark hills of Lake Superior's ice water came rampaging out of the thick snow and burst over the ZILLAH's bow in an unending succession as their water found its way through every crack and doorjamb. There was only one choice that the steamer's master could make...turn, and run back for Whitefish Bay.

As the steamer's laboring powerplant pulled the trio around, the gale lashed out at them. Spray was flung completely over the wildly rolling lakers and snow blew so hard that you could not look into the storm. Lifting on the seas and cork-screwing the ZILLAH's timbers twisted against one another and spit their caulking into the foaming lake. After what seemed to be an eternity she fell onto an easterly course and the waves began to mount the stern rail.

183

The groaning of the towing hawser was overpowered by the roar of the irate lake. Luck alone caused the MIZTEC and PESHTIGO to follow. Now, wallowing with the seas at their heels, the three oak lakers pushed toward Whitefish Point. Without a doubt, Walter Neal's memory spooled back to that autumn tempest in 1919 that left him floating on the MYRON's pilothouse roof not far from where he and the ZILLAH were now. Certainly the numbing sting of his once frost-bitten limbs came back clearly enough.

Onboard the PESHTIGO, Captain Campbell was doing his best to keep the schooner-barge properly aligned with the ZILLAH. Even in rough weather a barge has to be kept out of the towing steamer's propeller wash to keep the consort from yawing on the end of the towing hawser. Tonight, it was difficult just to see the MIZTEC and ZILLAH's lights, let alone attempting to keep her at the proper position from the steamer's wake. In fact, most of the time the steamer was simply swallowed by the snow and all that could be seen from the PESHTIGO's pilothouse was one or two of the MIZTEC's lamps as they rocked ahead. With the gale at their backs the storm-raked trio now made good progress toward shelter and soon would be able to round the point and retreat into the lap of Whitefish Point's lee. From the ice spattered window of the PESHTIGO, Lockman Harris kept an eye ahead in hopes of sighting the Whitefish Point light through the swirls of snow when, without warning, the lights of the MIZTEC went out. A heartbeat later, those aboard the PESHTIGO felt the waves lift her stern, twisting her from her course. Absent of cargo, the schooner-barge was being rapidly blown into the sea trough and now began to violently roll on her beam ends.

There was no time for Captain Campbell to concern himself with the fate of his brother over on the MIZTEC.

The MIZTEC came to her end without a witness.

The PESHTIGO was now apparently adrift and it was his duty to save his own command. Ordering the crew forward, the master of the drifting barge directed that the storm sail be set. This action would catch the wind and pull the schooner-barge's bow around bringing her out of the sea trough. Staggering with the rolling deck, the PESHTIGO's crew struggled forward amidst tidal waves of frigid Lake Superior as it came over the rail looking to take the boat and her desperate crew into her depths and leave not a crumb behind. Slipping and sliding on the icy deck, the crew of the schooner-barge would have made a comical sight had not their circumstances been so dire. Upon reaching the foreboom and storm sail, the crew found it encrusted in a thick cake of ice. With the haste and strength that only men facing certain shipwreck can muster, benumbed hands pawed at the frozen canvas and

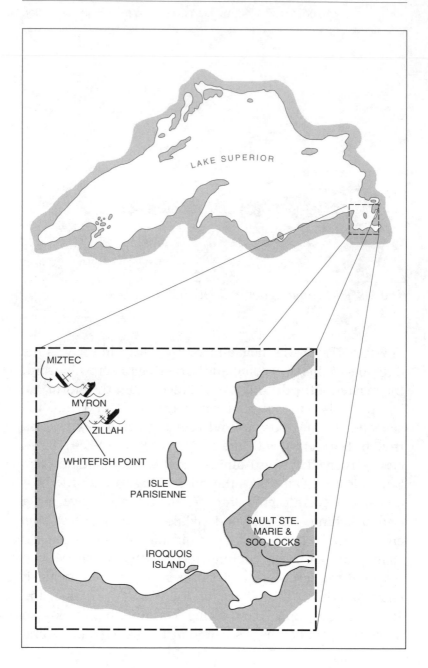

rigging as the barge broached and Superior came aboard again and again.

Free of the burden of her barges, the ZILLAH dashed ahead through the snow. Her barges had broken away less than a mile from Whitefish Point, leaving only a short distance to sprint to safety. It was perhaps this short distance alone that saved the ZILLAH, as she had been twisted to the point where her seams had opened and were badly leaking. Knee deep was the water in her engine room and her stokers would soon have been unable to keep her fires alive. As the wallowing steamer came to a listing repose in the lee of Whitefish Point, it became clear that Lake Superior had come within a whisker of claiming Walter Neal and the vessel that he sailed upon—again! The strings of happenstance had put him in the same peril as on the MYRON a year and a half earlier and within just a few miles of the grave of his former command to boot.

Through the night, the pumping out of the ZILLAH proceeded as the gale continued to blow. Locally, around the Soo, six inches of snow fell before the storm eased, peculiar for mid-May, even at Sault Saint Marie. Supervising the pumping operations, Walter Neal could see by dawn on Saturday that the ZILLAH would probably be able to get under way by afternoon. A search for her two missing barges was in order. Perhaps they were riding at anchor, or blown ashore, or worse yet—pounded to the bottom. Thoughts that there might be someone out there some where floating on the wrecked roof of a dead laker haunted the ZILLAH's mate, and it is a sure bet that he was itching to get out on the lake. Little did he know that the his worst fears were true.

Downbound early Saturday morning, the 390 foot tanker RENOWN of the Standard Oil fleet, was headed for

Whitefish Point amid the expiring gale. About three miles off of the point, the tanker suddenly plowed into a heaving field of wreckage. Checking her speed down to dead slow the RENOWN's master ordered all hands on deck as the tanker slid in among the flotsam. It was the wreckage of a wooden vessel, but as soon as the crew began to search the field, the RENOWN's momentum carried her clear of the debris. Apparently some old wooden laker had met her end in the previous night's storm, but all that was left for the RENOWN and her crew apparently was the flotsam. There was nothing left to do but press on to the Soo and report their find. Just as the tanker's screw started to churn ahead once again, there came a chorus of shouts from the deck crew. In the distance, among the wreckage, a man floating on a shattered cabin roof was sighted. Turning the RENOWN seemed to take forever, even with the will of every member of her crew pushing on her rudder. Agonizingly, she finally came about and headed back toward the stricken crewman. As the big tanker neared, the makeshift raft pitched with a wave, and this time the threads of happenstance broke. Unlike Walter Neal, 18 months before, this castaway rolled from his perch and was swallowed by the lake right in front of the tanker's horrified but helpless crew. Superior was not about to be cheated this time. With heavy hearts, the RENOWN's crew proceeded to the Soo to report their finding, and loss. If Walter Neal had any premonitions of someone re-living his ordeal, they were terribly true.

Pumping of the ZILLAH had concluded by late Saturday afternoon and with a belch of black coal smoke from her funnel, she headed back around Whitefish Point. A stiff wind was still blowing thick snow as the Blodgett steamer got under way. Shortly after rounding the point,

PHOTO COURTESY OF MILWAUKEE PUBLIC LIBRARY MARINE COLLECTION

From the tanker RENOWN another man floating atop a shattered pilothouse was spotted.

the ZILLAH's crew spotted one of their wayward consorts riding at anchor. Easing near the battered schooner-barge, it quickly became clear that she was the PESHTIGO. After she went adrift, her crew had managed to get the storm sail set and attempted to navigate through the night. At dawn, the reluctant daylight revealed that the schooner-barge was less than a half mile off of the rocks near Whitefish Point. Immediately Captain Campbell ordered the boat's hooks dropped—not an easy task on a schooner-barge. Splashing into the gray whitecaps the anchors at first simply dragged across the sandy bottom, then grabbed, bringing the PESHTIGO's bow to the winds. There she rode until the ZILLAH came for her. The waves continually assaulted her and the annoyed sky spit snow, but the boat survived. Now, as the ZILLAH lingered near, it was clear that the PESHTIGO had weathered the worst of her ordeal.

Megaphone shouts between the two boats confirmed that all aboard the schooner-barge were safe and her hooks were holding. With concerns shifted to the MIZTEC, the ZILLAH set out in another search.

Later that night, the crew of the PESHTIGO spotted the familiar lights of the ZILLAH once again headed toward them. The MIZTEC, however, was not following faithfully in tow. A search of the surrounding area had yielded only sparse patches of floating wreckage. As the sorrow-filled crews made fast the towing hawser between the ZILLAH and PESHTIGO, an atmosphere of black remorse that not even Lake Superior's mighty winds could blow away hung all around the two vessels. The MIZTEC would never be coming back, nor would the crew that she had taken to the bottom with her. Those who sailed the Blodgett boats were neighbors and close friends and this loss would be deeply felt for a long time.

The strings of happenstance had connected Walter Neal, shipwreck, Whitefish Point and the MIZTEC in a way that he could never have imagined, but had twice released him to return to the safety of his home on Erie Avenue. If, however, the southeast shore of Lake Superior and Whitefish Point's web of kismet happened to be finished with Captain Neal, it was by no means done with the Blodgett fleet. Later that same season, on the 11th of November, the P.J. RALPH was cast ashore just west of Grand Marais by the lake's treachery. With no small effort the steamer was pulled free and went on to sail another day. Not so lucky was the Blodgett schooner-barge J.L. CRANE four years later, as nearly to the day, she was swallowed whole with all hands by the angry lake just a dozen miles from the MIZTEC's grave.

August's calendar had flipped 25 days in the year 1926 and just five seasons had passed since the MIZTEC snapped from her tow. The ZILLAH was huffing upbound from the Soo locks once again. Walter Neal was not aboard the ZILLAH this season, having found demand for his skills and experience on a different vessel. However, serving aboard the elderly oak laker were three closely related sailors with more than one thread of shipwreck happenstance about to be woven between them. Tending to their duties aboard the ZILLAH were Charles Godspeed Heilbronn, and his twin brother George Godlove Heilbronn, elder by two hours, as well as George's son Calvin. The three sailing Heilbronns had a number of sea stories to tell, as do all lake mariners, but one was a tale of shipwreck that all had shared just two seasons previous.

It was the sweltering summer of 1924, August 5th to be precise, when the three Heilbronns had sailed out of the Saginaw River aboard the wooden lumber steamer MIAMI which was under the command of the venerable Captain Charles Garey. The MIAMI had spent many a winter roosting near the ZILLAH at her home port of Bay City, but with winter's ice being just a dim memory the MIAMI was busy on her way to Sprague, Ontario for rough cut lumber. As the little oak steamer pushed into upper Lake Huron, however, fire was discovered smoldering in her coal bunkers and shortly thereafter the steamer was being consumed by flames while her crew, including the Heilbronn men, took to the lifeboats. This was not the first command that Captain Garey had lost to fire on the lakes as the steamer WYOMING had been burned from beneath his feet in the autumn of 1904, a tale which he no doubt shared with the Heilbronns on the long trip back to the Bay City waterfront. After a brief stint with the gloom of unemployment the

Heilbronn mariners finally found gainful employment in the Blodgett fleet and now not only had a steady income, but a good yarn to share—in triplicate.

Lake Superior was delivering a taste of weather vastly different from that which saw the end of the MIAMI, as the ZILLAH beat her way up Whitefish Bay some two years later. A dense heap of limestone was crammed into the Blodgett boat's leaky belly as she began to feel the teeth of Superior's temper. This was a modest summer blow, by Lake Superior's standards, and had only managed to whip up rude whitecaps to beat at the ZILLAH's oak bow.

Just what causes a wooden laker to suddenly give itself up to the temperament of one of the fresh water seas will always be a source of speculation among boat-buffs. Perhaps it is the roll and twist of the hull in just the wrong kind of sea or that little bit of extra cargo placed aboard in quest of a few dollars more in profit, or maybe a circumstance as distant as a long forgotten battle with some of spring's ice-flows that suddenly causes hull timbers to open and let aboard the wanting lake. No matter the reason, long before Captain Peter Ward could bring the ZILLAH from Whitefish Bay and onto open Lake Superior, Chief Engineer George Heilbronn sent word up from the engine room that the boat was taking water—lots of water. In short order, the boat's pumps were overwhelmed and her engine room crew forced from their stations. Captain Ward ordered the ship's flag raised upside down on the forward mast—a universal signal of distress, then told all hands to man the lifeboats. The ZILLAH had a mind to go to the bottom, and no amount of effort on the part of the crew could stop her.

Fortunately, the nearby steamer WILLIAM B. SCHILLER as well as the Coast Guardsmen at the Whitefish Point station, recognized the Blodgett boat's plight and set the gears of rescue in motion. With the SCHILLER hovering near and the Coast Guard rowing in their direction, Captain Ward, the Heilbronn men and E. K. Hungerford, A. Routhons, William Breanham, John Helbrodt, Harry Morgan, D. Doun, John Riley and Clarence Lightfield began the process of abandoning the steadily set-tling ZILLAH. The entire event was photographed by one of the SCHILLER's crew, providing a rare glimpse of a laker snared in the web of happenstance. You see, the doomed boat elected to founder within a dozen miles of her fleet-mates MYRON and MIZTEC. Interestingly, the entire sailing brood of the Heilbronn family had survived together through their second shipwreck almost two years to the day after Lake Huron had put them out of work by taking the MIAMI.

Exactly why the ZILLAH suddenly decided to die on a modestly choppy Whitefish Bay will never be known. Captain Ward speculated that her careworn oak bottom had given way under the stress of her cargo, and his theory is as close as we can get to a cause. The reasons mattered little at half past noon on August 26th, 1926 when the ZIL-LAH rolled over onto her port rail and joined her fleet-mates on the bottom off of Whitefish Point.

It would be fairly easy to stretch the kismet among the Blodgett boats that rest wrecked near Whitefish and the crews that once worked upon them. The simple fact is that Mr. Blodgett pressed his over-worked vessels into service on long haul routes that often sent them around Whitefish Point, an area that has often been called "the graveyard of the lakes." As the era of the wooden laker drew to an end, the odds against the members of the Blodgett fleet grew larger. The fact that three boats from the same fleet ended up on the bottom within a dozen miles of one another within a seven year period was much more a result of old boats repeatedly passing the same area than any kind of local hoodoo. Additionally, the crews of wooden boats in the 1920s tended to stay with that type of vessel and the companies that operated them, so the fact that the same people were involved in related events is nothing more than happenstance as well.

In the years that passed, the Heilbronn men appear to have given up work in the maritime industry. The chances are that the great depression which spelled the end of what remained of the wooden lakers also deprived the senior Heilbronns of their desired workplace. In later years Adeline Heilbronn—keeper, of sorts, of the family tree, knew only that Calvin had been somewhat involved in sailing. The fact that the three men had survived multiple shipwrecks was a surprise to say the least. As of this writing, it is fully expected that while researching some other obscure adventure of wooden lakers, the names of the three Heilbronn men may pop up again.

Captain Walter Neal went on to command vessels in the magnitude of the Nicholson fleet. He retired from the maritime industry around the middle of the 1900s, (best information says in the late 1940s or early 1950s) as a lake pilot—often guiding vessels from the DeFoe shipyard in Bay City. One cannot help but wonder what thoughts went through Captain Neal's mind each time he guided one of the big Nicholson freighters across Whitefish Bay and over the resting places of the long lost wooden lakers that were once the tools with which he earned his living. Doubtless there would sometimes be the images of lumber laced waves of ice water, heartless freighters sailing off with no render of assistance, hours spent waiting for numb death, shattered tow lines, vanished shipmates and the boats that simply gave up to the clutches of the lake. These are the images that kept an old time skipper quiet as he leaned against the pilothouse windowsill and peered out across the blue-gray horizon of Whitefish Bay.

The Lights Are Bright

*I*t was a deep black night in the first week of December, 1992 as the 647 foot steamer J.L. MAU-THE pressed westward onto Lake Erie. The pilot-house was blacked-out with only the glow of the radar scopes and the compass repeater giving light. Slamming the heavy steel pilothouse door behind him, watchman Wally Watkins entered. "The lights are bright," he announced to the mate in report fashion. Around the pilot-house there were a few puzzled looks as Watkins stepped to the wheel and started his watch. Having started sailing over four decades before, Wally had retired officially more than a year earlier but just could not stand to sit idle "on the beach" and get old, so in the autumn of 1992 he asked and was allowed to ship-out again, "sorta' part time." What most aboard the steamer that night did not know was that as well as being a highly skilled vesselman, Wally Watkins was a link to the maritime traditions of the past.

"I don't get that," one of the guys in the pilothouse queried. "Every time you come on the night watch, you say that 'The lights are bright' thing... Where'd you get that; what's it mean anyhow?"

"Well you see," Watkins explained patiently, "in the old days when the watch came on at night, he'd always have to check the oil lamps that were used for the navigation lights. Then when he came into the pilothouse he'd say, 'The lights are bright,' to let the mate know he'd checked 'em." As the night watch dragged on Watkins kept the pilothouse entertained with a wealth of other long lost traditions that have been misplaced in the clamor of modern electronic lakes navigation. Unbeknownst to anyone in the pilothouse that night was that during this same watch they would pass near to the spot where another proud laker had gone to the bottom, even though—her lights were bright.

On the seventh day of August, 1902, Captain George P. McKay, the chairman of the Lake Carrier's committee on aids to navigation, issued a notice to all downbound boats on Lake Erie. Sent out across the wire services the alert was picked up by the Bay City *Times-Press* and headlined "Beware of the Wreck" and read, in part, "Keep a sharp lookout for wreckage of the sunken steamer CITY OF VENICE." This headline was a far cry from those printed about that specific vessel in the same city just 10 summers earlier. The notice went on to state, "The location of the wreck is 50 miles east northeast of the southeast shoal lightship." It was the very first notification of the vessel's fate in the town where she was born. This was also the lead into a set of puzzling circumstances that surround the cause of the big laker's loss to this day.

As you read this, it is important to keep in mind that at this moment that once proud hull rests silently in the chilly depths of Lake Erie. The length of her wooden keel stretched 301 feet. Once she had boasted 315 feet in length overall and 43 feet in beam. Prior to ending up on the bottom, her hull had measured a 26 foot depth. Steel strapping, arches and keelsons once supplemented the strength of the oak hull timbers. Dynamite had taken care of most of what was once the fine lines of a proud laker and little of her structure remains—only the imagination can bring back her appearance. Just forward of her after deck-house a steel engine house is constructed, and within it two

Scotch boilers—13 feet by 11 and one half feet in diameter that once produced the boat's steam to a maximum of 160 pounds—sleep, forever cold in Lake Erie's depth. A triple expansion engine with cylinders of 20, 33 and 54 inches in diameter on a 42 inch stroke sits inert with only an occasional fish to tend to its workings. Where coal and elbow grease once were the order of business, now only silt and mud are present. How this once proud lakeboat ended up where she is can easily be told here, but exactly why is quite another matter.

With some measure of pride, the Bay City *Tribune* announced "Six Boat Launches" in the headline of its West Bay City column on the 26th day of June, 1892. The kickers added that "One will occur each week at the Davidson Shipyard in this city." Indeed it appeared as if Captain James Davidson had another season of spectacular side-launches planned for the coming summer. Just a year before, the Davidson yard had turned out four giant wooden steamers in a row. Dubbed the "big four" by the local media, the oak hulled lakers CITY OF LONDON, CITY OF PARIS, CITY OF BERLIN and CITY OF GLASGOW had represented the prosperity of the West Bay City maritime industry. This summer, apparently, Captain Davidson was out to double that effort with three massive oak steamers, two big schooners and a tug poised on the ways. The fact was that the local newspapers were not saying more than most Bay City residents had known for quite some time. Spaced closely together, the soon to be born lakers had become a land-mark that was visible from nearly every corner of the city. Considering that Bay City was, in this era, the heart of the great lakes shipbuilding industry, visitors to the city looked on in awe at the wooden boats in the process of being built. Rising from a jungle of scaffolds, these six lakeboats were to be more than Captain Davidson's latest additions to his own fleet; they were also a slap in the direction of his local shipbuilding competitor, Frank Wheeler.

A rivalry between Wheeler and Davidson had always existed, and down the river from Captain Davidson's yard, Wheeler's shipyard employees were working on steel hulled vessels in direct conflict to Davidson's motto that lakers should be made of wood rather than metal. In fact, things between the two vesselmen had gotten rather ugly a year and a half before when Wheeler attempted to sue Davidson, alleging that Davidson was spreading rumors that damaged the Wheeler yard's business. Perhaps in an attempt to over-shadow Davidson's announcement of six boat launchings in six weeks, Wheeler announced on the same day that his huge plant for the construction of marine engines would soon expand to double its current size. The engine works had turned out its first product just over a year before, which was placed into the tug YULU that had gone to South America and engaged in the towing of mahogany logs. Unlike ship-building, the engine works were indoors and thus provided year-round steady employment for workers of skill. This alone was a major plus in the 1890's when many jobs of labor were out of doors and often a week's pay was dependent on the weather. Certainly this expansion to Wheeler's yard was news that could outshine Davidson's six launches in the eyes of the locals.

Oblivious to all of this competitive banter, hull number 48 sat poised on Davidson's ways. Painted black from her rails to the water line with a single stylish white strip run-ning the length of the hull and white on her prow, the first of the "big six" needed only a few finishing touches before she would slide toward the brackish Saginaw River.

Curiously, these oak lakeboats were only painted as far down as the water-line where the timbers were then left un-painted. It is said that the bare timbers, once wetted by the lake, expanded and better sealed the spaces between them. The deck-houses were finished in oak and white ash, making for accommodations of the finest quality. Steering gear as well as capstans and deck hoists were all steam powered to ease any task of heavy labor. Atop the boat's pilothouse, an "open-air" pilothouse was arranged with a classic wheel for steering and a pair of whistle-pulls. Looking much like a brass pump-handle mounted horizontally atop a large wooden table-leg, one of the handles was to blow the boat's whistle and the other signaled the engine room as an augment to the speaking tube.

In addition to all of the other accommodations, there was one striking feature that all three of the new steamers, including hull 48, sported that was quite out of step with vessels of this era; they had no masts other than a frail single spar forward to loft the running lights. In a time when most steamers of this size were wearing two or three heavy telephone pole sized masts, Captain Davidson reckoned that such rigging would be in the way of the swing of ore and grain loading chutes. He figured that eliminating these spars would speed loading and make his new steamers more profitable. Although this theory was quite sound, it was apparently so out of step with the maritime mind-set of the time that, although the new vessels went into service without masts, the spars were soon added back to each boat's structure—even though they served absolutely no purpose. On Tuesday, the 28th of June, 1892, the first of Davidson's six—the steamer CITY OF VENICE—was ready for her launching scheduled at four o'clock in the afternoon the following day. Surely Davidson himself was looking forward to a festive day ahead, as Wheeler scowled from his office window toward the banners and flags being hung at his competitor's yard.

Gray clouds and a depressing summer rain came with the next day. No doubt, Frank Wheeler rubbed his hands together and gave a slight chuckle as the hour for the launch drew near and the rain showed not a sign of stopping.

"This should throw a wet blanket on ol' Davidson's picnic," he would have smirked. Although this weather tended to dampen the festive atmosphere, still a throng of several hundred spectators gathered at the Davidson yard. The difference this time was that the crowd began to gather just one hour before the launch time, where normally these events stretched out for an entire day. At half past four the sounds of numerous hammers banging at the wedges beneath the boat began to overcome the patter of the rain. The excitement started to grow, as Captain Davidson was supervising the operation personally. A vessel is launched only once and the thrill was partly in seeing months of work come to life, but mostly in the suspense of what the immense hull would do when it was cut free and allowed to slide down the ways. There have been instances when a hull has started down bow-first or stern first and others where the new-born has nearly rolled over or gone astray, careening into crowds of on lookers. Still others have simply sat there and not moved at all. In one instance, the signal was given, the wedges were hammered out and the boat just sat there. Despite every effort to push or pull her off of the ways—she just sat there, refusing to launch. Finally everyone gave up and went home. When the shipyard workers returned the following morning, they found the boat happily sitting in the water—she had launched herself in

With a giant splash, the steamer CITY OF VENICE is born.

the middle of the night when no one was looking. That embarrassing event occurred at the yard of Frank Wheeler, much to James Davidson's delight. Certainly, when a launching was about to happen, even on a rainy day, folks showed up just to see what would happen. Now it was hull number 48's turn.

The West Bay City *Tribune* described the scene the best:

> *"Capt. Davidson, who stood a little way off, but directly in a line with the center of the boat watched the progress of the work at both ends with a critical eye, now hurrying up the gang at one end and now the ones at the other. Finally both gangs completed their work. There was a lull of a few seconds duration; Capt. Davidson then gave the signal to the men stationed at both ends of the boat, the ropes were cut and*

*the big black monster commenced its short trip down
the ways into the murky Saginaw, while the crowds of
people who lined the shore cheered lustily.*

*"Both ends of the boat struck the water at the
same instant and even the old timers united in saying
that the launch was one of the finest they had ever
witnessed."*

Without regard to the rainy weather, the CITY OF
VENICE had brightened the day at the Davidson yard. For
the better part of the next month, the big steamer went
through her fit-out and trials. On the sultry day of July 19th,
the lines were cast off and the CITY OF VENICE headed out
on her maiden voyage. Locking upbound at the Soo on the
20th, the newest member of the Davidson fleet pointed her
steering pole toward Duluth and a cargo of grain. Just three
days later, she passed back downbound headed for a Buffalo
delivery. On the way down it was found that she was shipping aboard a respectable quantity of water; her steam
pumps were started and in short order appeared to hold
back the flow. Arriving at Buffalo the new, but leaking, vessel was quickly unloaded and it was discovered that the leak
was caused by an auger hole left un-plugged at the shipyard.
Apparently the hole was above the water-line when the vessel was running empty, but when a cargo was put aboard,
the auger hole was submerged. The repair must have been
an easy one because the vessel was immediately back in service. On Tuesday, August 30th, 1892 she departed Duluth
with 102,042 bushels of wheat—the biggest grain cargo ever
carried by a wooden lakeboat. The record was set while holding a draft of 14 feet two inches. Saying that Captain
Davidson's new steamer was off to a good start would be an
understatement at the very least.

Departing the Soo Locks downbound, the CITY OF VENICE hauls another load.

Bringing our time machine ahead ten years to the first week of August, 1902, we slow to a stop on the fourth day of that month at the upper end of the Detroit River. With a burden of 3,690 tons of iron ore heaped in her cargo hold, the CITY OF VENICE is found approaching Belle Isle and the big city. It is lunch time and Captain Broderick had finished his afternoon meal and now took his proper place in the pilothouse so as to supervise the vessel's downbound slither to Lake Erie. Along the way the oak oreboat would pass riverside parks where shorebound residents took advantage of this beautiful summer day to picnic and stroll. Most Detroiters would not even be taking more than a casual notice of the passing lakers. Much more of the river front is taken up by the bustle of fresh water commerce and the fact is that the CITY OF VENICE simply melted into the crowd. Snoring ahead of the CITY OF VENICE the steamer ELIZA STRONG pulled a tail of schooner-barges and beyond her went the PARKS FOSTER and TUSCARORA as well as the rabbit boat D.F. ROSE and a string of her barges. Coincidentally, just ahead of the ROSE and within whistle distance of the CITY OF VENICE was the steamer PANTHER, another one of Davidson's creations. Although two years older than the CITY OF VENICE, she was indeed a sister and nearly identical in construction. The simple truth that no one at that moment was aware of was that this would be the last time that one of these vessels would ever be seen by any of those ashore—this was the CITY OF VENICE's final passage by Detroit.

McGraw Transportation had taken over the services of the CITY OF VENICE from Davidson by 1902, and her ownership and management was shared by Thomas and S.P. Cranage as well as J. Will McGraw of Bay City with a like interest held by F.S. McGraw and Edward Smith of Buffalo and Captain John S. McNeil of Chicago. Around three o'clock that same afternoon, the CITY OF VENICE exited the Detroit River and pushed onto an open Lake Erie. As the sun set, Captain Broderick had successfully zigzagged his boat through Pelee Passage and now had nothing between the tip of his steering pole and Buffalo but some 200 miles of Lake Erie. Turning over charge of his vessel to First Mate John Sullivan, an exhausted Captain Broderick went to his cabin for a well deserved sleep. Out of the open pilothouse window the view was that of a flat-calm Lake Erie and a clear sky with stars just beginning to shine. As watchman George Weir came on, he dutifully checked each of the vessel's navigation lamps to insure that each was glowing with proper intensity. "The lights are bright," would be the report to the mate. There was very little else to do as the night dragged on; the winds were calm, the lake was glassy and the stars sparkled as far as the horizon. It seemed as if you might see Buffalo if it were not for the curvature of the earth. In the pilothouse the crew made idle conversation as the CITY OF VENICE pressed eastward.

Shortly after midnight, the watch spotted a vessel ahead and off the starboard bow at the same time Mate Sullivan spied the oncoming boat. Since leaving the Detroit River, dozens of lakers had been seen and passed, this one appeared no different. Ever cautious, Sullivan went to the whistle-pull and blew a starboard to starboard passing signal. There was no answer to the echoing signal, as all that came back from the distant boat was silence. Figuring this odd, but not really a problem, Sullivan let the other boat draw more near. When the other boat was close enough that the CITY OF VENICE's whistle could not possibly be missed, Sullivan blew another passing whistle. There was no response. The opposing boat simply kept coming, and worse yet, appeared on a collision course with the CITY OF VENICE. Now a cold chill tingled behind Sullivan's ears and the alarmed mate tugged frantically at the whistle-pull for a third time. No response; the other laker just kept sliding silently closer. Sullivan's instincts were well founded—the nearing laker now started to show her red lamp, she was swinging starboard. With his hand never leaving the whistle-pull, the panicked mate now gave two quick blows and ordered the CITY OF VENICE swung starboard as well. Spinning the boat's wheel as fast as his arms could move, the wheelsman anticipated the order, but the hefty oak steamer just seemed to plod ahead. With a roar down the speaking tube to, "Back 'er! Back 'er!" Sullivan ordered reverse, but it would take a while for the engine to be put into reverse and much longer to actually start in the other direction. John Sullivan had done everything in his power to prevent a collision, but the opposing boat did little else other than starting to veer into his boat. Like a ghostly dreadnought, she came ahead from the middle of the night, as if no one at all was aboard.

So violent was the impact of the collision between the two lakeboats that everyone in the pilothouse was tossed from their feet as the pilothouse itself came crashing down on top of them. Sullivan could feel incredible pain in his back and chest as he squirmed in a fruitless attempt to free himself. In a bitter ice water swirl, the wrecked pilothouse and its struggling occupants were swept from the CITY OF VENICE as the mass of its iron ore cargo pulled the vessel to the bottom of Lake Erie.

Two days after the career of the CITY OF VENICE was forever ended, her assailant, the steel Canadian steamer SEGUIN, was in the hands of the U.S. Marshal at Cleveland. Having been libeled by the owners of the CITY OF VENICE, the SEGUIN was undergoing a series of surveys to determine, not only the extent of her damages, but also her value. The examination of the boat showed eight twisted plates and frames, most of which could easily be removed and rolled back into shape. That same day John Sullivan testified from his hospital bed as to his actions prior to the collision. The Cleveland agent for the CITY OF VENICE, Captain W.C. Richardson, listed those details in his petition to the court and the primary finger of blame was directed toward the SEGUIN's second mate, W.A. Lavigne. Captain J.B. Sims had left the steamer in the hands of Lavigne who had then managed to run down the

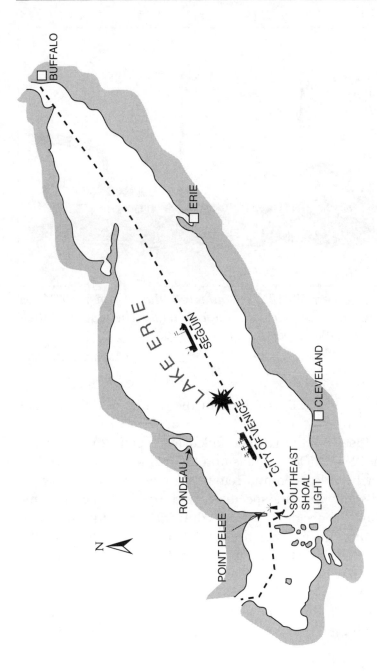

The steamer SEGUIN encountered the steamer CITY OF VENICE on a calm, clear Lake Erie night. The results of their meeting are unexpelained to this day.

—*Author's concept*

CITY OF VENICE, resulting in the deaths of three of that boat's crew.

Just why the Lavigne failed to respond to any of the CITY OF VENICE's signals and just plain ran her down has never been learned and remains a mystery to this day. In hind-sight we can speculate and try to build a frame around the accident, perhaps drawing a conclusion as to a probable cause. There are two highly likely causes for the SEGUIN's clash with the boat from Bay City without even a signal having been returned. This was an era when abuse of alcohol infected many a ship's department—on occasion including the pilothouse. There is the very real possibility that an intoxicated pilothouse watch was to blame for the collision. Additionally, the hour was late and the night was extremely clear and quiet—it is possible that the pilothouse crew simply fell asleep. The failure of the SEGUIN to respond to loud whistle signals sounded in close proximity, however, seems to discount this theory. All that Lavigne ever stated in public was that "The less said about it the better..."

Forever the wreck of Davidson's hull 48 will sit on the bottom of Lake Erie. Her workings were said to have been "cleared" to prevent their becoming a menace to navigation. Normally such "clearing" consisted of going out over the luckless vessel and dropping wads of dynamite on it; such was the eulogy for the CITY OF VENICE. Chairman McKay's warning to "beware of the wreck" was no longer needed, and the once proud vessel would fade into obscurity leaving the mystery as to the exact cause of her end to fade as well. All of that was probably just as well for W.A. Lavigne, who had the answers to the puzzle, but was probably much better off after the questions stopped being asked of how he collided with another vessel with all of her lights glowing brightly on a clear night. Only he could solve the poser of the CITY OF VENICE's wreck on that clear summer night in 1902—and he kept that explanation to himself until the end of his days.

Shadows in the Shallows

*A*pproaching Chicago's O'Hare airport, aircraft after aircraft is lined up by the approach controllers in a radar conga-line that often stretches a good distance out over Lake Michigan. One by one and more often two by two, the airliners head toward the runways in a high tech parade of mass transit that seems unending. From countless window seats the air travelers gaze out from above toward the lake below. In good weather aircraft from the south and east that are assigned to runway 22 left make their curving approach and cross the lakeshore over Gross Point. Likewise, when runways 27 are in use aircraft from the north and west pass over the same area, making the approach to runway 27 right. Below the approaching airliners, the blue freshwater sea shimmers until the color slowly turns toward the light brown of the sandy beach. The scene below passes quickly and it takes a sharp eye to spot the dark bullet-shaped shadow that rests in the shallows just off shore the suburb of Evanston. By the time that the realization of what the eye has caught below sinks in, the viewer is usually being unloaded at the busy airport and the question remains—was it a gathering of rocks in a suspicious shape, or was it the remains of a long forgotten shipwreck? Just what was that specter in the shallow water resting off shore one of the largest cities on the lakes? Was it really there—a tiny portal into the past visible only from directly above, or was it simply a trick played on the eye by the sun, the lake, and the populated shore? It is enough to make one want to charter another trip over the same area... in a slower airplane.

Captain Carelton Graves was a "marline spike sailor," meaning that he was capable of both fitting-out and rigging sailing vessels. As a youth his heels first clopped upon the deck of a lakeboat in 1846 when he shipped aboard the scow SWALLOW out of the harbor of Fairport. It was a natural progression for a member of the sailing family of Eli and Nancy Graves, which consisted of four sons—all of whom became vessel masters. Now, as he stood in the pilothouse of the wooden laker KEYSTONE, with the snow pelting at the windows the good captain had more than 50 seasons under his belt and had seen more nights like this than he could recall. Lake Michigan was serving up a hefty gale and all of the nasty garnish that goes with it. In these, the first hours of the fourth day of December, 1897, the waves boiled up in an ice water stew and came aboard the steamer making their best effort at becoming a general nuisance. The winds and seas would, of course, be no match for the likes of Captain Carelton Graves—a marline spike sailor.

Having been under Captain Graves' command since 1893, the KEYSTONE herself was somewhat of an enigma. According to Inland Lloyds Vessel Register of 1898 as well as the Duluth Evening Herald of 1897, she was launched in 1866 as the barkentine sailing vessel BRIDGEWATER. A barkentine, or "bark" on the lakes was a three masted sailing vessel whose two after masts were schooner rigged and whose forward mast was square rigged. As best can be told, the vessel came to grief of some kind in 1875 (one source says she was wrecked just outside of the Buffalo breakwater). Supposedly she was raised in 1880 and taken to drydock in Buffalo for the repairs that would put her back into service. But, Great Lakes maritime commerce in 1880 was rapidly changing from what it had been in 1866 when the BRIDGEWATER was born. The power of the sail was quickly being outmoded by the power of the steam engine— there was little room in such a competitive market for a bark. With this in mind there was no trouble in deciding to convert the beat-up barkentine into a steam powered propeller while she was in the dry-dock. In fact, this may have been the motivation for raising her in the first place— although there are no records that exactly describe such conjecture. When she came back into service in 1880, the boat had a whole new look—with all of the standard lines of a lumber hooker. Her fo'c'sle and after quarters were raised one deck and her spar deck was left to accommodate piles of fresh cut lumber. Additionally the newly converted steamer now carried the name KEYSTONE as well as the hope of a profitable career to come. Several seasons later, the boat's owner Thomas Axworthy had her configuration changed to a double decked bulker. In other words, her sides were raised to the level of her forward and after decks and a second spar deck was constructed atop the original. Her gross tonnage was now measured at 722 and her depth set at just over 11 feet. These dimensions were in perfect harmony to her 163 feet of length and 34 feet of beam to make her a handy vessel to her owner. By the blizzard-choked night in December of 1897 when Captain Graves found himself attempting to guide her by his instincts alone, the KEYSTONE was owned by Cleveland vesselman Frank C. Goodman. There is no doubt that with Captain Graves at the helm, the KEYSTONE continued to be a handy boat for Mr. Goodman.

Attached to the KEYSTONE's stern by several boat-lengths of towing hawser and swallowed completely by the blizzard was the schooner-barge JOSEPH G. MASTEN. The three masted former sailing boat was one year younger than her towing steamer, having been first enrolled on the 29th day of August, 1867. Her rig was listed as a barkentine, and she was assigned an official number of U.S. 13750. At 186 feet in length by 33 feet in beam and a depth of 13 feet, the MASTEN measured 620.52 gross tons and was launched from Quayle & Martin shipyard at Cleveland. In the spring of 1877 the MASTEN was taken to Buffalo where her rig was changed to that of a schooner. She returned to service on the first day of May, 1877 and worked as a wind-grabber until the economics of the industry forced her onto the end of a tow-line as a barge.

Both boats were hauling burdens of soft coal from Lake Erie's ports, the MASTEN having loaded hers at Lorain, Ohio then being towed to Huron, Ohio where the KEYSTONE was to take aboard her cargo. Both steamer and consort were owned by Cleveland vessel mogul Goodman, and as quickly as their holds were filled, the pair headed for Lake Michigan to deliver their loads. The KEYSTONE's load was bound for delivery at the port of Racine, Wisconsin. On the way to Racine a side stop would be made at Milwaukee where the towline to the MASTEN as well as the schooner-barge herself would be let go just outside of the harbor piers. A tug local to Milwaukee would then pull the schooner-barge to the unloading dock. Since the 29th of November, a whopping 100,000 tons of coal had been unloaded at that port by various lakeboats in an effort to stock-pile for the long cold winter to come. In just a matter of days the bitter winter winds and temperatures would turn the harbor waters into a solid sheet of ice—impassable to the coal carriers. Still, there were more than 40 coal boats scheduled to bring loads into Milwaukee before sea-

The steamer KEYSTONE was as illusive to photographers as her story is to historians. This image, although poor in quality is one of the only photos of her.

son's end. As the KEYSTONE and MASTEN departed, a combined sense of urgency to beat the seasonal freeze as well as the tired desire to bring what had been a long season of work to an end hovered over both boats like the gray winter clouds.

In these, the industrial revolution years before clean air concerns and the E.P.A., most spaces that were occupied by people were heated by coal. The best way to move this product around the region of the Great Lakes was by boat. Mountainous piles of the fossil fuel would grow on the river banks as the season grew late and then would dwindle through the long winter months as the snow swirled with the black smoke. Houses and shops would remain toasty warm until the temperate wafts of spring returned once again and the lakeboats could break their way clear to replenish the stockpiles.

Nearly two days after his departure from the coal dock at Huron, Captain Graves found himself "feeling" his way across Lake Michigan. The wind blasted from nearly due north and the snow was now coming down upon the KEYSTONE in a full blizzard—the night turned black in the choking snow. Atop the steamer's pilothouse her wheelsman stood bundled up in multiple layers of winter garb attempting to keep his eyes clear of the giant snowflakes. It was all that a man could do to just keep the boat on her compass heading; in fact it was all that he could do just to see the compass itself. All around the vessel the snow reflected the amber glow of the KEYSTONE's oil lamps; this was the era when most wooden lakers carried no electric lights.

At about the same time as Captain Graves was picking his way through the blizzard, another vessel master was guiding his boat safely out from under the same storm. Scheduled to unload her cargo at Milwaukee, the 192 foot steamer GEORGE W. MORLEY eased off of Lake Michigan with Captain Owen in command. Chicago would next be the MORLEY's destination and Captain Owen, like Captain Graves, was not the kind of man to let a bit of blizzard get into his way. It was his intention to be out from under the unloading rigs and onward to Chicago within a day— regardless of the weather. Unlike the KEYSTONE, the MORLEY's past is a matter of clear record. Frank Wheeler's West Bay City yard launched the steamer in April of 1887 and she went to work at the opening of that same season. Monikered with official number 85990 and hull number 37 the MORLEY measured 34 feet across her deck and 21 feet in depth. With a gross tonnage of 1,045 she was indeed a commanding presence on the lakes in her first years. On this snowy night in 1897, however, the MORLEY's elegant curves were highly obscured by the blizzard.

Using most of his mariner's senses, Captain Owen managed not only to make the dock—but to make the task appear routine. As the MORLEY's lines were made secure, the deck crew were in the advanced stages of opening the hatches. The process of unloading a lakes bulk carrier in 1897 was a slow one in most ports. Normally, a steam hoist was used to drop a large bucket into the vessel's hull, the cargo would then be either shoveled into the bucket by hand or the bucket itself would be rigged as a clam-shell to open and "bite" the cargo. The full bucket would next be hoisted from the hold and drawn shoreside to be dumped. Indeed there were all types of variations of unloading equipment around the lakes at this point in time. Rigs varied from steam powered clam-shells to horse-drawn hand filled buckets depending on how much the individual docks had invested in their equipment. Just what kind of rig worked the MORLEY's cargo is not on record, but it is certain that the process, by today's standards, was not fast.

While Captain Owen was retiring to his quarters aboard the securely docked MORLEY, Captain Graves was about as far from that comfort as one can get. It was his intention to hug up as close to the western shore as possible and hope that the land would break the wind and afford him some lee in which to run. Pulling the barge MASTEN with her belly full of coal was an effort in any kind of weather, but in these stiff winds and rough seas it had become a chore in the excess. A bit of lee would put far less strain on the towing hawser and cut the rolling of both boats significantly. In fact, this was the course of action that most masters would have followed in the same circumstances, and would work well—providing that one was

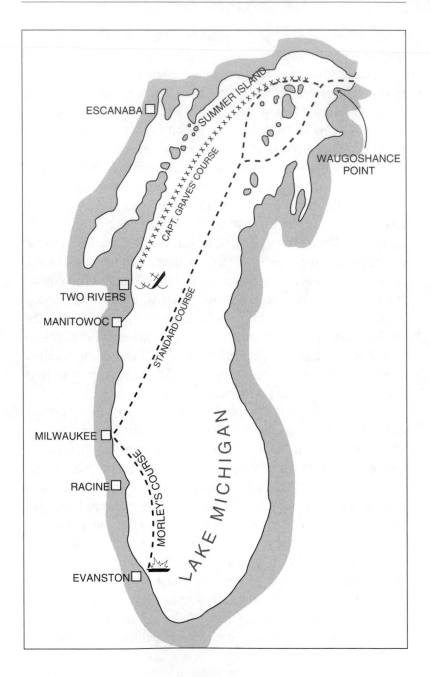

ESCANABA

SUMMER ISLAND

WAUGOSHANCE
POINT

CAPT. GRAVES' COURSE

TWO RIVERS

MANITOWOC

STANDARD COURSE

MILWAUKEE

RACINE

MORLEY'S COURSE

EVANSTON

LAKE MICHIGAN

on one's course. No one knew just how it happened; perhaps the winds were just a bit stronger than Captain Graves reckoned, or the steamer's engine was putting out just a few less revolutions, or just a bit less steam pressure was being produced other than that shown on the gauges—regardless, the KEYSTONE was off course, way off course.

Dawn brought little help toward the navigation efforts aboard the KEYSTONE. The method used in these times is commonly referred to as dead-reckoning. A simple technique, dead-reckoning involves basic time-speed-distance calculations. Using a known starting point, the navigator measures the distance to the next point and using a given speed, figures the time until reaching the destination or any known point along the way. Using this method, one should be able to find his way with no visual aid—simple. Well, simple until the navigator has to do the same task—considering wind-drift, currents and common compass errors. Toss in a blinding snow storm and you have Captain Graves' dilemma. He had kept the hope that daylight would bring better weather and visibility—it did not. In fact, the blizzard had grown worse and the pilothouse seemed immersed in milk white snow as all around the frozen precipitation cut visibility to zero. Surely Captain Graves figured on making his turn to the south, but the seas and wind had yet to ease, indicating his nearing the Wisconsin shore. Perhaps that was the cue that he was looking for to signal his next move in the dead-reckoning game—it is just the kind of a cue that a marline spike sailor would use.

Unfortunately, Captain Graves' first hint of the Wisconsin shore's nearing came when it thundered along the KEYSTONE's keel beneath his feet. There was no time to signal reverse, shout up to the helmsman to turn the wheel or even become startled—the bottom simply rose up and stopped the KEYSTONE cold. Unaware of the steamer's grounding a moment earlier, the schooner-barge MASTEN simply followed her own momentum. As the towline went slack in the snow-obscured distance, the MASTEN ran directly onto the shallows behind the KEYSTONE. Records, rare as they are concerning this wreck, are unclear as to whether or not the schooner-barge actually struck the steamer as she drove ahead onto the shoal. It is probable that the MASTEN did hit the KEYSTONE as both found the beach, and it is also probable that she damaged her bow in the process. Spinning out of control, the MASTEN rotated 90 degrees and came to rest perpendicular across the KEYSTONE's heels. Now Captain Graves' boat was blocked from even attempting to back off the shoal. Worse yet, the seas slammed broad-side to the MASTEN and caused her to grind against the stern of the steamer. Planking twisted and seams opened as each wave rocked the schooner-barge.

Looking back from the modern end of our periscope through time, we would see that the records of what happened from this point are less than sketchy. As best can be told, the two boats "went on" six miles north of the Two Rivers lifesaving station and 600 feet off shore, just north of Manitowoc. And when the snow let up, there they sat, squatting in the surf. Since the spot of the grounding was within sight of the Two Rivers Point lighthouse, it is safe to conclude that when the blizzard lifted, the light-keeper had a good view of the wrecks. In short order, word was spread that two wrecks were ashore and the tugs ARCTIC and PANKRANTZ as well as the local lifesavers were reported dispatched to the scene at two o'clock on Saturday afternoon, December 4th, 1897. At about the same time the tugs HAMMEL, NARSTE and HILL departed from Two Rivers with the rescue of the vessels in mind. For Captain Graves the whole ordeal must have been a supreme embarrassment—imagine a mariner of his ilk running his steamer and her consort smack into the state of Wisconsin. It was an awkward position for a marline spike sailor, awkward for certain.

A small crowd gathered on the wind-swept beach. Even the bitter December wind could not outmatch the urge to watch a real shipwreck, and the locals had gotten the word quickly. The tugs hauled at the stuck KEYSTONE for most of the day, and it became clear that she had her bottom anchored in what was described as "quicksand." Apparently the sands off the point are very loose and shift constantly with the ebb and flow of Lake Michigan. Both boats were now rapidly settling in the sand trap. By nightfall, the KEYSTONE had been freed and only the rescue of the MASTEN remained. The lifesavers did their best work, running lines between the schooner-barge, the steamer and the tugs, then manning the MASTEN's pumps. It was a losing battle, the seams continued to open, the sands continued to shift and the lake continued to devour the schooner-barge. At eight o'clock that night the lifesavers removed the crew of the MASTEN and transferred them to the safety of the KEYSTONE. The following morning the lifesavers returned to the battered boat and removed all of the cabin furnishings—the JOSEPH G. MASTEN was being left to the lake.

On Sunday, as the MASTEN squatted in the sands off Two Rivers Point, the GEORGE W. MORLEY departed for the city of Chicago. Once more the old adage that nothing good can come from a trip started on a Sunday was ignored as Captain Owen directed the MORLEY onto Lake

Michigan. After all, the trip down to Chicago from Milwaukee was somewhat of a milk-run, taking just over half a day to complete. Shortly after nightfall the steamer would be secured to the dock taking on her next cargo. It was a sailing distance of just over 80 miles, and no sooner had the MORLEY cleared Milwaukee then Captain Owen took on a south, southeast heading. His course would take him about eight miles out into the lake and well clear of Wind Point near Racine. The trip quickly turned into a typical late season passage. What had been a blizzard the previous day was now just a series of marauding snow-squalls in the gray distance. Down in confines of the MORLEY's engine room, Chief Engineer Chapman had all of the boat's workings running like a fine pocket-watch. Despite the freezing temperatures outside, in the firehold, the thermometers constantly hovered above the 100 degree mark. There were no fans, no electric lights and there was no escape from the hot, dirty work. An occasional waft of cool air would come down through the windjammers and illumination was gotten via the sky-lights in the daylight hours and simple oil lamps at night. Like every other laker, the work went on around the clock.

By evening the MORLEY was north of Evanston when the finger of happenstance reached out. For no good reason at all, a single oil lamp in the engineroom exploded. Like a small bomb, the bursting lamp spread flaming droplets of oil into every corner of the wooden laker's engineroom. In an instant the seeds of conflagration were planted and weeds of flame seemed to instantly sprout. There is no enemy greater to the mariner at sea other than fire. Even in modern times, with steel ships, halon and carbon dioxide flooding systems, a fire aboard a vessel can rapidly turn to disaster. In 1897 the crew of a wooden vessel had little more than bucket brigades and steam hoses to fight the flames. The crew of the MORLEY did not have even that much to use in saving themselves. A careful audit of the vessel's equipment would show that she was lacking one of the primary fire fighting tools of her day, because there was not a single fire bucket aboard.

Nearly as soon as the fire could be reported to the pilothouse, the flames were gaining control of the engineroom. Chief Chapman had only time enough to set the throttle at "full ahead" crank up the pressure and tie the safety valve closed before being forced from his post. The MORLEY would either run ashore or blow up, that is, if the fire did not consume her first. Topside, the crew mustered at the firehose in an already losing battle. Captain Owen had put the wheel hard over and the steamer was plowing toward land. It would be a seven mile sprint to beach the MORLEY—nearly an hours steaming time. For the length of the run for survival, the steamer's crew worked at the fire, until the hose itself was destroyed by the flames. Now all that was left was to hang on and wait to go over the side. For a time it appeared as if the distant horizon was drawing no closer, but just as all appeared lost the beach loomed near off the steering pole. Like a floating, flaming wooden train wreck, the GEORGE W. MORLEY piled into the shallows. Less than 300 feet from shore one and three eighths miles south of Gross Point, the steamer found the place where she would rest forever. Ashore, the Evanston fire department had been alerted, along with the local lifesaving crew. The wreck had driven ashore only one half mile south of the lifesaving station, and the station lookout had spotted the blazing lakeboat a long way out. Plenty of time had been available to put out the alarm and as the MORLEY rammed ashore both the lifesavers and the fire department were waiting. So close was the wreck to dry land that a number of the crew went overboard and waded to the beach. Others were picked up by the lifesavers and shuttled ashore in their surfboat. Now the MORLEY just sat there burning.

To a professional, or even volunteer fire fighter, there is nothing more motivating than a structure that is burning. For Evanston Fire Chief Harrison's men, even a flaming lakeboat represented a call to duty. Remarkably, the fire department managed to reach and board the MORLEY in the same manner that her crew had abandoned her—they waded over. After going to battle with the flames, the Evanston firefighters actually started to make progress against the inferno. It was only then that Captain Owen flew into a rage and insisted that a boiler explosion was immanent. He insisted that the firefighters must leave the MORLEY immediately, lest they be blown to kingdom come. At the time Captain Lawrence O. Lawson of the lifesavers was also aboard the burning steamer. He found the contention that a boiler explosion was about to happen to be silliness, but Captain Owen insisted. Eventually he invoked his authority as captain and expelled every last person from the vessel. Ashore, Chief Harrison was told of the captain's conclusion, and he too was astounded. In his opinion there was absolutely no chance of such an explosion. Nevertheless, Captain Owen ordered the MORLEY abandoned by every living soul, and she was left to simply burn to her bottom planks.

In the days that followed, the lake managed to sweep apart most of the charred remains of the MORLEY. Meanwhile, 140 miles to the north, the MASTEN was suffering a similar fate. Stuck firmly in the quicksand the waves managed to beat her until the barge's seams opened completely and she slipped beneath the surface. Some accounts say that the MASTEN "slipped off onto deep water," while others claim she was swallowed by the shifting sands. According to the Door County *Advocate* of December 18, 1897, *"The MASTON (sic.) has settled out of sight and at last reports there was five feet of water over her bones."* No matter, by the following year the MASTEN had disappeared completely, and the MORLEY's engine works had been salvaged by the Dunham Towing and Wrecking company of Chicago. Like so many others in the annals of Great Lakes maritime lore, both boats ended their careers as easily overlooked shadows in the shallows.

This, however, is not the end of the story—as far as Lake Michigan and the marline spike sailor were concerned. In the second week of September, 1898—less than a year after the KEYSTONE was run into the state of Wisconsin, Captain Graves guided her out of Cleveland. Piled in her hold was 1002 tons of coal headed for Manitowoc. Captain Graves piloted the steamer up the Detroit and St. Clair rivers through the expanse of Lake Huron and into the Straits of Mackinac. Somewhere in that neck of the lakes something went very wrong. Just exactly what happened, why it happened and even where it happened is lost in a vortex of loose facts, minor details and missing evidence. In fact the best account of the event that can be found is a single paragraph printed in the Duluth Evening *Herald* on September 20, 1898—it reads in part as follows:

THE KEYSTONE BURNED.

Cleveland. Sept. 20-(Special to The Herald.)—The steamer KEYSTONE, which went ashore on Big Summer Island, near Escanaba, afterwards burned to the water's edge, according to a telegram received from Captain Carter (sic) Graves today. The KEY-STONE is owned principally by the National Bank of Commerce of Cleveland, but the captain has an interest in her. There is no marine insurance on the steamer, but she was fairly well covered as to fire with Gibbs & Joys of Milwaukee. Her insurance valuation was ($)17,000. Her cargo of 1002 tons of coal for Manitowoc was shipped by Turney & Co. of Cleveland and was fully insured through Smith, Davis & Co. of Buffalo.

Oddly this account of the end of the KEYSTONE presents more questions about the vessel than it answers. If Captain Graves was on the way to Manitowoc, how on earth did he run onto Big Summer Island? It is at the entrance to Green Bay and more than 20 miles off any course to Manitowoc. Running into it would require steaming nearly due west of the downbound track for a couple of hours. There are other questions to be found in the research of the KEYSTONE's end. At least one lead seems to point in the direction of Waugoshance Point. Located at the west end of the Straits of Mackinac, it is supposed that the steamer ran ashore there and burned. Some diving has been done in the area, but there is no evidence yet found that indicates that the KEYSTONE is there. Nothing also points to her being on or near Big Summer Island; of course, her carcass could have been ground to her keel by nearly a century of ice flows. The once hard working lakeboat may, like the MAS-TEN and MORLEY, be just a shadow in the shallows by now. Some sort of storm activity is normally blamed for an "off course" loss such as this, but according to local records, the only storm in the approximate time-frame of the reported loss occurred nearly a week before. Additionally, the Escanaba paper gives no mention of the KEYSTONE's fetching up, or of her burning. Such an event would have surely dominated the local marine column which details losses and events all around the lakes. Then there is the added possibility that the information is out there, but this author has yet to stumble across it. Just exactly what happened to the boat, as well as where and when the occurrence took place, is at this time—a puzzle.

For the marline spike sailor, his five season command of the KEYSTONE may have ended, but his days on Lake Michigan had not. Over the years that followed it is likely that he found more than a few commands among the jumble of the lakes maritime industry. In the spring of 1907, before the winter ice had released its grip on the lakes, Captain Harry May purchased and took possession of the lumberhooker ARCADIA. But, Captain May had little or no experience as the master of a steamboat, so he turned to the most experienced of his peers that he could find—a marline spike sailor... Captain Carelton Graves. When the ARCADIA started her season at Manistee on the sixth day of April, 1907, Captain May was in command and Captain Graves was aboard as pilot. A brutal spring gale swept Lake Michigan and the tempest lingered for nearly a full week. When the gale ended the ARCADIA had gone missing, and the marline spike sailor had gone with her, a fitting epitaph for someone whose life was spent on the fresh water seas—perhaps.

A flight along the coast from Chicago, north to Washington Island can show the sharp-eyed observer more than two score of those bullet-shaped shadows that may once have been lakeboats. In fact, all around the lakes the shadows in the shallows appear, and strangely most of these wrecks in the wading depths are not identified. When a boat went down in deep water, it would remain safely in the depths until modern divers could find the wreck. In many cases, there is enough left of the vessel to make identification possible. Sometimes the boat's name can be read directly from the wreck. When a wreck occurred in shallow water, however, the waves almost immediately break the boat up. The very next winter's ice then proceeds to distort and grind away all but the basic shape. All that remains for the future research historians are some confused newspaper accounts, an official document or two and occasional foggy photos in some collector's file.

One may ask how the facts of the loss of a boat such as the KEYSTONE can become so obscured? The simple fact is that the information does not exist because the records were never kept. Like her captain, the KEYSTONE simply went away. Where Captain Graves slipped through a crack in the lake, the KEYSTONE slipped through a crack in history. As lost in the sands of time as the MASTEN is in the sands off Two Rivers Point. Only the MORLEY remains where we can put our finger on her—in 10 feet of water off Evanston. The mystery as to why Captain Owen elected to let her incinerate herself is indeed on a par with the puzzlement surrounding the location of the KEYSTONE; the happenings that caused the MASTEN to sink and what became of Captain Graves.

In July of 1967, a large hunk of wooden hull, complete with a hawspipe for an anchor, washed ashore at nearly the same point where the MASTEN was lost. Originally, the local media incorrectly speculated that it was part of the steamer VERNON. That being the most famous local wooden wreck, it was probably the only vessel name that those in the media could equate with the hunk of lakeboat. When the VERNON was discovered, however, it was found in deep water, intact—no one in the media bothered to retract the earlier error. There are several dozen wooden lakers off the point that the piece may have come from, among them the MASTEN. Today, the big hull piece is on display at the entrance to the state park at Two Rivers Point where anyone can just go up and touch lakeboat history. They are in a far better position than those who fly into Chicago and look down to see the bones of the MORLEY below. Both observers are left, as are we, to ponder the shadows in the shallows of the lake beyond.

Ellis' Rules

*T*here are times when the events and adventures of the people and vessels that worked the Great Lakes seem to drift, lost among the din of life and the passing of time. When we are lucky, a story will surface and provide us with an open window to the distant past and a look at the life of someone who worked the common toil of the lake's maritime industry. Such an opportunity can allow a glimpse at a shipwreck that has been long forgotten. Sometimes it takes the quest of a single individual digging over a great deal of time to uncover the bits and pieces of a tale that can easily be overlooked. Such is the case in the saga of Mary Carstensen, Gary Hill and the schooner-barge MONTANA.

It was a joyful evening indeed at Grandma Lempke's house; in fact, the whole residence seemed aglow. The year was 1972 and grandson Gary Hill was finally home from the army. A number of Gary's relatives had gathered at Florence Lempke's home to catch up on family events, both recent and distant. It was the kind of evening that only those who have found themselves stuck far away from family and home can appreciate. Every voice, laugh, sound and smell says that those long home-sick days are finally at an end. It is the kind of an evening that you do not forget.

Through the night the conversation bent in the direction of reminiscences of family yarns and inside jokes. At one point Grandma Lempke told grandson Gary of an adventure that her mother, Mary Carstensen, had experienced more than 80 years before. Florence recalled her mother having told of being shipwrecked up by Alpena sometime around 1890—the yarn was of a schooner that went ashore, and broke in two as the water turned red. Her story was brief and very short on details, but it would be enough to send Gary on a scavenger hunt of family history that would stretch out for more than two decades. About a year after Grandma Lempke casually related her story, Gary began to ponder the hows and wheres of Mary Carstensen's shipwreck. He wrote letters, and gathered the pieces of what was becoming the typical jigsaw puzzle that is characteristic of a long lost shipwreck. He found the name of a schooner-barge wrecked near Alpena in 1890 that was under the command of a captain from Mary Carstensen's local area and was carrying a load of iron ore—mix it with water and the surf turns red. All of the pieces seemed to fit, but after 20 years of searching, only one detail was missing... actual written proof that Mary Carstensen was really aboard that particular vessel.

The era of the wooden oreboat was one of striking contrast to today's "information age" where every movement of nearly every business and its employees is recorded and tracked by computer. In our time, we all have come to live with social security numbers, photo licenses, credit bureaus and every other form of personal tracking that can be concocted. In 1890, however, the story was far different. Persons were often born with no record at all, there was no government bureaucracy to reach into the individual's pocket, in fact—income taxes and the I.R.S. were still more than two dozen years into the future. Thus, there was no need for records to track the individual citizen or small business. In the Great Lakes maritime industry, people of labor often roamed from one vessel to another, perhaps working several vessels in a single season. Pay was always in cash which was doled out by the mate or more often the captain—who was, on many occasions, also the vessel owner. The able bodied sailors would sometimes sign aboard under an assumed name, that is, if they were asked to sign aboard at all. Then came the instances when the crewman was not able to read or write and was required simply to "make your mark." The only other time when a signing of papers was common would be when the crewman was discharged or paid off at the end of his service. When a vessel met with its end, the few records that had been kept were often lost with the boat. Any specifics as to who exactly was aboard was left churning in the waves to disintegrate in the lake. Such was the era that found Mary Carstensen aboard the schooner-barge MONTANA.

Mary spent her youth in the Ohio port city of Oak Harbor, located at the western end of the Portage River. As well as being the point where Penn Central railroad meets the Norfolk and Western, the tiny town has long been a hub of regional commerce. The boats with their tall masts and hulls worn by the battles with wind and sea had become Mary's only vice. After all, these were the same boats that sailed off onto the lake that she loved so much. The dreams of distant ports of call and the freedom of sailing away on the intoxicating expanse of the beautiful blue lake probably made for a welcome escape for a lady constrained by the Victorian starched-collar era that was young Mary's time. Schleswig-Holstein, Germany was where the birth cries of newborn Mary were heard on the 11th day of August, 1864. Three summers later, Peter and Nomina Carstensen, Mary's parents, elected to change their lives and join the waves of immigrants seeking prosperity in America. They packed up what precious possessions they were able to

Mary Carstensen, c. 1886

drag across the Atlantic Ocean, and the Carstensen family made the harsh pilgrimage to the United States. The family arrived in June of 1867, and settled in the town of Rock Ridge, Ohio. On March fourth, 1880 Mary's Mother, Nomina, passed away and at age 16, Mary was left as lady of the house. This must have been a smothering responsibility; today we can barely imagine what her days were like as she tended to the chores of Carstensen home and family.

Sometime during the 1887 season, Mary's brother, Martin, took a job on the schooner-barge MONTANA out of the port of Sandusky, Ohio. The MONTANA was under the stringent command of Captain James S. Ellis, a resident of the vessel's port city. Captain Ellis was an archetype of his era, and ruled over his boat with an authority that bordered on tyrannical. There were rules on the MONTANA and these were imposed and directed by Captain Ellis—without question. Such may be the reason why the MONTANA was suddenly in need of a ship's cook, either when Martin Carstensen came aboard or shortly thereafter. It was, in fact, Martin who made the connection between his sister Mary and the MONTANA. Looking back, the thought may come to mind that a skipper of Captain Ellis' starch would have no place on his boat for a female, after all it was a man's world. In reality, Captain Ellis was a man steeped in tradition, and it had always been within tradition to have either a male or female cook serving a lakeboat. So, Martin was sent to Oak Harbor with the Captain Ellis' offer: if Mary wanted to cut her shorebound ties and take the job as cook aboard the MONTANA, it was hers... under Ellis' rules—of course.

We can only picture the scene as Mary Carstensen, in the company of her brother, made her way to the MONTANA for the first time. The probability is that the two met in Sandusky—the MONTANA's frequented home-port. In keeping with the times there was no official record of the event, but without doubt the schooner-barge and the German-born immigrant did come to meet and Mary Carstensen's life started into a new direction. The schooner-barge was indeed a world foreign to the 22 year old maiden. For a resident of Oak Harbor in 1887, the trip to Sandusky in itself would be an event, but the MONTANA now represented a door to places and adventures unimagined. Everything about the boat must have seemed different and exciting. The tall masts reached toward the sky, supported by a spider-web of rigging; thick ropes were strung slackly to the dock as if there was no need at all for them to hold the boat. Crossing the gangway to board the boat was a trek that bordered on being frightening and once her feet hit upon the deck planking, Mary was swallowed into the world of the wooden schooner. There was a smell of soaked wood and musty canvas broken only by the breeze off the water, and ropes seemed to be everywhere. The faces of the crew appeared worn, unfriendly and a bit frightening—Mary focused her gaze downward in spite of herself as her brother lead her aft toward the captain's cabin. Martin's knock at the captain's door was followed by a protracted silence, but when the door was opened Mary Carstensen would have come face to face with Captain James Ellis and his rules.

If dreams of the open sea had been foremost in Mary's thoughts, her first moments in the presence of the MONTANA's master brought such ponderings to an unexpected halt. First and foremost on Captain Ellis' list of rules would be that while onboard the vessel, Mary would be restricted from speaking with any member of the crew—including her brother Martin. Additionally, the ship's new cook was not to leave the boat at any time unless escorted by Captain Ellis. Such harsh rules appear authoritarian in the extreme to us looking back today, but there was probably good motive to his unorthodox restrictions. Those who commonly crewed the boats of sail on the lakes in the 1880's were sometimes members of the lower levels of society, and the waterfront stops where vessels often unloaded were probably dangerous places for an un-escorted lady. Thus we can conclude that at least part of Captain Ellis' constraint on his new cook was for her own safety and his peace of mind. On the other hand, his rules offer us a glimpse into the enigma of this particular master of vessels.

When Captain Ellis introduced Mary to her galley for the first time, she would find the workspace cramped, at best. Schooner-barges were equipped with a single wood-burning stove on which all of the tasks of meal preparation were performed. A meager complement of cooking and cleaning utensils were supplied, and there was no such thing as refrigeration. At the center of the of the tiny room, a long table and bench seats seemed to take up every inch of space. Most of the lighting was provided by an overhead sky-light, which was supplemented at night by a few oil lamps. Running water was produced by fresh water being stored in casks on the deck-house roof and tapped when needed, garbage and dishwater were simply tossed overboard. For its day, the MONTANA's galley accommodations were spartan, even by lakeboat standards. To Mary Carstensen, the whole scene must have been a cramped, cluttered, filthy nightmare.

Mary's quarters were probably not much better than the galley. She would find a room the size of a walk-in closet with a single narrow bed and bare mattress; or if there were sheets they would presumably be nothing that she would wish to sleep on. A small and well-worn dresser with pitcher and bowl would undoubtedly round out the fixtures. A single window the size of a newspaper page and near-by oil lamp provided illumination to the claustrophobic quarters but did little to brighten the gloom. As the new cook surveyed her new home, she must have already felt a million miles from Oak Harbor. There was no space it seemed, and certainly no accommodations for the needs of a lady. Doubtless, Martin had cautioned her to only bring what she could carry because of the vessel's tight quarters, but this was far from what she had envisioned. As the door closed behind her the room seemed to shrink even more... if she could concoct curtains, at least she would have privacy. She would have to find other items in order to deal with the special needs of a lady.

A cook's job on the lakes in 1887 was much the same as today—to provide good food for the entire crew at designated meal times plus have something available at all times for those who roam into the galley in the off hours. Today, the modern laker sports stainless steel cooking facilities that rival the best restaurants, and has dining areas larger than the MONTANA's whole deck-house, but the job remains basically the same. As Mary would immediately discover, a lakeboat works around the clock, seven days a week, from the time the ice begins to open in the spring until winter freezes the lakes once more. The boat's cook does the same. On the lakers of Mary's day breads and biscuits had to be mixed from scratch then baked in a wood- or coal-burning oven where only the control of the draft could be used to regulate the temperature. Pots and pans had to serve multiple purposes, meaning that a good cook needed to juggle the cookware in order to prepare each meal—planning would be critical. Captain Ellis probably made it quite clear that the MONTANA was a workin' boat and he expected Mary to operate a workin' boat's galley, in spite of its fixtures. Before many second thoughts could well up within her, Mary's ears caught the sounds of shouted commands and rousting about on the deck. Her career at sea began as the MONTANA got under way.

Coincidentally, the MONTANA was almost the exact same age as Mary Carstensen. Launched at Clayton, New York in the spring of 1864, the boat was given her first enrollment on April 26th of that same year, making the MONTANA just four months older than its new cook. Officially the vessel's papers were issued at French Creek, New York, District of Cape Vincent, listing her as number 16340 "Schooner-Wood." John Oades was her builder and although there was no record of her dimensions when launched, a measurement taken the following spring listed her as being 138 feet in length, 27 feet and seven inches across her beam and 11 feet in depth. Her sails were raised on two masts and she had a gross weight of 345.59 tons— all of these measurements made her just the right size for

transiting the old Welland canal. Oades was a prime con-
tractor for the construction of boats for Detroit shipping
czars H. Esselstyn and Company through the 1850s and
1860s and that is where the MONTANA went to work.
Esselstyn fleet vessels were easily identified by the prefix
"MONT..." attached to each name. Such lake vessels as
MONTMORENCY, MONTPELIER, MONTCALM, MONT-
GOMERY, and MONT BLANC made up the MONTANA's
peers. Shortly after she went into service the MONTANA,
along with her fleetmates, were swallowed by Detroit shipping baron John Pridgeon's massive company and found
themselves laboring along "Pridgeon's line" across lakes
Huron and Michigan.

Autumn of 1890 caught the MONTANA in the employ of
Sandusky vesselman F.A. Hubbard, and making most of its
money on the end of a towing hawser attached to the tug
CRUSADER. Mary Carstensen had apparently found a way
to live and work under Captain Ellis' rules, because she was
nearing the end of her third season on his boat. The weather
was quiet and the thermometer hovered at 41 degrees on
Tuesday evening the 21st of October, 1890, but where the
St. Clair River meets Lake Huron, the scene was anything
other than quiet. In the hour of six p.m., an armada of lakeboats pushed upbound past Port Huron and onto the open
lake. Spear-heading the freshwater flotilla was the steamer
CUBA, with the MONTEAGLE and TORRENT plowing in her
wake. The DONALDSON and her barges came next, with the
D. LEUTY and ONAPING and their barges following close
behind. No sooner had these boats set their course than the
steamer ROBERT WALLACE and her consort DAVID WAL-
LACE pushed past Fort Gratiot with the steamer TEMPEST
and her barges in trail. Amid the lingering black haze of coal
smoke, the traffic continued with the CHICAGO, TOLTEC,

MIZTEC, CITY OF ALPENA, JOHN EDDY, JOHN SHAW, NEWELL A. EDDY, OSCAR T. FLINT and ARMENIA. Amid these upbounders, only the A.P. WRIGHT was able to sneak past, downbound, in the last 10 minutes of the hour. More than two dozen lakers had passed in the space of just one hour. The poor ship-reporter hardly had the time to put a new point on his pencil before the next wave of lakers came steaming. Leading the hour of seven o'clock upbound the ship-reporter listed the WESTFORD and her barges followed by the SPARTA, SUMATRA and SAMONA. Compared to the previous sixty minutes this was a relative calm in the traffic as the clock struck the hour of eight. Continuing the parade came the CHARLES A. EDDY, J.P. CLARK and barges, followed by the WILLIAM H. GRATWICK and ROCHESTER. At half past the hour, the tug CRUSADER plodded past with the MONTANA and perhaps as many as four other schooner-barges tightly moored to her heels. In keeping with the times, the ship reporter recorded the tug, but conveniently ignored the barges.

Escanaba was the tug CRUSADER's destination and a cargo of iron ore awaited Captain Ellis' boat. The entire month of October had consisted of unsettled weather, and the massive upbound fleet that the CRUSADER and MONTANA were caboosing had taken advantage of this break to dash for their next port while the calm conditions prevailed. Sailing when the weather was placid was always the best course of action when the CRUSADER was towing, considering that the burden of barges gave the vessels an over-the-bottom speed that was somewhat similar to a snail's crawl. In any kind of weather the tug and her barges made slow but steady progress, and it was always the "but steady" part that made for a slim, but tidy profit for the vessel owners such as Captain Ellis.

Over the next few days the MONTANA and her tug would stroll up Lake Huron and through the Straits of Mackinac toward Escanaba. Arriving at the crowded ore dock the diminutive schooner-barge would have to wait her turn to load. Taking her proper place, the MONTANA simply blended into the forest of masts. The barge's cargo would be bound for her home port of Sandusky—not what the modern lakeboat observer would normally consider to be a bustling steel port, but this had become the boat's regular shuttle. When it came the MONTANA's turn under the ore chutes, some $4,000 worth of ore was dropped into her hold. Dense as the red ore was, it took up less than half of the boat's cargo space, but lowered her hull deep into the water.

Pre-dawn on Sunday morning November 2nd, 1890, found the tug CRUSADER and the MONTANA downbound just below the Mackinac Straits. When she departed Escanaba, the tug had four other schooner-barges sharing the tow with Captain Ellis' boat. This meant that the tug and the MONTANA would have had to wait around in Escanaba for the other barges to load, which would be consistent with the time lapse between the CRUSADER's upbound passage on October 21st and her position now, on November 2nd. Lake Huron was in one of her most foul November moods in the darkness of the first hours of Sunday morning. A whipping wind brought a mix of rain and snow raking across the contemptuous seas of the lake's surface as the temperature hovered near freezing. Aboard the MONTANA, Mary Carstensen had her galley set for a typical rough autumn passage down. After two previous Novembers on the Great Lakes, she knew just how to prepare her utensils and other cooking implements so as to prevent their being tossed by the rolling boat. Additionally, the maiden cook also had adapted to life aboard the MON-TANA. From Ellis' rules to stocking up on the bottles of lady's items, Mary had learned to make the MONTANA her home during the shipping season. What Mary had not pre-pared for was just how and where this season, as well as her career on the Great Lakes, would end.

As the CRUSADER and her charges approached the waters north of Alpena, the winds increased to gale force and the seas began to come up. The tug's captain soon found that the lake had become much more than he wanted to be out on with a tail of schooner-barges and the weather-wise skipper elected to run for cover. The closest shelter was Middle Island located between Presque Isle and Thunder Bay. It was the tug's intention to ease up behind the island and let it block the winds and seas to provide lee for the CRUSADER and her tow. With the waves beginning to board and sweep her deck, the CRUSADER labored toward Middle Island. Lake Huron was now coming aboard in gray billows of icy cold water that sought out every open-ing, using them as intrusion points. Water found its way into each corner of the tug and worked through the hull to the bilges where it was pumped overboard. Near dawn the tug drew up under the island's lee and at last found a degree of shelter from the gale. The vessel tow behind the CRUSADER swung with the wind and settled in weather-vain fashion behind their tug.

Aboard the MONTANA, the scene was probably one of storm-bound routine. As a tow-barge, the vessel and crew had spent many a wind-beaten hour in lee of a convenient island, and this morning should have been no different. Sometime during that ugly Sunday morning, (there are no records as to exactly when), the storm winds suddenly shifted and robbed the CRUSADER and her ducklings of their valued shelter. There was no option for the tug's master now; he was forced to strike out once more and attempt to find a better spot behind Middle Island. No sooner was the slack of the towing hawser taken up by the pulling tug than Lake Huron reached out to play a spiteful trick on the hapless lakeboats. With the winds now in conflict to the waves a confused sea had developed. Once pulled out onto that sea, the boats each began to roll and twist at the towline. If Lake Huron could not get to the boats, it could surely take advantage of the towing hawser.

It is most probable that Mary Carstensen was either in her galley or, much more likely, in her cabin, as the MONTANA was pulled back into the waves. From her ice-blurred window, Mary's only view was of the gray lake as its horizon humped and twisted in an icy boil outside. Suddenly, the creaking wooden deck slanted in a alarming manner beneath Mary's feet while the familiar sound of big seas boarding the MONTANA thundered beyond her cabin. The schooner-barge was broaching and being blown into the sea-trough. Unknown to the boat's cook was the fact that the tow-line to the CRUSADER had been overcome by the stress of the wind and waves and parted like seamstress' thread. The MONTANA, like the rest of the tug's tow was now adrift.

With their umbilical cord to the tug severed, the schooner-barges now were forced to take to their own against Lake Huron. The captains of each barge ordered storm sails hoisted and reverted their boats back to their natural state, that of schooners. Flapping eagerly with the November winds the aged canvas of the once proud sailing vessels grabbed the winds and began their struggle to pull their crews to safety, or at least put the storm to their heels until the CRUSADER could round them all up once more.

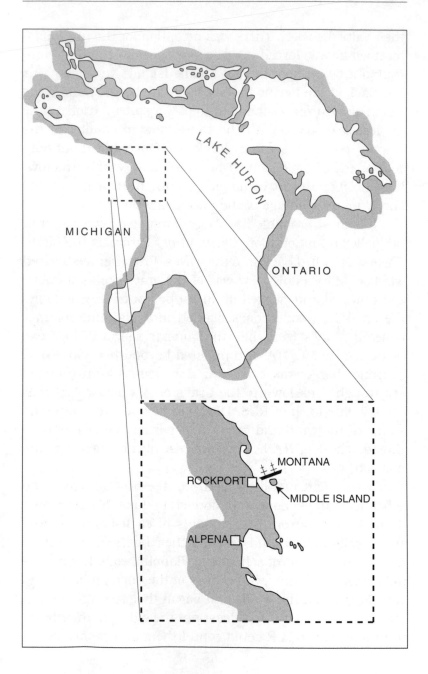

This was true of all of the tug's barges except for the MONTANA; for some reason she alone was having difficulty coming under her own power.

Maneuvering with the dexterity that only a tug can manage, the CRUSADER set back for her tow. Through the snow squalls it was difficult to tell from the tug which barge was which, or even how each was handling the difficulty. Rolling and pitching madly, the tug came about and punched its way through the waves toward the wayward barges. Down within the tug's engineroom the scene was that of a netherworld. Even when the weather was calm, the act of stoking the tugs' boilers in the cramped engineroom was done with the engine crew's bellies at the furnace and backsides at the bunkers as temperatures hovered over 100 degrees. Aside from the fires beneath the boilers only an oil lamp or two provided the light to work by. Now as the tug tossed in the billowing waves the deck grating seemed to tilt and spin as bilge water slapped up in filthy spikes. Lake Huron continued to come intruding aboard the tug, now making its way down the companionway to the engineroom. There the lake water mixed with the tug's hot engine works and made steam that added to the engine crew's misery. Despite the inhuman atmosphere, the engine crew stoked on; they had no idea what was going on topside, but they could tell from the motion of the tug that it was not good. From the tug's tiny pilothouse her captain spun the wheel as he set his sights on the recovery of all of the drifting barges—but Lake Huron had other ideas.

Listing in a fearful manner, the MONTANA was batted by waves, the likes of which Mary Carstensen had never felt before. What the frosted view out of her cabin window could not tell her was that this new punishment was being delivered by the breakers just off Middle Island. With the tremor of an earthquake and the sound of thunder, the schooner-barge was spit onto the rocks of the island by a maniacal Lake Huron. Smashing like a china cup, the MONTANA's oak hull shattered on the shoal as all aboard were thrown from their feet. The tug CRUSADER had come up short in her effort to recover the MONTANA, and Mary had been cast into an adventure at sea that she had not considered when she signed aboard as cook—she was shipwrecked!

The scene had started with each schooner-barge fending for itself, but after they had gained their own control, the vesselmen began looking about for their companions. Apparently the CRUSADER had managed to re-capture one vessel, and three others had sail up and were making good way toward Alpena, but a single glance toward the MONTANA revealed she had run smack onto a reef one quarter of a mile north, northwest of the Middle Island lifesaving station.

There are no written records of exactly what transpired immediately after the MONTANA was slammed onto Middle Island, but a few sketchy accounts of the event can be found. Using a bit of imagination, and what few written descriptions do survive, we can easily picture the scene that followed the stranding. The schooner-barge was not "high and dry" on the beach; being deeply loaded with ore, her hull would have found the bottom a few hundred yards off shore having the wild churning ice water surf between her crew and dry land. A swim to shore would have been suicidal and with the waves breaking over her, the boat showed every sign of breaking up. Coming out on deck, Mary found the lake heaving up high and crashing over the MONTANA's rails. The water turned red as it swirled within the iron ore cargo, giving each wave a strange and frightening appearance. It was a sight that Mary Carstensen would never forget. Winds screamed through the vessel's rigging and the snow continued as the boat began to twist and groan in an odd way. Looking forward it was clear that the bow was rolling and sagging in one direction as the stern seemed to go in the other. Beneath Mary's feet, loud creaking sounds, like those from a giant oak tree being cut down, were heard as well as felt. Clearly, the MONTANA was coming apart.

At the Middle Island life saving station, Captain McKenzie could not help but be aware of the wreck that Lake Huron had just deposited on his doorstep. The tug EFFIE L. had also been alerted and headed to the scene. Drawing as near as she dared, the EFFIE L. quickly found that the winds and seas were far too wicked for her to make any effort toward the MONTANA. Now it was time for Captain McKenzie's "storm warriors" to go to work. Crews of the U.S. Life-Saving Service spent endless hours practicing their rescue drills in wait for the day when the waves would put mariners in peril, and on the Great Lakes that day was never far ahead. Parting the breakers, the lifesavers launched their surfboat. With all of the passion that was woven into their calling, the surfmen pulled at their oars—this was it; the mighty lake was out to swallow the crew of the MONTANA and only Captain McKenzie's men could thwart it. All around the rowing lifesavers, the breaking white-capped seas roared as bitter wet snow pelted at their oilskins. Each time a new wave was met, it took the liberty of introducing itself by leaping over the bow of the surfboat and sloshing among the crew's benumbed feet. It was hard pullin' to say the least, but this was what the men of the U.S. Life-Saving Service trained and lived for.

Garbed in layers of her warmest clothing, Mary Carstensen waited, semi-sheltered in the MONTANA's swamped deck-house as the surfboat approached. Now she faced the most terrifying move of her life. Going over the rail of a foundering vessel into a tiny surfboat pitching wildly in the surrounding seas wearing pants and a shirt was a dangerous ordeal. Attempting the same venture wearing the heavy cotton petticoat and dress appropriate to the era—as well as to Ellis' rules—would appear a near impossibility. With the surfboat banging against the MONTANA's twisted hull and the lifesavers beckoning, it became Mary's turn to go over the side. Imagine, if you will, the amount of courage and moxie that it must have taken for this sheltered maiden to go over that rail. Howling wind would have ripped at her hair and pulled at her skirt as waves reached up aching to clutch and carry her off—the journey to the arms of the waiting lifesavers would not have been a "ladylike" affair. A single slip on the iced-over wooden surfaces would plunge Mary to her doom in the cold, cold teeth of Lake Huron. This was a horrifying moment that has, in some cases, caused seasoned lake mariners to stiffen with panic and submit to going to their fate with the vessel. Peering over the side, the choice for Mary was simple: tempt destiny and crawl over that frozen oak rail, or stay behind and be lost. The lifesavers called to her, coaxing, as the members of both crews attempted to stabilize the surfboat in the thrashing red waves in wait of the cook's decision, while beneath her button shoes the MONTANA moaned in its death throes.

On April 11th, 1994, more than a century after the wind-teared eyes of that shipwrecked maiden cast their gaze toward the ore-stained waves off Middle Island, Gary Hill carefully packed all of the information that he had gathered concerning the wreck of the MONTANA and slipped it into a large envelope. With some amount of resignation the accumulated data of two decades worth of searching was sent to this author. Gary's quest had taken him to the General Services Administration in Washington D.C., National Archives, Institute for Great Lakes Research, Alpena dive shops and historians, Ohio newspapers and contemporary researchers such as Dave Swayze and myself. No where, however, could he find, in writing, a record that the tale handed down to him was that of the MONTANA and his great grandmother. So many dead-ends were met. A fire in 1936 for example, destroyed all of the Alpena newspapers previous to 1899. Perhaps, if a crew roster had ever been kept at all, it had been printed there and is gone forever. Now Gary forwarded his accumulated documents in the hope that the story could be told. All of the facts fit: the barge's home port and master, the place and date of the wreck, and Mary's home town—all that was missing is that written proof that she was actually, physically there.

It is most likely that written proof of Mary's tenure on Captain Ellis' boat does not exist. Either the record was never kept, was lost with the wreck, or simply lost in the passing of time. But one very telling detail in her story says that Mary Carstensen was indeed on the wreck of the MON-TANA—within the account of her ordeal that she passed to her daughter, Mary stated flatly that "the water turned red..." The fact that shipwrecks involving cargoes of natural iron ore often stain the waters red is common knowledge only to those who have witnessed such wrecks or have spent a good deal of time researching the same. Odds are that a common housewife of the Victorian era would not be able to weave such an obscure detail into a fictitious yarn. A sea-going cook who had experienced an actual oreboat wreck would state this detail as common fact without thinking much about it. Mary was there, and saw it with her own eyes, of this there is no doubt.

All eight of the MONTANA's crew, including Mary Carstensen, were successfully removed from the wreck in a single trip by the Middle Island lifesavers. Then a second trip was made by Captain McKenzie's boys to recover as much of the crew's possessions as possible. The seas now washed completely over the wreck, and the lifesavers scurried about the vacated cabins, scooping up whatever they could carry. It was a messy task, as the lake swirled nearly knee-deep and carried off every loose article that it could. The ship's documents probably were taken by the lake at this time, and perhaps the crew roster that Gary Hill would seek a 100 years later, floated casually past as the lifesavers sloshed around attempting to rescue a pair of trousers and a hat or two. In the hours ahead the lake purged all of the MONTANA's cabins, including Mary's galley and stateroom. Away went her cooking utensils, bedding and all of those special things that made Mary's room a lady-like place.

For six days the crew of the MONTANA were "succored," or provided with room and board at the Middle Island lifesaving station. Normally, the stations in remote locations, such as Middle Island, were constructed with quarters to temporarily house shipwreck survivors. These usually consisted of a single "spare room" measuring about 12 feet by 24 feet with a number of cots. Such accommodations must have been unpalatable in the extreme for the lone shipwrecked female who was still under Ellis' rules. For reasons unknown, the days dragged on and the castaways remained at the station. Just why they were not taken to Alpena is not known, perhaps Captain Ellis was holding out at the station in hopes that the MONTANA could be freed, and would then need his crew to work her. Or maybe Ellis simply did not have the means to charter a tug to shuttle the group to the harbor. Additionally the facts seem to indicate that the storm persisted for a few days. Without regard to such speculation, all that is on the record is that the crew's stay stretched out to six days. It is said that it was Mary who finally put her foot down and demanded that she as well as the rest of the crew be taken to civilization. Threatening to "walk across the water" to get to Alpena if no one was willing to take her there by boat the plucky cook led a minor dry-land mutiny. This ended the succor as well as Mary Carstensen's career on the Great Lakes.

By the 11th of November, 1890, Mary was probably back at home and the MONTANA was given up as a total wreck. Marked "abandoned" her enrollment was dropped at Sandusky and she was left on the shoal at Middle Island, broken amidships. The tug EFFIE L. was charged with salvaging as much of the wreck's machinery as possible and began the work as soon as the weather permitted. It would appear that this was the end of the story, but as with many such tales this was not the case for the MONTANA, or Mary Carstensen. The MONTANA eventually was raised from the shoal and it is thought that she was towed to Bay City, Michigan for extensive repairs. By 1892 she was back in business as a schooner-barge under the ownership of Bay City vesselman N. Barkwell and went on working until 1910, when she sank on Lake Erie.

It is worth pondering that the moment when Mary Carstensen decided to go over that icy ship's rail may have been a turning point in her life. Later she broke from Ellis' rules and spoke up for herself and the others to have them taken to the mainland from Middle Island. Next, just 51 days after she was shipwrecked, Mary was wed to George Paulsen. Exactly how and when they met is not known. The

Mary Carstensen — George Paulsen, c. 1890

two newlyweds took up residence in Oak Harbor, and eventually parented four children. Mary never worked upon the Great Lakes again, although her sense of the romance of going to sea seems to have remained with her. She often said that had she not settled down into a family life, she would have liked to have sailed the oceans and gone to visit other countries. Mary lived with her eyes toward the distant waters until September 26th, 1936. It is the research effort of Gary Hill that has been woven here into the saga of his great grandmother's adventure on the lakes. Although the conclusion has been drawn within this text that Mary Carstensen was, in fact, aboard the MONTANA, it is certain that her great grandson's effort to find that written proof will continue. Perhaps he will stumble upon that shy collector of Great Lakes memorabilia who just happens to have such a piece of record stashed away. Or maybe some "boat-nut" will read this text and dig into an area that we have not, and find that crew roster with Mary's name on it, sharing this data with Mr. Hill. Gary Hill has found out what those of us who spend so much time digging into the history of the Great Lakes know so well—the adventure into the past is very much like mining. The researcher must continue to dig; sometimes the effort yields nothing, but there are pockets of gold just waiting to be found.

Presently, groups of volunteers scurry around Middle Island like ants before a hard rain and the sound of hammers echo across the rocky landscape. Cement for sidewalks is shuttled from the mainland in five gallon buckets and work is at a fever pitch from June through August. It is the restoration of the Middle Island light keeper's quarters as well as the lifesaving station, and all is being done under the close watch of Marvin Thuit—the owner of most of Middle Island itself. In 1989 Marvin acquired the 10.2 acres adjacent to his property on which the light station is located. The current plans are to restore the structures to their condition in the 1905-1939 era. Additionally, the establishment of a bed and breakfast in the keeper's quarters will allow the members of the Middle Island Light Keeper's Association to soon be succored on the island themselves. It is true that they will have a great deal better accommodations than Mary Carstensen had, but perhaps while looking out toward the shimmering blue lake, those who visit the island may consider that stormy November and the moment that a Victorian era maiden's life changed. At the Association's new headquarters and museum on U.S. 23, a few miles north of Alpena, shelves are lined with artifacts and old bottles found around Middle Island. Upon examination it is clear that some contained lady-like material, and the thought occurs that one of these small bottles may have contained some special substance that made life aboard the schooner-barge MONTANA bearable for Mary Carstensen more than a century ago.

A Sutton's Bay Pirate

*V*isiting the tiny resort village of Sutton's Bay, Michigan today, the tourist will be relieved to find it a peaceful place far removed from the bustle of most vacation spots. Located just north of Traverse City, the town looks out onto the hypnotic blue expanse of the western finger of Grand Traverse Bay. It is just the right distance north of Traverse City to escape any influence of the big town to the south. In the months of winter, Sutton's Bay becomes a snow-bound wonderland where those who love the cold weather sports and arts seem able to find a place to keep that season all to themselves. In the summer months, the tree-lined main street through town sees the open doors of dozens of upscale unique shops and stores. Additionally, the water-front is garnished with a fine marina and dive-shop... but still, the crowds of visitors find a quiet pace that makes a fine summer's day seem to last a week.

Walking the streets of Sutton's Bay while a gentle summer breeze from off water combs the shade, it is hard to imagine this as a place that would breed a pirate. After all, when the term "pirate" comes to mind we imagine a sword slashing, bandanna-capped cut-throat with a patch over one eye pillaging merchant ships for their treasure. Surely, such a person could never have come from the serenity that is Sutton's Bay. But, on September 25th of 1911, that is just what happened.

Mart Bailey never intended to become a pirate; in fact, the Sutton's Bay resident spent the vast majority of his mariner's career as a hard working ordinary vesselman. Having worked many of the jobs that elevate someone up through the ranks of mariners, Bailey managed to gain experience along with income. By the shipping season of 1911, he had the credentials of a lake pilot, and in September of that same year found himself employed in that very position aboard the steamer MANISTEE. Knowing this we would conclude that such was hardly the root cause that would drive a person to piracy, and for the most part this assumption would be correct. It is probable that had it not been for James Ferguson, Mark Foote and "King Barleycorn's favorite brew"—"Mark, the pirate of Sutton's Bay," would have never come to be.

It was Tuesday, September 19th, 1911 and the break-bulk carrier MANISTEE was firmly moored to her Chicago dock. Not to be confused with the MANISTEE that was lost with all hands on Lake Superior in the 1880's, this vessel had been given the name in 1905 and remained primarily in the Lake Michigan trade. In his quarters aboard the steamer, First Mate James Ferguson paced about like a man awaiting a sentence. Occasionally, Ferguson would edge up to his cabin window and peek out toward the dock and waterfront beyond. Shortly the figure of a man the stature of whom most would not want to tangle with, would appear and the nervous mate would have to perform one of the least pleasurable of his duties. The walking, talking dilemma that Ferguson had to deal with was none other than Mart Bailey. Although a hard-working and all around good fellow, Bailey had a taste for liquor, often bringing his intoxicated state aboard ship. By now the MANISTEE's captain had reached his limit of overlooking such conduct and told Mate Ferguson in no uncertain terms that the fermented pilot had to be fired. Ferguson, although in complete agreement with the vessel's master, was not looking forward to that bit of dirty work. He knew too well that Bailey, when angered, probably had the girth to do some damage.

For Ferguson, it was the waiting that was the hard part; the hours ticked past but Bailey had yet to appear. The pilot had been ashore since the boat's arrival. In fact, no sooner had the steamer put her lines ashore than Bailey went "up the street" to patronize a familiar tavern. Now, it was nearing the time for the lines to be cast off and Mate Ferguson was sure that Bailey would soon come staggering back aboard. Perhaps somewhere in the back of his mind Ferguson held out the secret hope that the drunken navigator would fall so far into the bottle that he might miss the boat. This, however, was not the direction that the hands of fate were determined to travel. As certain as clockwork, the image of a drunken Mart Bailey came stumbling toward the MANISTEE's gang plank. Figuring that firing the hefty pilot between decks would not be the smartest move, the mate elected to stop Bailey on deck. Being in the confines of the steamer's companionway with a drunken, wrathful, freshly-fired crewman, Ferguson reckoned, might just get him clobbered. As Bailey stumbled up the gangway, he came face to face with a determined Ferguson who, in very few yet extremely clear terms, fired him. Unfortunately, Bailey would have much preferred to be dismissed in private and in his intoxicated state equated the mate's actions with the worst level of insult. Ferguson's well laid plan exploded in his face, as did Bailey who proceeded to pummel the mate and toss him about like a flour sack.

Apparently, the commotion soon drew the attention of nearby law officers who joined in the fracas. We can gain an insight to Bailey's construction by the fact the he was soon getting the better of three police officers and Mate Ferguson. Just how the drunken crewman was over-powered and exactly how many men it took to subdue him is not on record, but the group eventually overcame the inebriated mariner. Later, Bailey found himself piloting a stone-walled damp cell at the county jail. There he sat until the following Monday when he was brought before United States Commissioner Mark Foote. With head held low, Bailey gave his best attempt at an excuse for his actions by explaining his interpretation of Ferguson's methods and how he had been driven to becoming angry. Admitting that he had been drinking, Bailey added that he could not recall fighting. Unfortunately, there were three bruised police offi-cers in attendance as living proof that Bailey's recall was faulty. Commissioner Foote was not impressed by the entire ordeal. In consideration of the pilot's direct and vio-lent insubordination toward the vessel's mate, the honor-able commissioner ordered that Bailey be held over for the Grand Jury on $1,000 bond... under the authority of the piracy act!

As the heavy cell door slammed behind him, Bailey did not realize just what the commissioner's words meant. While cooling his heels in the lock-up, Bailey may very well have been the world's only living pirate, certainly he was the only one on the lakes. In modern times, many decades after "the pirate Mart" had his legal problems resolved, we find not a trace of piracy in his home town of Sutton's Bay. There are no cannons, or treasure chests on display to mark the town as the place that was once the residence of one of the few certified pirates on the Great Lakes. Surely, Mart Bailey's predicament has been long forgotten—which is just how he would have preferred it.

Breakfast at the Owl Cafe

aptain John Sinclair gave the "finished with engines" signal as the oak-hulled lakeboat OSCAR T. FLINT hovered to a dead stop on the calm waters of Thunder Bay just outside of Alpena, Michigan. Following faithfully behind, the barge NELLIE REDINGTON was in tow and came to rest at the end of the slackened towing hawser. It was November 24th, 1909, the day before Thanksgiving, and the boat's chief had been having fits over one single accursed steam valve and air pump since nearly the beginning of the trip. Finally the matter had degraded to the point where steam would have to be let off and the engine shut down so that the pesky valve could be properly repaired. Shortly after the captain had signaled his having finished with the engine, the a cloud of steam hissed loudly into the autumn air nearly swallowing the stern of the vessel as the chief dumped the pressure. Now the FLINT sat dead in the water with no steam-pressure to power her engine and worse yet, no steam to run through her radiators and heat her cabins.

A cargo of limestone from Kelley's Island on western Lake Erie was piled in the FLINT's hold while 500 barrels of salt that had been shipped at St. Clair, Michigan crowded her deck. The whole load was bound for Duluth, and although the REDINGTON was without cargo, her master, Captain Keenan had requested 800 tons of limestone aboard at Kelley's Island in the expectation of a heavy November sea on Superior. Two million board-feet of fresh lumber waited on rail cars to be put aboard the FLINT and REDINGTON as soon as they reached Duluth and unloaded their limestone. Now Captain Keenan's trip was delayed not by weather, but by the machinery of her towing steamer, the FLINT. As he watched the steam dump from the FLINT, Keenan could not help but smirk a bit; his barge might not have a power-plant but surely his people would have a better night than those aboard the idled steamer. After all, the schooner-barge was always at work without the benefit of a steam engine, so her crew knew all too well how to get along with the cold.

Upper Lake Huron is never balmy in the last week of November, and even "Indian summer" is driven into hiding by the approaching of winter. It seemed as if the steam had no sooner been released than the cabins of the FLINT became as cold as a walk-in icebox. There was heat in the galley, however, as the cook's big coal-burning stove had no need for the steamplant. Naturally, it did not take long for most of the crew to begin gathering in the dining quarters as the ship's cook and his second occupied themselves with the production of hot stuff to keep the crewmen warm. Among those stopping by the eating quarters was wheelsman Hurlsley, who had only recently shipped aboard the FLINT. As most of the galley-talk probably speculated over the Thanksgiving feast that the cook would prepare for the next day, the new wheelsman stood quietly in the background. While the others chuckled and loudly joked in the din of pre-holiday cheer, Hurlsley's thoughts would occasionally drift out the galley window, across Lake Huron and toward an event that was not too far away—in both time and distance. Only five months before, he had been walking the decks of another steamer at an Alpena dock, very near this same spot on Thunder Bay. Now, out there just a few miles away, rested his former boat.

It was Friday, the last day of April, 1909 and the package steamer RUSSIA had been loading a deck-cargo of bagged cement for the entire day. From the boat's pilot-house, Captain John C. McLean had kept a "weather eye" toward Lake Huron which had put on her uncivil and gray disposition for the moment. Snow squalls swirled across the scene all day while the dock workers carted the bags aboard against a stiff wind. Winter it seemed, was unwilling to let go of its cold grip on the lake as it overpowered the onset of spring. On deck, the RUSSIA's crew, including Hurlsley, kept busy securing the cargo. Just before dinner time, the work of loading the cement had been completed and Hurlsley as well as his shipmates made their way to the galley for coffee and the chance to get the warmth to return to their benumbed fingers.

A respectable spring gale had been blowing for most of the past two days, but now Captain McLean reckoned that the worst had passed and the weather was right for getting under way. Without the benefit of modern weather reports and forecasts, Captain McLean had only his barometer and mariner's savvy to guide him. Having the opportunity to look back through the years, we can say that his decision was well founded and the bad portion of the storm was indeed passing. In fact, the strongest portion of the gale was currently striking far to the north on Lake Superior. There the steamer SCHOOLCRAFT was plowing from the Soo with the schooner-barge GEORGE NESTER in tow. In command of Captain George DeBeau, the NESTER was running light and carried a crew of six. The steamer and her consort had passed upbound through the Soo on Wednesday morning and was near the Huron Islands when the gale reached out for her. With a single swift stroke, the storm plucked the barge from her steamer and tossed the luckless craft onto the island's reef at 11:45 Friday morning. Minutes later, the schooner-barge was being beat to pieces by the surf. Alerted by the Huron Island lightkeeper Frank Wittie, the lighthouse-tender MARIGOLD set out to the rescue. Towering waves and a wind made of iron thwarted the MARIGOLD's effort as not even a lifeline could be put aboard. The lighthouse-tender and her crew could do nothing more than stand by helplessly as the NESTER broke up and took all of her crew to their doom. So close had the MARIGOLD ventured toward the foundering schooner-barge, that one of the tender's crew had been struck by the NESTER's wreckage—inflicting a broken shoulder. The risk was fruitless; the 207 foot NESTER and her crew were gone to Lake Superior.

Unaware of the events up on Lake Superior, Captain McLean guided the RUSSIA from Alpena and onto an ill-tempered Lake Huron just about 12 hours after the NESTER's story came to an end. Among those aboard the RUSSIA, there was one person who was not a member of the crew; in fact, Alexander Mathews had paid to be aboard the steamer. His job with the McMorran Milling Company of Port Huron had required that he travel to Duluth, and the best way to get there in 1909 was obviously by boat. Just how Mr. Mathews was connected with a passage aboard the RUSSIA we do not know, but the Duluth-Port Huron run was the RUSSIA's normal route and was certainly going his way. With an occasional side trip to pick up a profitable deck-load, the steamer was making a fair profit for the Port Huron and Duluth Steam Ship Company. During the 1908 season, passenger accommodations were added to the vessel's other deck houses and Mr. Mathews would be her first paying passenger of the 1909 season. The RUSSIA had been at the fit-out dock for most of the week and as she prepared to start the 1909 season, Mr. Mathews came aboard. His itinerary was Port Huron to Duluth with an intermediate stop at Alpena, but had he known the true stormy schedule of his trip, Mathews would probably have stayed at his desk.

The first iron plates of the RUSSIA were placed at Buffalo, New York in 1872 by the King Ironworks. As hull number 12 she measured 231.7 feet in length, 35.7 feet in beam and 13.3 feet in draft. When she came from the builder's yard the vessel could take 2,000 tons of bulk cargo through six hatches. Her steeple Compound engine provided the power of 600 horses through the drive of 20 and 40 inch diameter cylinders each with a 36 inch stroke. This steam power-plant turned twin screws that rotated at 72 revolutions per minute when the boat was at full-ahead. Some sources have concluded that the RUSSIA was, by virtue of her name, related to the passenger steamers JAPAN, INDIA and CHINA. The fact is that she has a far different family tree. One of four sister ships the RUSSIA's kin were the steamers JAVA, SCOTIA and CUBA. All of the quadruplets had been designed for the package and bulk trade between Buffalo and Chicago having both side ports and deck hatches. By 1909, the JAVA was resting at the bottom of Lake Michigan after foundering in 1878 and the SCOTIA had been lost off of the Keweenaw in 1884. Now only the RUSSIA and CUBA, renamed IONIC, remained.

Snoring onto an unsettled Lake Huron early on Friday evening, April 30th 1909, the RUSSIA spewed thick billows of black coal smoke from her stack. Pressure from her two boilers was up near 135 pounds as the twin propellers shoved the boat full ahead. It was shaping up to be a loathsome night, and Captain McLean was of a mind to make the protected waters of DeTour and the lower Saint Marys

Years of searching may soon find the wreck of the RUSSIA.

River as soon as possible. So the order was sent down to the firehold not to spare the coal and "let 'er go." Apparently all was in order with both the deck cargo and the load of assorted general merchandise. The preceding storm had left behind a considerable swell that the RUSSIA was taking on her port bow. A twisting roll of the sort that could only bring annoyance to the mariners had now become the steamer's swagger. Asleep in his stateroom, passenger Mathews was being rocked asleep by the very same roll that was causing Captain McLean to grind his teeth.

Apparently, this was going to be a lumpish but routine trip to the head of the lakes. Passing Presque Isle, the RUSSIA just rolled along on the course for DeTour like an old tub. Captain McLean made certain that the watchman kept a close eye on the deck cargo as well as the load below decks. Not long after the Presque Isle light was fading over the stern, however, there came an abrupt change in the state of affairs aboard the RUSSIA. Without warning, the steamer took an abrupt list to her port side. In fact, so pronounced was the heel that Captain McLean thought that the vessel was in immediate danger of capsizing and ordered the crew on deck to trim the load. Just how long the desperate chore of moving the bags of cement took is unclear, but after a good deal of elbow grease, the load was shifted and the RUSSIA appeared to take on a more even keel. With no small sense of relief, the boat's crew returned to the shelter of the deck house when the hand of providence reached out once again and pushed the steamer over. This time, the deck below the feet of the RUSSIA's people suddenly canted to starboard, and to such an alarming degree that some of those left on deck were nearly tossed over the rail.

For a series of heart-beats, every man aboard the RUSSIA stood frozen, holding his breath and afraid to move a muscle. It seemed as if the entire vessel was teetering on the brink of eternity, and the movement of a single hair would send her over. Indeed, the scene was surreal as the big steamer pushed her way along under full steam, lights aglow and listed so far over that her rails nearly touched the waves. When the fact that the boat was not going to instantly turn turtle became apparent, Captain McLean gave orders to muster everyone on deck. They had just spent what seemed like eternity piling the bags of cement powder on the starboard side and now those same bags would have to be thrown overboard. Sensing that there may well be something more afoot in this situation than a simple shifting of the deck load, McLean also ordered the pumps started and the engines reversed. Unusually, the pumps came up dry, indicating no leaking in the boat's double bottom, but the list grew more pronounced.

Struggling to the pilothouse, Captain McLean glanced at the needle on the list indicator, but the gnomon-like device had pegged long ago. Rustling his charts and using his fingers as dividers, the master quickly calculated his position as being about 12 miles below DeTour—easily within rowing distance. With that in mind, he gave the order to abandon the RUSSIA to her own ends. By the time all hands were top-side, the steamer's deck-rails were awash in Lake Huron and it was clear that she was determined to founder. With all of the others, wheelsman Hurlsley grappled at launching the two lifeboats, while passenger Mathews stood by feeling fairly helpless among the crowd of lakemen. Launching the lifeboats with the vessel in this extremely odd attitude was no easy task, and it was at this point that the only injury in the RUSSIA's saga occurred. While putting one of the yawls over, Captain McLean's fingers were smashed, but his was the only trauma inflicted in the escape. As best can be told from the accounts, the lifeboats began pulling away at approximately 11 p.m., and about 20 minutes later the RUSSIA rolled completely on her side. Hatches gave way and decks burst as Lake Huron invaded the open spaces of the steamer. In the darkness beyond the lifeboats, the RUSSIA went down as the lake's surface rose up in a churning mound, peppered with assorted items of her cargo. Three hours later, the yawls rowed into DeTour Village and all of the RUSSIA's people were safely delivered to dry land.

On the Wednesday following the wreck, Alexander Mathews was making his way through the lobby of the Hickler House at Sault Saint Marie. Nearly a week had passed since he departed Port Huron and he was still stuck halfway between his destination and departure point with only the clothing he had been wearing on the night of the wreck. There in the lobby the castaway was met by a tight-vested man in a bowler hat who asked if he had been aboard the RUSSIA. Responding that he had indeed been there, Mr. Mathews was stopped in mid sentence when the man pulled a note pad from his pocket.

"I've had enough of you fellows!... " Mathews bellowed, realizing that the man was a reporter from the Sault Saint Marie *Evening News*. Shaking his head and batting his hand in the reporter's direction Mathews attempted to break away from the now pressing newsman, "...A fellow down at Port Huron got hold of me and what he printed in his paper was a fright."

Through a bit of comforting chat, the newsman was soon able to calm Mathews and get him conversing about the events on Lake Huron five nights earlier. What the reporter found out was that Mathews had been asleep through most of the events and thus could give few details. Scratching what few bits of information he had managed to squeeze out of Mathews, the newsman ambled out of the hotel. For a moment he paused looking at what information he had accumulated and wondered—just what did happen to the steamer RUSSIA?

Seven months after the RUSSIA turned turtle and went to the bottom, her former wheelsman stood on the deck of the OSCAR T. FLINT waiting for the steam to come up and the heat to return to his cabin. As the evening grew late, members of the crew shuffled off to their respective quarters and curled up under every blanket that could be found. Everyone knew that the next day would bring heat and a Thanksgiving feast, but what they did not know was just how much heat and how little feast there would be.

Sometime in the early morning of Thanksgiving Day, 1909, (no one knows exactly when), smoke started to fill the FLINT's forward areas. As the smoke slithered beneath Captain Sinclair's cabin door and found its way to his nose, the pungent fumes woke the slumbering captain faster than a kid with a trumpet. Exploding from his bed, the startled master leaped to his door and ripped it open. His worst fears were confirmed: the companionway was a thick fog of smoke. Apparently Captain Sinclair was the only one residing in the forward quarters and as soon as he assured himself of that fact, he dashed aft in his bare feet to alert the rest of the crew. Just what they were going to do, aside from abandoning the FLINT, was unclear. The problem was that the boat had no steam up. No steam meant no pumps and no water pressure to fight the fire. Other than toss cups of coffee at the flames, the crew could do little more than gather their belongings and take to the lifeboats.

Fishermen at the North Point Fisheries spotted the blaze out on the bay, from there a phone call was made to Alpena and in turn the Thunder Bay Island lifesavers were alerted. As they launched their motor surfboat, the tug RALPH cast off out of Alpena, also headed for the FLINT. From the docks of Alpena and the beaches of Thunder Bay Island, residents were beginning to take notice of the growing tower of dense smoke emanating from the anchorage. What was developing was a Thanksgiving day event that no one had expected.

Born to the Great Lakes at St. Clair, Michigan in 1889 the OSCAR T. FLINT was a product of shipbuilder Simon Langell. She had been built to the specific order of A.R. Sinclair & Company, measuring 226 feet in length, 37 feet in beam and just over 15 feet in draft. At 1124 gross tons the FLINT could haul a maximum of 1,000,050 board-feet of lumber. A fore and aft compound steam engine powered the boat using 26 inch and 48 inch diameter cylinders with a 40 inch stroke turned her screw and supplied propulsion. Now, 20 years after she had been launched, the FLINT was about to go up in flames.

Taking to the lifeboats, the FLINT's crew lowered themselves to the surface of Thunder Bay. Abnormal for northern Michigan in the end of November, the winds on this Thanksgiving morning were dead-calm and the waters of the bay were glassy flat. Once aboard the yawls, the crew had little trouble escaping the FLINT. By the time that they had pulled a safe distance from the steamer she was rapidly consuming herself and the heat from her combustion radiated over the distance. The crewmembers could feel the burning vessel as they worked to widen the gap between their yawls and the FLINT. By the time that the tug RALPH and the Thunder Bay Island surfmen's motor lifeboat pulled onto the scene, the wooden steamer was becoming a floating bonfire. A resigned heave tossed a line from the surfmen to the FLINT's lifeboat and with the connection secured the lifesavers putted toward Alpena towing the yawl. A short distance away the tug RALPH took a like connection to the other yawl hauling its occupants to safety.

Once back on dry land, the FLINT's people were gathered together and made their way to the Globe Hotel. Captain Sinclair made the best of the situation by invading the Owl Cafe and ordering up breakfast for his crew. Since the fire had started forward, the crew had plenty of time and had managed to rescue most of their possessions. The single exception to this was Captain Sinclair, who had ended up with only what clothing he had been wearing. Unfortunately, the captain's wardrobe at the time of the fire had not included shoes, so he found himself shuffling around the Owl Cafe in his socks.

After he had finished his Thanksgiving day "feast," wheelsman Hurlsley sipped at his remaining coffee. So far this season he had survived two shipwrecks. First there had been the RUSSIA to start the season, and now the FLINT. He had also been an eye witness to two of the many small puzzles in the annals of Great Lakes maritime history. The RUSSIA had rolled over and gone to the bottom 57 miles north of where Hurlsley was now seated—and no one knew why she had done so. Now, the FLINT was going up in flames and again, no one knew exactly why. As Hurlsley's former job burned out on the bay, he glanced around the cafe. Most of his shipmates were rehashing their escape. The whole room was a cacophony of loud conversation and back-slapping speculation as to how the FLINT had burst into flame. "Maybe," Hurlsley thought to himself, "it's time to quit for the season."

Sources

Entanglements

REF; Bay City *Tribune*, 11/14,15, 16, 17, 21, 22/1883

Statement of the circumstances of the AKELEY disaster by Chief Engineer Driscoll, AKELEY file, Canal Park Museum, Duluth, undated author unknown.

Correspondence with Kenneth Pot, Michigan Maritime Museum, South Haven, Michigan, 6/19/1995

Coast Guard City, USA. *A History of the Port of Grand Haven*, Seibold

Grand Haven *Tribune*, 12/21/1979

Correspondence with the Tri-Cities Museum, Grand Haven, 6/21/1995

Life-saving Service—Table of wrecks, season of 1883-'84

"*Historic Grand Haven and Ottawa County*," Lillie

Spring Lake Community Centennial publication 1869-1969, Kitchel

"*Shipwrecks of the Straits of Mackinac*," Feltner

"*Shipwreckd*," Swayze

"*History of the Great Lakes*," Mansfield

"*Wreck Ashore: The United States Life-Saving Service on the Great Lakes*," Stonehouse

Through the Cracks in History

REF; E-mail from Dave Swayze who had gotten the vessel passages from the Detroit *Free Press* for Chicago 9/23&24/1911 at the author's request.

Bay City *Tribune*, 7/26, 30/1893 9/26, 27/1911 10/7, 8, 9/1911

Bay City *Times*, 9/23, 25,/1911 10/4, 11, 12, 17/1911 11/15, 16/1911

Detroit *Free Press*, 9/26, 27/1911 10/8/1911

Duluth *Herald*, 9/29/1911 10/4/1911

Marine Engineering 6/1898

"History of Bay County" published by the Bay City *Tribune*, 1883

Correspondence with James Hunter, Director/Curator, Huronia Museum, Midland, Ont. 2/22/1994

"An Inventory of Marine Disasters in the Vicinity of the Christian Islands, Georgian Bay," Folkes

Transportation Safety Board of Canada, Correspondence #1300-1 11/21/1994

"Namesakes 1900 1909," Greenwood

"Namesakes 1910 1919," Greenwood

"Georgian Bay, an Illustrated History," Barry

"Wrecks and Disasters," Shipley/Addis

"Great Lakes Ships We Remember" Vol. I & II, Van der Linden

"Shipwreck!," Swayze

"History of the Great Lakes," Mansfield

"Vessels Built on the Saginaw," Swayze, Roberts, Comtois

Ice Follies

REF; Detroit *Free Press*, 2/12, 13, 14, 15, 17, 18, 20,/1899

Duluth *News Tribune*, 2/12/1899

Duluth *Evening Herald* 2/11/1899

"Vessels Built on the Saginaw," Swayze, Roberts, Comtois

"The Great Lakes Car Ferries," Hilton

"Namesakes 1900 1909," Greenwood

Inland Seas Vol. 4, No.2, *"The Ships That Made Milwaukee Famous,"* Dowling.

"Ships and Shipwrecks in Door County, Wisconsin" Vol.1, Frederickson

Personal observations from aircraft

A Mooring of Family

REF;   *"Namesakes 1900 1909,"* Greenwood

"Vessels Built on the Saginaw," Swayze, Roberts, Comtois

"Shipwreck!," Swayze

"Hauling Wind and Heaving Short, Language of Lakemen" Pott, Michigan History Magazine Nov. Dec. 1992

Bay City *Times Press,* 11/28/02, 12/1/02

Bay City *Daily Tribune,* 11/28/02, 11/30/02

SILVANUS J. MACY's Master sheet, Institute for Great Lakes Research.

E-mail from Dave Swayze concerning the MABEL WILSON's wreck 1/7/1996

Which Boat Are Ya Waitin' On?

REF;   Bay City *Times Press* 11/29/1902

Bay City *Tribune* 11/30/1902, 12/2, 3/1902

"Namesakes 1900 1909," Greenwood

"Namesakes 1910 1919," Greenwood

"Vessels Built on the Saginaw," Swayze, Roberts, Comtois

"Great Lakes Ships We Remember" Vol. I & II, Van der Linden

"Shipwrecks of the Straits of Mackinac," Feltner

"Shipwreck!," Swayze

"History of the Great Lakes," Mansfield

"Wreck Ashore: The United States Life-Saving Service on the Great Lakes," Stonehouse

Footnotes to the Storm

REF;   Duluth *Evening Herald,* 9/1, 2, 4, 5, 6/1905

"True Tales of the Great Lakes," Boyer

"Went Missing," Stonehouse

"Lake Superior Shipwrecks," Wolff

"Namesakes 1900-1909" Greenwood

"Namesakes 1910-1919" Greenwood

"Davidson's Goliaths" Cooper & Jensen

Three Button Coat

REF; Bay City *Times Press*, 6/1, 3, 5, 6, 9/1893

Bay City *Times*, 6/1/1893

Bay City *Daily Tribune*, 6/3, 7/1893

"Namesakes 1910 1919," Greenwood

"Great Lakes Ships We Remember" Vol. I & II, Van der Linden

"Shipwrecks of the Straits of Mackinac," Feltner

"Shipwreck!," Swayze

"History of the Great Lakes," Mansfield

"Hauling Wind and Heaving Short, Language of Lakemen" Pott, Michigan History Magazine Nov. Dec. 1992

Matchsticks

REF; Oswego *Daily Palladium*, 9/26, 27, 28/1916

Toledo *News Bee*, 9/26/1916

Toledo *Blade*, 9/26/1916

Duluth *Herald*, 9/26,27/1916

Chicago *Herald*, 9/27/1916

"Namesakes 1910 1919," Greenwood

"Namesakes 1920 1929," Greenwood

"The Bay of Dead Ships," Reich

Correspondence with the Institute for Great Lakes Research.

Bohemian

REF; Bay City *Times*, 6/2-7, 24-26, 28 ,30/1880 7/2, 3, 4, 6-11, 13-17,19-24, 26-30/1880

Bay City *Evening Press* 8/12/1880

"Namesakes 1900 1909," Greenwood

"Namesakes 1910 1919," Greenwood

"Shipwreck!," Swayze

"History of the Great Lakes," Mansfield

"Wreck Ashore: The United States Life-Saving Service on the Great Lakes," Stonehouse

"Vessels Built on the Saginaw," Swayze, Roberts, Comtois

Letter from Dave Swayze, 10/4/1993

"History of Bay County" published by the Bay City *Tribune,* 1883

Inland Lloyds Vessel Register, 1885

The Fang of Mud Lake

REF; *The Evening News,* Sault Saint Marie, 9/22, 25, 27/1909

Duluth *Evening Herald,* 9/14, 17, 20, 23, 24, 25/1909

MONTEAGLE's Master Sheet, Institute for Great Lakes Research

"Freshwater Whales," Wright

"Namesakes 1900-1909," Greenwood

MONTEAGLE's file, Canal Park Museum, Duluth

Phone conversation with Tom Farnquist, Great Lakes Shipwreck Historical Society, 9/9/1994

Library of Congress Great Lakes photo file

Beeson's Marine Directory 1910

Just What Became of Them?

REF; Huron *Times,* 11/10/1893

Bay City *Tribune,* 11/8, 10, 11/1893

Bay City *Times-Press,* 11/9/1893

Personal visit to the Point aux Barques lighthouse 7/1995

"Wrecks and Disasters," Shipley/Addis

"The Great Lakes Car Ferries," Hilton

"Great Lakes Ships We Remember" Vol. I & II, Van der Linden

"Shipwrecks of the Straits of Mackinac," Feltner

"Shipwreck!," Swayze

"History of the Great Lakes," Mansfield

"Wreck Ashore: The United States Life-Saving Service on the Great Lakes," Stonehouse

Threads of Happenstance

REF; Bay City *Times Tribune* 5/14, 16, 17, 18, 21/1921 8/18, 30/1926

Copies of telegrams, letters and certificates belonging to Captain Walter R. Neal from the files of the Great Lakes Shipwreck Historical Society provided by Tom Farnquist

"Namesakes 1900 1909," Greenwood

"Namesakes 1910 1919," Greenwood

"Namesakes 1920 1929," Greenwood

"Namesakes 1930-1955," Greenwood

"Propellers," Shipley/Addis

"Wrecks and Disasters," Shipley/Addis

"Great Lakes Ships We Remember" Vol. I & II, Van der Linden

"Shipwreck!," Swayze

"History of the Great Lakes," Mansfield

"Wreck Ashore: The United States Life-Saving Service on the Great Lakes," Stonehouse

"Lake Superior's Shipwreck Coast," Stonehouse

"Vessels Built on the Saginaw," Swayze, Roberts, Comtois

"Stormy Seas," Wes Oleszewski

"Sounds of Disaster," Wes Oleszewski

Phone conversation with Tom Farnquist 3/2/1994

The Lights are Bright

REF; Bay City *Tribune*, 6/26, 29, 30/1892 7/17, 20, 21, 28/1892

Bay City *Times*, 8/5, 7, 8, 11/1902

Duluth *Daily News*, 7/20, 21 , 23, 24/1892, 8/30/1892, 9/1, 13, 14/1892

Lake Superior Weekly Tribune 7/29/1892

"Fresh Water Whales," Wright

"Dive Ontario Two!" Kohl

"Namesakes 1900 1909," Greenwood

"Namesakes 1910 1919," Greenwood

"Namesakes 1930-1955," Greenwood

"Great Lakes Ships We Remember" Vol. I, II & III, Van der Linden

"Shipwrecks of the Straits of Mackinac," Feltner

"Shipwreck!," Swayze

"History of the Great Lakes," Mansfield

"Vessels Built on the Saginaw," Swayze, Roberts, Comtois

Author's trip on the J.L. MAUTHE, 12/1992

Shadows in the Shallows

REF; Duluth *News Tribune*, 12/5, 6/1897

Detroit *Free Press*, 12/5/1897

Marquette *Daily Mining Journal*, 12/6/1897

Bay City *Tribune*, 12/8/1897

Duluth *Evening Herald*, 12/8/1897 & 9/20/1898

Master sheet for the JOSEPH G. MASTEN, Institute for Great Lakes Research

Inland Lloyds Vessel Register 1898

Merchant Steam Vessels of the United States register 1898

Information from the collection of historian Dave Swayze

"Shipwreck!," Swayze

"History of the Great Lakes," Mansfield

"Wreck Ashore: The United States Life-Saving Service on the Great Lakes," Stonehouse

"Namesakes 1900 1909," Greenwood

"Propellers," Shipley/Addis

"Shipwrecks of the Straits of Mackinac," Feltner

"Vessels Built on the Saginaw," Swayze, Roberts, Comtois

The Telescope Sept.—Oct. 1990 *"The Wind That Wouldn't Die,"* Gebhart

Shipwreck data form, Wisconsin submerged cultural resources survey, JOSEPH G. MASTEN

Annual report, United States Life-saving Service, 1898

Wisconsin Sentinel, 12/5/1897

Correspondence with David J. Cooper, State Underwater Archeologist, State Historical Society of Wisconsin, 11/1995

Personal conversation with C. Patrick Labadie, Director, Canal Park Museum, 11/11/1995

Map of shipwrecks of Two Rivers Point by Conrad Swiggum

Ellis' Rules

REF; *"Namesakes 1900 1909,"* Greenwood

"Namesakes 1910 1919," Greenwood

"Shipwreck!," Swayze

"Wreck Ashore: The United States Life-Saving Service on the Great Lakes," Stonehouse

Alpena *Argus* 11/5/1890, 8/12/1891

Alpena *Pioneer* 11/7/1890

Michigan Labor Journal 11/8/1890

Bay *City Tribune* 10/23/1890

Listing from the collection of John McConnell 4/22/1994

Letter correspondence between Mrs. Betty J. Werner and Mrs. A. Hendrickson 1/3/1974

Letter to Gary Hill from Dr. Richard J. Wright, Institute for Great Lakes Research, 3/9/1984

Letter to Gary Hill from Dave Swayze 4/7/1994

Letters from Gary Hill 2/7/1994, 3/22/1994, 4/11/1994, 5/1/1994

Register of Wreck Reports Received from Life Saving Stations, 1891, forwarded from the General Services Administration, 3/16/1982

MONTANA's Master Sheet, Institute for Great Lakes Research

Phone conversation with Marvin Thuit, President of the Middle Island Light-keeper's Association and owner of Middle Island 8/19/1995

Direct conversation with Dan McGee, Keeper of Presque Isle Light 8/13/1995

Phone conversation with Martha Long, Great Lakes Historical Society, 1/26/1995

A Sutton's Bay Pirate

REF; Detroit *Free Press*, 9/26, 27/1911

"*Namesakes 1900 1909*," Greenwood

"*Namesakes 1910 1919*," Greenwood

"*Lake Michigan*," Quaife

Author's visit to Sutton's Bay 8/5/1995

Breakfast at the Owl Cafe

REF; Duluth *Evening Herald*, 5/1/1909

Detroit *Free Press*, 5/2/1909

Sault Saint Marie *Evening News*, 5/1,6/1909

Marine Review, May 1909

Marquette *Daily Mining Journal* 5/3/1909

Alpena *Argus-Pioneer* 12/1/1909

Beeson's Marine Directory 1910

RUSSIA's Master Sheet, Milwaukee Public Library

Correspondence with Bill and Ruthann Beck, Thunder Bay Divers

Correspondence with Paul Ehorn, Wreck Diver and Historian

"Great Lakes Ships We Remember" Vol. I, II & III, Van der Linden

"Shipwrecks of the Straits of Mackinac," Feltner

"Shipwreck!," Swayze

"History of the Great Lakes," Mansfield

"Lake Superior's Shipwreck Coast," Stonehouse

"Ships Gone Missing," Hemming

"Isle Royale Shipwrecks," Stonehouse

"Went Missing," Stonehouse

"Vessels Built on the Saginaw," Swayze, Roberts, Comtois

Other Sources

"Around the Bay," Thornton

Index of Vessels

Acknowledgements

*W*ork on the earliest of chapters within this text was started in 1992, and over the time that has passed since then the individual stories have taken anywhere from four years to a single month to research and write. In that kind of time-frame, many individuals have given input—both large and small. In my effort here to acknowledge the efforts of those who have helped, some may be left out. So, I would like first to express thanks to anyone whose help was given, but whose name may have been left out in this section.

Next, recognition must go to the people who make their living, or volunteer their time in the effort to preserve our maritime history. Often I have called upon these individuals for help, and every time they have jumped into the task. The tales presented here could never have been completed without the aid of, Kenneth Pot—Michigan Maritime Museum, James Hunter—Director/Curator, Huronia Museum, Tom Farnquist—Great Lakes Shipwreck Historical Society, David J. Cooper—State Underwater Archeologist, State Historical Society of Wisconsin, map maker Conrad Swiggum, C. Patrick Labadie—Director, Canal Park Museum, Martha Long—Great Lakes Historical Society, Bill and Ruthann Beck—Thunder Bay Divers, Paul Ehorn—Wreck Diver and Historian, Robert Stasser—Reference Librarian, Bay City Branch Library, Marvin Thuit—President of the Middle Island Light-keeper's Association and owner of Middle Island, Dan McGee—Keeper of Presque Isle

Light, Lauren Hafner and Ethan Barnett—Tri Cities Museum, Donna Geisler and Robin Flory—South Haven Public Library, Karen Rose—Escanaba Public Library. Credit in the greatest sense must be given to these individuals as well as those who work in their support—whose names always seem to be overlooked.

Next on the long list of people who deserve thanks are those who I like to call my "boat-nut" friends. These are the collectors, shutter-bugs and all around fans of the lakeboats, without whose energy and enthusiasm the long process of bringing this book to press would have been possible. Boat-buffs such as D.J. Story, Dave Swayze, Don Comtois and Dave "the bullet" Willett who fight the daily struggle to keep history alive as well as keeping their wives from throwing out the "good stuff." The collectors such as Ralph Roberts and Ken Thro who have assembled personal museums of incredible value after decades of pains-taking effort. Then there is the dean of wooden and other lakeboats, Pat Labadie—Director of the Canal Park Museum in Duluth, Pat is the only person that I know of who cuts the pages from my books and re-binds them in loose-leaf fashion for easier reference. Knowing the level at which Pat works, that action is indeed a compliment... thanks Pat.

Not to be forgotten are all of those who staff the assorted libraries to which I have sent a letter containing assorted dates and a check in request of microfilm photocopies. Each time my request has been answered and sometimes forgotten history has been discovered. Thanks must go to the whole staffs of the Bay City Branch Library, Oswego Public Library, Port Huron Public Library, Bayless Library—Sault Saint Marie, Escanaba Public Library, as well as the Milwaukee Public Library.

Finally, there is the dose of gratitude must go to my family. My mom, Sue, my dad Walt, sisters Jeanine and Karen as well as my brother Craig. Thanks also to my in-laws, the Anderson family, "Andy," Akie and Karen. All of these folks have, at one time or another, been forced to put up with my boat-nut ways to a insufferable extent. The one person who has been forced to the greatest limit of tolera-tion, however, has been my wife Teresa. I cannot express enough gratitude for having this amazing woman in my life. She completely understands every aspect of being wed to an author and often puts up with charts and documents spread across the living room, late-night dashes to the computer for the capture of a sudden brain-storm, week-ends away from home for book-signings and the unending research, talking to myself and silent pondering. The fact that you are reading this text can be credited in a large way to the world's most understanding, tolerant and clear thinking spouse—my beloved wife Teresa.

About the Author

W. Wes Oleszewski was born on the east side of Saginaw, Michigan in 1957. He attended Nelle Haley and Webber public schools in that same city through grade 9, at which time his family moved to the town of Freeland, Michigan. He graduated from Freeland High School in 1976.

Through most of his youth Wes kept a passing interest in the vessels of the Great Lakes that was second only to his fascination with the space program and areas of aviation. When accepted for enrollment at the Embry-Riddle Aeronautical University in 1977, Wes' career turned toward aviation, leaving room in his life for a diversion deeper into Great Lakes maritime history. Such diversion was often needed during the ten years of difficult work that were required for him to earn his way through the university. By 1987 Wes had earned a Bachelor of Science Degree in Aeronautical Science with pilot certification through commercial pilot with multi-engine instrument rating. Additionally Wes earned the Student Leadership and Involvement award, served on the university's Precision Flight Demonstration Team leaving as Chief Pilot, collected awards and honors for ten years of outstanding service to the university and worked as the editorial cartoonist for the "*Avion*" newspaper from 1978 until his graduation.

Such, however, was not enough—in the summer of 1986 Wes was earning money to return to school by working days as a film delivery driver and nights as a part-time

Author Wes Oleszewski seen here "hard at work" at his "other" job as an airline pilot.

clerk at Land and Seas gift shop, at that time in Saginaw. While there he noticed that every book on the shelf was already in his own personal library. Also it seemed as if the most recently published material consisted simply of lists and data—no one was telling the tales anymore. With that in mind Wes sat down the next day during his lunch hour and began writing his first book on a legal pad. No one ever told him how it was done, and better yet—no one ever told him that he couldn't do it. For the next year he assembled the true stories of the obscure adventures of the lake mariners, the tales that everyone else had overlooked. Over the summer of 1987, while Wes attended classes in a redoubled effort to graduate, his soon-to-be-wife Teresa transferred the hand written text into computer text. That same summer Wes sent the text off to a well-known Great Lakes publisher, who promptly rejected it. In 1990 the exact same text was sent to Avery—who immediately published it as "*Stormy Seas.*"

Since that first book hit the shelf Wes has written and Avery has published "*Sounds of Disaster,*" "*Ice Water Museum*" and "*Ghost Ships, Gales and Forgotten Tales.*" Currently Wes has more than 40 stories in research and can produce a book every year. Aside from writing and working at his other job as an airline pilot, Wes finds time to travel around the Great Lakes region visiting book stores to sign copies of his work, researching local maritime history, and his favorite side-trip... speaking to classrooms of students from the elementary level up. Often the enthusiastic boat-nut can find Wes perched on the canal wall at Duluth, shooting video tape under the bridge at Port Huron or hanging out on the west observation platform at the Soo locks... like most professional pilots, he gets around.

As of this publication, Wes has logged more that 4,000 hours of flying time, most of that in airline category aircraft. He holds the highest pilot certification issued by the FAA— the Airline Transport Pilot certificate, and has passed every airman's written test offered by the FAA. He is currently living on the east coast and employed as an airline pilot based in the midwest. Work is already under way on his sixth book.